The Global Spread of
Fertility Decline

The Global Spread of Fertility Decline

Population, Fear, and Uncertainty

JAY WINTER & MICHAEL TEITELBAUM

Yale

UNIVERSITY PRESS

New Haven and London

Published with assistance from the Kingsley Trust Association Publication Fund established by the Scroll and Key Society of Yale College.

Yale University Press books may be purchased in quantity for educational, business, or promotional use. For information, please e-mail sales.press@yale.edu (U.S. office) or sales@yaleup. co.uk (U.K. office).

Set in Minion type by Newgen North America.
Printed in the United States of America.

Library of Congress Cataloging-in-Publication Data

Winter, J. M.
    The global spread of fertility decline : population, fear, and uncertainty / Jay Winter and Michael Teitelbaum.
        pages cm
    Includes bibliographical references and index.
    ISBN 978-0-300-13906-8 (cloth : alk. paper)
    1. Fertility, Human.   2. Demographic transition.
    3. Population.   I. Teitelbaum, Michael S.   II. Title.
    HB901.W56 2013
    304.6′32 — dc23

                                                2012049847

A catalogue record for this book is available from the British Library.

This paper meets the requirements of ANSI/NISO z39.48-1992 (Permanence of Paper).

10 9 8 7 6 5 4 3 2 1

Contents

Preface

This book, the third in a series of collective reflections we have written on population movements in historical perspective, represents the fruits of a friendship and collaboration of three decades and more. It is rare for a historian and a demographer to join together to try to unravel the complex strands of population change and the political and ideological framework within which it occurs. It is rarer still for such a partnership (and the friendship on which it rests) to last intact for the better part of two working lives.

Following *The Fear of Population Decline* (1985) and *A Question of Numbers: High Migration, Low Fertility, and the Politics of National Identity* (1998), the present book takes the discussion of population and politics into the twenty-first century. There are many continuities evident in the three studies. The most salient is the way, over thirty years, discussions of fertility touch fundamental questions of values and aspirations. As a result, the rhetoric of population debates tends to take on a life of its own. Exaggerated claims and fears proliferate, and unjustified inferences are drawn from data poorly understood (if at all). In this highly charged field, there is room for considered and calm reflection on fertility trends and their consequences. Leaving the subject to the ideologues is simply not an option.

Extending the geographical range of our earlier analyses shows continuities of another kind. The study of fertility decline in Europe is now a well-established research subject; and yet, after decades of work by many researchers, it is clear that the old notion of "modernization" as the fundamental economic process driving fertility declines is no longer a sufficient basis for understanding fertility trends from Ireland to Russia. In this domain, politics matters. The same is true when we turn to fertility trends in Asia. In both cases we need to place greater emphasis on political processes as fundamental elements framing fertility declines to low levels.

The same is true in those areas not covered by this book. In large parts of the Middle East and Africa, fertility has remained high, but we must leave to others the task of explaining such matters. We expect that convincing interpretations will need to go beyond strictly economic issues, but we note that in demographic matters as in other domains, globalization is a patchwork trend evident in some areas and not in others. In all of them, politics, from the family to the neighborhood to the town to the city to the region to the state, is an integral part of demographic history. This book tries to show how this is so.

The authors are grateful for the help colleagues and friends have offered us in the gestation of this book. In particular, we have profited from the suggestions of Robert Wyman, Davidson Gwatkin, Adrian Drixler, David Washbrook, Emmanuel Sivan, Sheldon Garon, Gerhard Heilig, Patrick Gerland, and Hania Zlotnik. Their command of specialist literature and data sources in various languages was invaluable to us in avoiding some of the errors that a book of this breadth self-evidently risks.

For any remaining errors, the authors return to the statement in their 1985 book, *The Fear of Population Decline:* Each author blames the other.

Jay Winter
Michael Teitelbaum
Guilford, Connecticut
April 2012

Globalization and Demography

Over the past decades, there has been an ocean of ink spilled about the process that has come to be known as "globalization." While the term itself rose to high public and academic visibility during this period, some have argued that the process that it denotes goes back centuries, even millennia.

Globalization has become a highly contentious subject, with the word itself carrying diverse meanings that are deployed as cudgels by proponents and opponents alike. It is now common to see one or another position characterized as "pro-globalization" or "anti-globalization," and in some cases activists describe themselves as such.

But what does it actually mean? While the term is sometimes used very broadly to connote simultaneous integration of the world's peoples and systems along dimensions of economics, politics, technologies, and cultures, it is more often discussed in more narrowly economic terms. In the 2004 book *In Defense of Globalization*, a title indicative of the growing attacks then underway, trade theorist Jagdish Bhagwati concentrates upon the relatively recent integration of national economies into a nearly global international economy, marked by free trade, free flows of capital, expanded foreign direct investment, increasing international migration, and the dissemination of technologies. These, he argues, have led to increasing prosperity and well-being.[1] We share many of these views but aim in this book to add a demographic dimension to them. Declining fertility and rising international migration are both features of globalization to which we need to attend. To understand contemporary fertility and migration, we need to focus on significant political as well as economic phenomena.

This book is intended to help put the politics back into our understanding of the shape, timing, and ramifications of globalization in the particular setting of fertility decline and international migration. Doing so helps us distinguish between recent history and earlier phases of globalization, marked by very different political and demographic regimes.

By politics we mean that network of power relationships extending from the family to the neighborhood to the village or city to the region and to the nation/state beyond it. It is in these networks of unequal actors that the linkages among economic forces, social structures, and cultural practices are negotiated. Politics certainly means governmental action and policy, but the outcomes of such initiatives always entails interpretation, implementation, and deflection. Intentions and outcomes are never perfectly aligned, especially when considering delicate and complex questions associated with fertility decisions. Though it is true that state actors now have unparalleled tools of communication and intelligence gathering, we should not assume that they and they alone dictate events, however much they would like to do so. Resistance, misinterpretation, and inertia on the part of individuals, families, clans, religions, bureaucracies, and others have their roles to play in population history, as in other domains. The key point is that politics matters in this field as in all others; in a nutshell, we present an alternative to the view that in any straightforward way economic change "produces" demographic outcomes.

Instead of economic determinism, we emphasize the significance of uncertainty—political, social, and economic uncertainty—in the history of fertility decline. We place the perception of risk, understood in political, social, and economic terms, at the center of this study. As defined by Ulrich Beck, a "risk society" is one in which there is no way individuals and couples can anticipate accurately the risks they face in an uncertain world. Among those risks are the consequences of child-bearing for a man and a woman whose futures are clouded with doubt on many levels. Women who forgo childbearing entirely or who decide to have only one child may well do so to manage the risks of an uncertain future, which could be constrained by family responsibilities. There is no way to know how great these risks are; that is part of the problem. But it is hard to deny that they exist and are evident at many levels—ecological, economic, and political—in places and at times in which supports for the well-being of individuals and families are either absent or under severe threat in many parts of the world. The "risk society," Beck argues, is not an option but an inescapable structural condition of industrializing or industrialized societies, now stretching across the globe.[2] One facet of the unfolding of the "risk society," understood in many ways, is—with notable exceptions—the globalization of fertility decline.

Two Globalization Waves, Divided by a Century

While they acknowledge earlier periods of increased international integration prior to the mid-nineteenth century, historians generally agree that there have so far been two modern "waves" of globalization, divided by a century: from 1880 to 1914, and from the mid-1980s to the present. The "first wave" of globalization was a dominant phenomenon at the turn of the twentieth century. By convention it is said to have originated gradually and incrementally beginning in the 1880s, and to have ended with a bang in 1914—as the Great War exploded into massive destruction of the globalized order that had grown rapidly during the preceding three decades.

The drivers of the powerful forces of the first wave took many forms: political, military, economic, technological, cultural. During that period much of the world was dominated by Great Britain and its semi-global British Empire. The Royal Navy, larger and more powerful than any other fleet, assured the peace and the relative safety of international transport and expanding global trade. Late-nineteenth-century technologies played a central role, too, as new modes of transportation and communication sharply reduced the cost and time involved in international trade. The global service sector—shipping, insurance, and banking—was based in London, the financial capital of the world, and British know-how and manufacturing techniques helped to industrialize the world.

Expansion of international trade was very substantial, driven by new and far more efficient means of bulk transport via steam power, and by the rising attractiveness of international investment that could be protected by the political power of the hegemon, Great Britain. Between 1850 and 1913 the carrying capacity of British (and world) shipping increased more than tenfold, with more than one-third of that increase occurring in the thirteen years before the Great War. The volume in merchandise exports as a percent of GDP rose in western Europe from 8.8 percent in 1870 to 14.1 percent in 1913. In the same period European per capita income rose by 1.3 percent per year, compared to 0.5 percent per year in the classical period of the industrial revolution, between 1820 and 1870. From the late nineteenth century onward European production and trade outstripped population growth, and income inequality increased between the less-developed and the industrialized world.[3]

Then as now, British bankers and businessmen tended to work in English, which, given Britain's imperial power, was the language in which most of the world's trade was conducted. Both economic necessities and the substantial outflow of British people to countries of European settlement, from Australia and New Zealand to Canada and South Africa, created a British diaspora linked by family ties and a common culture. In this period, English became a world language for business, a full century before the Internet reinforced the hegemony of English as the lingua franca of international exchange.

The beginning of the "second wave," of globalization may be (somewhat arbitrarily) located in the mid-1980s, and it is still in motion today. Like the first wave, it too was undergirded by forces that were simultaneously political, economic, technological, and cultural.

The origins of the second wave can be traced to the end of World War II. In 1944, a General Agreement on Trade and Tariffs (GATT) was created as part of the "high politics" of the 1944 Bretton Woods agreements among the soon-to-be-victorious Allies. The GATT was one of three new global institutions constructed to avoid the mistakes of the post-1918 period and to manage international monetary and financial affairs after the Second World War. The other two were the International Bank for Reconstruction and Development (IBRD), commonly known as the World Bank, and the International Monetary Fund (IMF). The intent of the GATT was to facilitate international cooperation via trade liberalization; its most immediate targets were the protectionist tariffs and other measures of the 1930s that were then still formally in effect.[4]

The first wave of globalization was protected by British power for the benefit of British prosperity. The second wave was similar, with the United States being the shield and a beneficiary of postwar recovery and rapidly expanding investment and trade. The political stakes were heightened by the early onset of the Cold War, which made economic competition between the two power blocs a "test" of which system worked better. Long before the collapse of the Soviet Union, the Communist system failed that test, and that outcome was both a reflection of intrinsic problems in the way "state socialism" operated and of the strength of the competing, increasingly globalized system constructed outside the Soviet Bloc after 1945. International trade politics in the non-Communist world prepared the ground for the leap forward beginning in the 1980s in information technology and other developments associated with the second wave of globalization.

This outcome was not at all inevitable, nor was it a seamless story of capitalist success and Communist failure. The Cold War made multilateral trade policy politically difficult to sell in the highly charged domestic political arena of the 1950s in the United States. Not surprisingly, the GATT had a notably "hesitant start" (in the delicately phrased words of the World Trade Organization—WTO—which inherited its role). The GATT agreement contained provision for a proposed new international regulatory agency, the International Trade Organization (ITO), as a specialized agency of the United Nations. The draft ITO charter was ambitious. It extended beyond world trade disciplines to include rules on employment, commodity agreements, restrictive business practices, international investment and services. The aim was to create the ITO at the UN Conference on Trade and Employment in Havana, Cuba, in 1947.[5]

The effort floundered, and by 1950 the ITO was effectively still-born. This premature death followed a decision by the United States government, the postwar hegemon that had led the campaign for post-war trade liberalization, to decline even to seek ratification of the GATT by the US Senate in view of clear indications that a ratification vote would fail.

Notwithstanding the failure of the ITO, the GATT weathered the storm. In particular, its small secretariat persisted, organizing a decades-long series of "trade rounds"—a set of agreements reached via lengthy and often difficult international negotiations and conferences. A list of the many "rounds" is provided in table 1.1.

As is evident in table 1.1, the early rounds focused on reduction of the protectionist tariffs adopted during the prewar Great Depression; these discussions included only small numbers of participating countries. The 1964–1967 Kennedy Round in Geneva, named after the assassinated US president, addressed antidumping measures as well. It also engaged considerably more country participants than the earlier rounds, including some former colonies that had only recently become independent states.

It was not until the Tokyo Round, a series of conferences and negotiations that stretched over much of the 1970s, that agreements regarding reduction of "nontariff" barriers to trade were negotiated. The Tokyo Round also addressed so-called "framework agreements," which provided more ambitious strategies and principles for dialogue about liberalizing trade and investment. In addition to tariffs, nontariff barriers, and framework agreements, the Tokyo Round also addressed trade in services, protection of intellectual property, dispute settlement, and controversial provisions regarding trade in textiles, garments, and agriculture. The Tokyo Round included participation for the first time of more than one hundred countries. It was the gradual accession by increasing numbers of countries to agreements reached during the Tokyo Round that ushered in and helped sustain the second wave of globalization, beginning during the first half of the 1980s and accelerating in the following decades.

Table 1.1. GATT and WTO "Rounds," with Years, Initial Locations, Subjects, and Number of Participating Countries

Years	Place & Name	Subjects Covered	Number of Countries
1947	Geneva	Tariffs	23
1949	Annecy	Tariffs	13
1951	Torquay	Tariffs	38
1956	Geneva	Tariffs	26
1960–1961	Geneva ("Dillon Round")	Tariffs	26
1964–1967	Geneva ("Kennedy Round")	Tariffs, antidumping measures	62
1973–1979	Geneva ("Tokyo Round")	Tariffs, nontariff barriers, "framework agreements"	102
1986–1994	Geneva ("Uruguay Round")	Tariffs, nontariff barriers, rules, trade in services, intellectual property, dispute settlement, textiles, agriculture, creation of World Trade Organization	123
2001–present	Doha ("Doha Round")	Agriculture, nonagricultural market access, trade in services, intellectual property, trade and development, trade and environment, trade facilitation, WTO rules, dispute settlement	157

Sources: From World Trade Organization, *Understanding the WTO: The GATT Years: From Havana to Marrakesh* (Geneva: World Trade Organization, 2009), fig.1.1; see also "Members and Observers" and "The Doha Agenda" (Geneva: World Trade Organization, 2012); available online at http://www.wto.org/english/thewto_e/whatis_e/tif_e/tif_e.htm.

The Tokyo Round was followed by the even more ambitious political agreements to facilitate economic globalization embodied in the GATT's Uruguay Round. At these meetings a broader range of issues was included under the rubric of trade. The Uruguay Round also created the World Trade Organization, a formal organization that replaced the small secretariat that had staffed the GATT; the GATT was not an organization per se but instead an agreement on rules. In effect, the WTO represented the final triumph of those who had failed in 1950 to establish the International Trade Organization.

The current round of negotiations about globalization, known as the Doha Round, has been underway since 2001. It has not (yet) been able to achieve new agreements. As may be seen, the number of participating countries has grown still further, and the range of topics being negotiated has also become far broader. It is anyone's guess what the ultimate outcomes will prove to be.

Like the first wave of globalization, the second wave since the early 1980s has also been heavily influenced by, and in turn has heavily influenced, trends in technology, economics, and culture. If the archetypal technologies affecting the first wave were the telegraph, railroad, and steam-powered bulk shipping, those of the second wave have been telecommunications, television, and cable; rapid and low-cost air travel; quantum improvements in shipping by both sea and air; and, ultimately, computers and the Internet. These in turn have contributed to the growth and reach of truly multinational corporations, which may be technically headquartered in a particular country but which in fact operate in a global manner.

The financial sector too has taken advantage of technologies that have allowed development on a massive scale of split-second transfers of capital and currencies around the world, with very low-cost and secure electronic linkages among hundreds of central banks and thousands of financial institutions in all parts of the world. Meanwhile, in one important developed region the embrace of the euro as a common currency for most of Europe has lowered the costs and risks of trade, while at the same time reducing the power of individual governments over the levers of economic policy and, in particular, their previous control of their own currencies.

There can be no doubt that all of these forces and others since the 1980s have had very large impacts upon the volume of international trade, capital flows, foreign direct investment, expansion of multinational firms and their reach, and constraints upon governments' ability to regulate their own economic patterns. Here are a few quantitative indicators:[6]

- Total exports have increased by tenfold over those around 1950.
- More than $1.5 trillion a day now moves across borders, versus only $15 billion per day in 1973.
- Foreign investment in 1997 exceeded $400 billion in 1997, or seven times the level in real terms of the 1970s.
- Between 1983 and 1993, cross-border sales of US Treasury bonds increased from $30 billion to $500 billion per year.
- International bank lending grew from $265 billion in 1975 to $4.2 trillion in 1994.

One important question—one that cannot be addressed here other than in rudimentary form—is whether the second wave of globalization from the 1980s to the present may also be marked by some of the same unanticipated developments that contributed to the fading of the first globalization wave around the turn of the twentieth century. In both cases, political leaders of the hegemonic power(s) believed that the palpable domestic prosperity created during the early liberalizing decades of the globalization drive could continue to grow indefinitely, if only they could continue to spread the reach of globalization. In both case, increasingly prosperous private corporate and financial interests exploited the short-term incentives provided by globalization to export their technologies, manufacturing, and employment-generating and other activities to lower-cost settings. In both cases, free trade arguably provided the conditions for the creation of competitors, which threatened to overtake the economic advantage of the prior hegemon. In 1914, that threat helped pave the way to war. In the early twenty-first century, international tensions are evident, though the risks of their precipitating war are less due to the common threat of nuclear disaster.

Demography and Globalization

For our purposes here, it is important to recognize that both the first and second globalization waves have had powerful impacts upon the volume and pace of international migration. It is likely no accident that the first wave of globalization, 1880–1914, was coterminous with the classical period of mass migration, especially from eastern and southern Europe to the New World. Over precisely this span of thirty-four years, from 1880 to 1914, an estimated 30 million persons moved from their countries of origin to another, representing some 2 percent of the estimated 1880 world population of about 1.4 billion. For tens of millions of these, the primary destination was the United States. Between 1880 and 1914, on the order of 21 million immigrants were admitted to the United States for permanent residence. Nearly all came from Europe, and primarily from southern and eastern Europe.[7]

The second wave of globalization, which we locate here as spanning from the 1980s to the present, has similarly been a period of large and accelerating international migration. The United Nations Population Division has developed the most credible estimates of these movements. It reports that as of 1990 the "stock" of international migrants totaled about 155 million persons, obviously a large number but still representing less than 3 percent of the much-expanded global population; of these 155 million, about 53 percent could be found in developed countries.[8] By 2000 the UN estimated numbers had grown to some 179 million, an increase of about 15 percent in that decade, of which 58 percent were resident in developed countries. Ten years later, in 2010, the number had increased to 214 million, or about a 20 percent increase, with 60 percent resident in developed countries.[9]

While the two waves of globalization both have been accompanied by major expansions of international migration, they differed in significant ways in terms of the geographies of migrant origins and destinations. Much of the 1880–1914 migration emanated from Europe and landed in the New World (United States, Canada, parts of Latin America) and in Australia and New Zealand. During the current second wave of globalization, the largest migrations have come from Asia, Latin America and the Caribbean, and increasingly from Africa. The main destinations of these large numbers of international migrants have been the industrialized countries of North America and Europe, along with petroleum-exporting countries concentrated in the Middle East. Hence the migration trajectories of the first globalization wave were largely east–west; now the trajectories are in new directions: south–north, and from the Far East eastward to North America and westward to Europe.

Converging Demographic Phenomena

Now that we have offered an extremely brief survey of conventional views on globalization, it is time to turn to the specific focus of this book. There is a demographic component to globalization since the 1980s, one which distinguishes this phase from the first phase located in the 1880–1914 period.

The current wave of globalization is framed by two powerful demographic phenomena:

- First, the (semi-) globalization of fertility decline to low levels, that is, the wide spread of low fertility rates across an increasing proportion of the world's countries and populations. To be sure, fertility decline has been much later and far slower in some parts of the world than in others. In some areas, especially in the Middle East and sub-Saharan Africa, high fertility rates have been sustained over this period.
- Second, as we have noted earlier, there have been dramatic increases in the volume of international migration, heavily from developing countries, and consequent increases in the stock of such migrants resident in the industrialized world and in oil-exporting countries. Migrants are now more mixed (in terms of national origins, race, ethnicity, religion, and so on) than ever before.

Moreover, recent migration has taken place against the backdrop of very rapid political changes, accompanied time and again by violence, some international, some transnational, and some subnational. Security issues of a kind unknown in the 1880s—for instance, concerning the traffic in weapons of mass destruction or of the objectives of radical Islam—frame the subject of international migration in new and (for some) ominous ways.

Taken together, the convergence of these two demographic phenomena in some world regions with low fertility and substantial in-migration can have demographic and political effects of a substantial and even "dramatic." kind.[10] Let us start with fertility.

The (Semi-) Globalization of Fertility Decline

Over the rough time period since 1985, there have been declines in fertility rates to low levels in an increasing proportion of the world's countries and populations. Low fertility had been registered during the Great Depression of the 1930s and evoked much concern about the future among political elites.[11] However, such anxieties largely evaporated in the postwar period, as low prewar fertility rates rebounded to much higher levels. Fertility rates rose dramatically in the United States, Canada, Australia, New Zealand, and markedly though not as spectacularly in Europe. In the United States there was a baby boom; in Europe what may be termed a baby "boomlet."

This was not the only demographic process in evidence after 1945. The fertility decline that has now become a semiglobal pattern was evident first in central Europe, especially in Germany, and in East Asia, led by Japan and then by the four "Asian Tigers" (South Korea, Singapore, Hong Kong, and Taiwan). In some of these countries, very low fertility rates appeared (or reappeared) as early as the 1970s. Fertility declines occurred many years later in southern Europe, where in some cases fertility declined rapidly and to levels even lower than in central Europe.

In many parts of the developing world, there were fertility declines from high to moderate but not to low levels. And in some parts of the developing world, especially in parts of Middle East, West Asia, and sub-Saharan Africa, there have been sustained levels of high fertility.

Despite these substantial variations, it is fair to say that globally since 1980 the phenomenon of low fertility levels has been transformed from that of the uncommon to the common—not by any means universal, but no longer unusual. Demographic globalization is uneven and incomplete, but as a rough generalization, it is clear that low fertility is now the rule and not the exception among the nations of Asia, Europe, and the Americas. Africa and the Middle East are mixed regions, with some states retaining high or very high fertility regimes.

Fertility decline is in no sense global, but it is a globalizing phenomenon. And in this second wave of fertility decline, many countries have reached unprecedentedly low levels. This too is one reason to distinguish the first and second waves of globalization. Now countries registering high and volatile levels of in-migration are also countries whose fertility rates are substantially below the replacement level of 2.1. Some demographers use, as a rule of thumb, a total fertility rate (TFR) of 1.5 as denoting very low fertility, and 1.3 as "lowest low" fertility. These are arbitrary distinctions, but they do point to one salient fact. Whichever figure is used, it is clear that many industrialized countries have now entered a fertility regime without precedent in their history.

The spread and pace of fertility decline to below replacement has been far more rapid than anticipated by most experts. In 1960 there were only 5 countries with fertility rates below the replacement level of 2.1, whereas by 2000–2005 this number had ballooned to 64 countries, i.e. 35 percent of the 185 countries tracked by the United Nations. Together these 64 countries accounted for populations of some 2.4 billion, or nearly 40 percent of the world's population.[12]

One well-informed assessment[13] concluded that by 2003, some 21 countries had total fertility rates below 1.3, below the arbitrary demarcation point for "lowest low" fertility.[14]

Is Very Low Fertility a Permanent or Transitional Phenomenon?

The advent of very low fertility as a widespread global phenomenon is recent. Whether it will prove to be long lasting is the subject of considerable speculation and controversy. Are these very low fertility rates intrinsic to modern societies, or a more temporary phenomenon related to transitional developments among their populations?

On such subjects we necessarily lack the distance and data needed to permit assessments of the trajectories and patterns of fertility rates in either 1945–1965 or 1965–1985. We can now say that much of what are now called the postwar baby booms proved to be short-term phenomena, not too different from the short-term fertility "spikes" that had been anticipated following the end of the war and demobilization of large numbers of soldiers. In a few cases, however (in the United States, Canada, Australia, New Zealand), the postwar baby booms were just that: unanticipated, sustained increases in fertility that were large in magnitude and lasted for nearly two decades. In the decade between 1947 and 1957 the total fertility rate of the United States rose to wholly unanticipated levels (for example, 3.7) before the declines of the 1960s and the subsequent baby bust. With some degree of confidence, we can also say that the subsequent large fertility declines of the 1965–1985 period appear now to be long-term phenomena.

But what can we say about the pending future? Perspectives on this question vary and have significant political implications. They matter, since assumptions about the long-term nature of very low fertility govern the construction of demographic projections, which themselves form critical components of public policy planning on pensions, health care, taxation, and education. The Commission of the European Communities (also called the European Commission), for example, has prepared a Green Paper entitled "Confronting the Demographic Challenge: A New Solidarity between the Generations," which calls both for measures intended to raise fertility rates (see following discussion) and adjustments in a wide range of societal policies affected by rapid shifts in age structures in the 27 European Union (EU) member states.[15]

Much of the debate about the future of low fertility is based upon arguments drawn from theoretical perspectives. Prominent among these are neoclassical economic theories put forward under various rubrics, including "rational choice theory" and the "new home economics."[16] The critical and overarching assumption of those propounding these interpretations is that individuals should be understood to be making rational choices with respect to their demographic behaviors, including fertility, marriage, and migration (though perhaps less so with respect to their mortality). They also assume that individuals and couples have full access to the information necessary to make such rational choices. Their decisions about childbearing are interpreted as balancing the costs and benefits of having a child or a given number of children on the basis of their own circumstances (employment, income, wealth, time, aspirations) in relation to their "preferences" regarding children. Choices based on emotion or love are not relevant in this framework.

There is a large literature based on this approach, and there are many criticisms about its assumptions, of which a full discussion here is not possible. For our purposes the key issues relate to how this perspective would anticipate the likely future tendencies among populations with low and very low fertility rates and, related to that, the extent to which policy actions by governments would or would not have potential to influence such rates upward. Early versions of these neoclassical interpretations argued that rising real incomes (such as those that have occurred in most countries with low and very low fertility rates) would be expected to increase the demand for children. However later formulations added that rising income might be translated into demand for higher "quality" children rather than higher quantity.[17] Hence, in this perspective the implications of rising income for fertility rates appear to be uncertain.

Other writers within this general neoclassical perspective have focused more heavily on conflicts between employment and family responsibilities. Here one useful concept is "opportunity costs" imposed by childbearing, that is, the loss of family income forgone as a result of parental time and effort devoted to children. Such forgone income could result from a decision not to engage in remunerated employment at all, to reduce the number of hours worked, or to seek employment in lower-paid occupations that are more compatible with family responsibilities. Schoolteaching, for instance, follows daily and annual schedules compatible with those of children. Some medical specialties allow greater control of schedules than do others: Choosing dermatology or dentistry could be more compatible with the demands and uncertainties of family life than other health-care careers such as surgery, emergency medicine, or obstetrics. This professional choice matrix evidently applies to highly educated populations and has limited relevance in other contexts.

Beginning in the 1980s, another school associated more with demographers and sociologists than with economists began to put forward the concept of a "Second Demographic Transition." In this view, low and very low fertility rates are a product of powerful value changes embodied in postmodern societies.[18] In the words of one of the founders of this perspective, the basic idea

> is that industrialized countries have indeed reached a new stage in their demographic development. A stage characterized by full control over fertility. And, as couples appear to lack the motivation to have more than one or two children, fertility declined below replacement level. While there may be an element of postponement of births involved in the very low levels of fertility currently observed, signs are that fertility will continue to stay at a level below that required for the replacement of generations. This will result in a new demographic imbalance. . . . The gradually increasing disequilibrium apparently generates a compensatory trend in the third demographic factor of the classical demographic balancing equation: migration.[19]

Van de Kaa has pointed to at least fifteen features of this transition, which he usefully summarized as follows.

1. Decline in TFR due to reduction in fertility at higher ages: decline in higher order birth rates
2. Avoidance of pre-marital pregnancies and 'forced' marriages
3. Notwithstanding that, the mean age at first marriage continues to decline for a while
4. Postponement of childbearing within marriage, fertility among young women declines, lower order birth rates decline, this accentuates decline in period TFR
5. Increase in judicial separation and divorce (when allowed)

6. Postponement of marriage largely replaced by pre-marital cohabitation, increase in age at first marriage
7. Cohabitation becomes more popular, marriage postponed until bride is pregnant, increase in pre-marital births, increase in mean age at first birth
8. Legislation permitting sterilization and abortion further reduce unwanted fertility: fertility at border ages of child-bearing declines further
9. Cohabitation gains further support, is frequently also preferred by the widowed and the divorced
10. Cohabitation increasingly seen as alternative to marriage, extra-marital fertility increases
11. TFR's tend to stabilize at low levels
12. TFR's increase slightly where women who postponed births start their fertility careers; increase of lower order birth rates at higher ages of childbearing
13. Not all postponed births can be born in years of child-bearing remaining
14. 'Voluntary' childlessness becomes increasingly significant
15. Cohort fertility appears to stabilize below replacement level[20]

It is worth noting that the creators of the Second Demographic Transition concept initially saw it as an irresistible and fairly uniform process associated with powerful economic and social changes of all advanced industrial (and "postindustrial") societies. In a metaphor drawn from the overwhelming forces of nature, Van de Kaa argued that the Second Demographic Transition could "be compared to a cyclone irresistibly sweeping south from Scandinavia and gradually engulfing the South of Europe before turning East and, most probably, to other parts of the developed world."[21]

Later, as empirical evidence of much greater diversity of fertility patterns emerged, and as the early declines of fertility to very low rates in Scandinavia reversed and fertility rose to higher levels than anticipated, the framers of the Second Demographic Transition theory responsibly modified the expectations implied by this meteorological metaphor. They noted that differences in history, culture, and economic and social conditions were such that there could be less certainty about just how uniform and predictable fertility declines to low levels would be. But the expectation remained that once such fertility declines did occur, it was likely that low levels of cohort fertility would continue indefinitely.

One of the problems with such bold theoretical arguments is that they rarely have predictive force. Efforts to test the predictive value of these and other theories about low fertility have regrettably not shown great explanatory power. Nor, it seems, have they done well in their common anticipation that the very low ("lowest low") fertility rates recently reported registered would persist over the long term. Goldstein, Sobotka, and Jasilioniene present data on this topic up to 2007, and conclude *tentatively* that the very low fertility rates seen in well over twenty countries in recent years now appear to be rather short-lived and temporary phenomena driven primarily by a pattern of postponement of childbearing among younger cohorts relative to older cohorts. This "cohort-driven 'postponement transition'" leads to a pattern of later births, whatever the total number of births in the younger cohorts. Thus, period and cohort fertility rates diverge. This transition in turn produces a distortion (or "depression") in the annual, or "period," total fertility rate that is misinterpreted to reflect real declines in average family size.[22] Their conclusions are tentative and cautious, noting first that the latest data available are for 2007 and hence do not reflect any effects of the global economic crisis and rising unemployment that ensued. It is still too soon to be sure whether this modification of the Second Demographic Transition argument will stand up to further scrutiny.

In later chapters, we examine some of these arguments and elaborate a sociological variant of them. The sociologist Ulrich Beck has pioneered the study of what he terms the "risk society." He has in mind an alternative to the standard theory of modernization, developed by Max Weber and other sociologists, who held that modern societies are molded by unavoidable forces creating an "iron cage" of bureaucratically controlled polities. Beck sees a flaw in this argument. Educated populations can see through the pretense of rule by "experts" who make decisions on the basis of inadequate knowledge.

When we see that such experts are no better than the rest of us, and sometimes significantly more deluded by their own self-importance, we have the chance to turn against the supposedly inexorable forces governing our lives. We manage risks in many ways, he argues, and one of them is in our strategies of family formation. Changing fertility patterns in some countries may, therefore, be responses to risks that seem to be out of control—environmental risks, political risks, economic risks. In chapter 2, we develop this argument in the European case, but it may have a bearing on the rest of the story we tell in this book.

The reason that this is so is that most theories of fertility decline have been economistic. That is, they deduce from economic conditions aspects of demographic behavior. Beck's "risk hypothesis" makes family formation a function not only of economic indicators but also of social, environmental, and political uncertainties that have not diminished in recent years. It is less a theory than a framework of analysis, which does what this book argues we need to do: put the politics back into the study of globalization in general, and into our understanding of demographic movements in the second wave of globalization in particular.

This is necessary for a host of reasons. One of the most fundamental is that demography is a subject with important political dimensions, in the sense that governments respond to demographic trends in a host of ways. Let us consider some of them.

Government Policies and Their Impacts

As noted earlier, in recent years numerous governments have concluded that the low fertility rates in their countries present difficult challenges to their economic and social systems. The 2005 Green Paper produced by the European Commission highlights such concerns, especially with respect to social protection systems, pension systems, workforce, education, and health care. It describes "three essential priorities" for Europe in these words:

- Return to demographic growth. We must ask two simple questions: What value do we attach to children? Do we want to give families, whatever their structure, their due place in European society? Thanks to the determined implementation of the Lisbon agenda (modernisation of social protection systems, increasing the rate of female employment, and the employment of older workers), innovative measures to support the birth rate and judicious use of immigration, Europe can create new opportunities for investment, consumption and the creation of wealth.
- Ensure a balance between the generations, in the sharing of time throughout life, in the distribution of the benefits of growth, and in that of funding needs stemming from pensions and health-related expenditure.
- Find new bridges between the stages of life. Young people still find it difficult to get into employment. An increasing number of "young retirees" want to participate in social and economic life. Study time is getting longer and young working people want to spend time with their children. These changes alter the frontiers and the bridges between activity and inactivity.[23]

With respect specifically to measures that might increase fertility, the Green Paper notes:

Europeans have a fertility rate which is insufficient to replace the population. Surveys have revealed the gap which exists between the number of children Europeans would like (2.3) and the number that they actually have (1.5). This means that, if appropriate mechanisms existed to allow couples to have the number of children they want, the fertility rate could rise overall, even though the desired family size varies considerably from one Member State to another.

The low fertility rate is the result of obstacles to private choices: late access to employment, job instability, expensive housing and lack of incentives (family benefits, parental leave, child care, equal pay). Incentives of this kind can have a positive impact on the birth rate and increase employment, especially female employment, as certain countries have shown. . . .[24]

And indeed a substantial number of low-fertility countries have adopted direct or indirect, or explicit or implicit, policy measures intended to increase fertility. The various theories about the sources of low fertility, outlined briefly earlier, offer some insights into the feasibility of policy interventions to increase low fertility rates. For those adhering to the perspectives of neoclassical economics, conclusions about policy matters generally follow from the key assumptions. If, as assumed, individuals and couples are rationally balancing the costs of an additional child against the benefits, it would follow that reductions in the cost of children would have the same quantity-enhancing effects as rising income. Hence, both direct public expenditures to subsidize the otherwise-private costs of childrearing (crèches, child care, preferential access to subsidized housing, child health care), and transfer payments that would increase their income (child allowances, birth bonuses) would be expected to increase at the margin that prospective parents' demand for children.[25]

With respect to those who emphasize the fertility-reducing impact of conflicts between parental employment with the demands of childrearing, the preferred policy levers naturally tend to focus on measures to minimize these conflicts, for example, via mandating that employers provide parental and/or emergency leave for family responsibilities, extended vacation/holidays compatible with children, full-day kindergarten and after-school programs provided by public schools, and so on. While such measures may neither increase parental income nor reduce the costs of childrearing, they might reduce the conflicts between work and family responsibilities.

Those adhering to the Second Demographic Transition interpretation tend to be more skeptical as to whether governmental policies such as subsidies or transfer payments surrounding childbearing and childrearing could have much impact on increasing low fertility rates. They see low fertility rates as a consequence of fundamental changes in values that are driven by postmodern social and economic trends. These forces are so powerful as to defy countermeasures based on government subsidies and transfer payments. Proponents also have tended to argue in favor of government policies to increase immigration, in the belief that the government cannot do much about native-born fertility rates and that increased levels of immigration will be needed to compensate for what they anticipate to be permanently low levels of fertility.[26]

Again, careful assessments of a wide range of policies recently adopted by governments to raise fertility have not yielded consistent outcomes. The most recent summary by researchers at two prominent European research groups concluded as follows: "Our tentative findings suggest that (i) there are instances where policies seem to be plausibly related to the rise in fertility (Estonia in 2004 and Russia in 2007); (ii) there are cases where fertility gains appeared in the absence of any major policy changes (Spain before 2007, Russia in 2000–2004), or where policies were instituted after the rise in fertility started and thus have no obvious role in facilitating it (Czech Republic); and (iii) there were policies which do not seem to have any discernable influence on fertility (Singapore and, until recently, Japan)."[27]

Two elements of recent economic and demographic experience have tended to receive insufficient attention in many discussions of governmental interventions intended to increase very low fertility rates. Both involve precisely the demographic groups that almost universally produce the bulk of a society's births: young adults. The first relates to employment, unemployment, and underemployment. In many of the countries experiencing very low fertility, the levels of unemployment and unstable employment among young adults of reproductive age (say, twenty to thirty-four) are strikingly high, far higher than for the older cohorts that are less likely to be bearing children. The Green Paper reports that the 2004 EU unemployment rate for those under twenty-five was 17.9 percent, compared with 7.7 percent for those twenty-five or over. Those under twenty-five were, unsurprisingly, also at higher risk of poverty.[28]

The second element is the reality that the real cost of housing, normally required for the establishment of a new nuclear family, has been rising over the past few decades in most industrialized countries. In some cases (for example, Spain, UK, US, Ireland) these increases have been so rapid as to have produced housing "bubbles" that recently have been punctured, initiated by the meltdown of speculative "subprime" mortgages in the United States, leading to subsequent instabilities in global financial markets. During periods of rapid real increases in housing prices, older cohorts that are owners or statutory tenants of housing have been relatively protected from the consequences, whereas many younger cohorts approaching the ages of independence have found themselves priced out of the housing market. In addition to prices, the availability of affordable mortgage lending varies substantially across industrialized countries, with more ready access in the United Kingdom and the United States and much less access in, for example, Italy.

If one were asked how to design a government policy to encourage its young adults to postpone marriage and childbearing, two effective recommendations would be to (a) raise the levels of unemployment and employment instability of entry-level workers in their twenties, and (b) inflate the real cost of housing and housing finance, with special impacts on young adults not already in owned or rented housing. Of course no government has deliberately pursued such policies, but the realities that have emerged are exactly those.

Dissensus on Migration as a Counterforce to Low Fertility

As noted earlier, the European Commission has encouraged expansion of immigration as one of several recommendations designed to "return to demographic growth."[29] However, there is little consensus about this strategy, which touches sensitive issues of national identity at a time of global insecurity. Immigration is an intrinsically divisive question in most countries, in part because it is so intensely political. Hence, seeing immigration as a way to compensate for fertility decline is to invite an explosive political and social reaction. And yet the two subjects—immigration and low fertility—are impossible to ignore in many parts of the world. We will return to this matter later.

In addition, the effectiveness of any policy decisions—their capacity to change behavior—often is limited. The demographic realities are fairly clear: Increased immigration can indeed increase the rate of demographic growth. Yet increasing immigration is not a powerful tool for addressing the demographic "aging" effects of low fertility. Moreover, substantial migration to countries or regions with low or very low fertility can have very large effects on demographic size and composition while also having negative effects in particular upon the employment and housing prospects of young adults in the prime ages of childbearing potential. Hence, such approaches may have unanticipated negative feedback effects while at the same time presenting serious political costs for governments that pursue them.

These realities were well illustrated by a 2000 report by the United Nations Population Division entitled *Replacement Migration: Is It a Solution to Declining and Ageing Populations?*[30] The report produced hypothetical scenarios for several low-fertility countries, projected to the year 2050, calculating the number of immigrants that would be required to

- Prevent a decline in the total population size;
- Hold constant the size of the population between ages fifteen and sixty-five;
- Hold constant the ratio of working age to "dependent" population (defined respectively as fifteen to sixty-four and over sixty-five);
- Hold constant the "old age dependency ratio" (defined as persons over sixty-five to those between fifteen and sixty-four).

The core conclusion of the UN report was straightforward: Countries with very low fertility rates are unlikely to be able to use immigration policy as a tool to halt demographic aging. Such a policy ". . . seems out of reach because of the extraordinarily large numbers of migrants that would be required."[31]

In the case of Germany, the scenario projection for a constant ratio of working age to "dependent" population implied the admission of 188 million immigrants by 2050; these hypothetical immigrants and their heirs would then account for some 80 percent of the population of Germany. For Italy, the comparable numbers under this scenario would be 120 million immigrants, accounting for 79 percent of the projected

2050 population of Italy. For the EU as a whole, the scenario would require 700 million immigrants by 2050, who would in that year account for 75 percent of the EU population. For Japan, the same scenario implies 553 million immigrants by 2050, accounting for 87 percent of the 2050 population in Japan.[32]

The negative political reactions to this report were not only predictable, they also showed how rapidly discussions of demography trigger the expression of anxieties related to national identity and to fears of the future of indigenous populations living alongside already large immigrant communities. If more immigrants arrive, some say, what will be left of our country? The fact that such fears are almost always exaggerated does not diminish their force.

Much of the reaction to the 2000 report was due to obvious misinterpretation by the press and politicians, who seemed to read the report's numerical findings as UN recommendations for increased immigrant admissions, rather than as outputs of hypothetical scenarios that demonstrated the insufficiency of an acceptable immigration policy to meet the specifications of the scenarios. *Le Monde*'s coverage of the report even changed its interrogative English subtitle (*Replacement Migration: Is It a Solution to Declining and Ageing Populations?*) into a declarative statement in French ("*Replacement Migration: A Solution to Declining and Ageing Populations*"[33]). Alarmist press coverage spread across Europe, in Germany, Belgium, Netherlands, and elsewhere. *Le Figaro* headlined its story "The Report that Alarmed Europe."[34] The French minister of the interior Jean-Pierre Chevènement forcefully criticized the report, and the European Union's representative to the United Nations complained that its publication should not have been allowed without prior permission from member governments, although UN Secretariat reports have never required such permission.[35]

Beyond Hyperbole: What Are the Links between Fertility and Migration?

Once we move beyond the polemics, it is possible to identify a number of elements that we need to understand in order to appreciate the national and regional narratives we describe later in this book.

First, the high or rising fertility rates and declining rates of infant and child mortality of the immediate postwar period led to increasing rates of demographic growth around the world, along with a shift in age compositions toward higher proportions in younger age groups. Both rising growth rates and young age structures were especially pronounced in many parts of the developing world, where fertility was generally much higher to begin with and in which there were parallel rapid declines in previously high rates of infant and child mortality.

Second, high fertility rates began to decline in the 1960s but with great variation across countries and regions. Those countries in which fertility declines were rapid registered shifts toward higher average ages, whereas those in which fertility declines lagged experienced continuing high and sometimes rising proportions of children and youth in their age structures. Migrants, and especially international migrants, were disproportionately young adults, most commonly in their twenties. Rapid growth in the size of a country's population of young children led, with a delay of about two decades, to similarly rapid growth in the age groups with highest likelihood of migrating. Countries with sustained high fertility and declining mortality rates in the 1970s and 1980s therefore saw rapid expansion of their young adult populations in the 1990s and after. Those in which high fertility continued into the 1990s and beyond would see similar expansion of their young adult populations prospectively into the 2010s and 2020s.

Third, the global economy over this period was marked by rising economic differentials between the wealthy industrialized countries and much of the developing world, with this generalization complicated by the wealth of the oil-exporting countries and the rapid economic advance of the largest single developing country, China.

Hence, trends in both demography and in economic differentials tended toward increases in the potential favoring international migration. "Potential" of course does not mean "actual." The volumes and directions of actual international migration are affected by many other elements, including especially the policies adopted by governments in countries of migrant destination.

Fourth, many of the barriers that historically had restrained international migration to levels well below its potential began to erode.

Widening access, both physical and financial, to high-speed, long-distance transportation expanded with the growth and declining real cost of air travel. Information about the attractions of high-wage countries reached even remote villages via television, radio, films, and satellite communication. A powerful disincentive to long-range international migration—long-term separation from family and kin—faded through rapidly expanding means of cheap and easy international communication.

A number of nodal migration points emerged: Mexico and the Caribbean to the United States; the Maghreb to southern Europe and on to central and northern Europe; South Asia to the United Kingdom and the Middle East; East Asia to the United States, Canada, Australia, and Europe. As has long been the case, the patterns of migration were guided by a complex of elements: economics, history, language and culture, physical contiguity, air transportation routes, military connections, earlier migrations, networks of migration intermediaries, and so on. No single or simple migration model emerged: Migration patterns were as diverse as might be expected on the basis of human behavior, connections, and history.

Thus, we are confronted by two substantial demographic realities, each of which is not explicable in terms of one single theory or approach. Both fertility decline and migration are phenomena imbedded in the social, cultural, political, and economic predicaments and difficulties faced by hundreds of millions of men and women. To understand them, both separately and as phenomena bound together in time and place, we need to adopt an ecumenical approach. With that in mind, we offer a few thoughts on some parts of the political implications of these demographic events.

The Transformation of Strategic Demography

In previous writings we coined the concept of "strategic demography," primarily in reference to the standard strategic view before the development of nuclear weapons that the size of a country's or empire's population, and hence the potential size of its armies, carried great significance for its power relative to other contenders.[36] In the era of massed armies charging one another's positions, the raw number of "boots on the ground" really did matter, especially if political elites were prepared to incur mass casualties, such as those in the stalemated trench warfare of World War I or the German invasion of Russia in World War II.

As the technology of warfare changed during World War II, and as decolonization struggles produced the "irregular" warfare modes of Southeast Asia and elsewhere in the 1960s, the crude size of a country's population and army began to matter less in strategic terms than ever before. This is not to say that there now is no strategic significance to the fact that countries such as China and India have populations of more than a billion while their neighbors are far less populous. It does mean, though, that nuclear weapons, effective air power, and other changes in the way war is waged have changed the significance of population size in equations of power.

The period from 1985 to the present has also been one of genuinely radical transformation of the postwar political and strategic system. The most dramatic shift was the collapse of the Soviet Union and the Warsaw Pact around 1990 and the resulting end of the Cold War. This had obvious and major implications for strategy, including the expansion of the North Atlantic Treaty Organization (NATO) to former Warsaw Pact countries.

In 1985 the European Union was still in its infancy. Now the original EU fifteen have expanded to twenty-seven member states, and the Maastricht Treaty and Schengen Agreement (along with the unratified Lisbon Treaty of 2007) have brought a possible confederation into focus, even as the problems experienced by the euro posed new challenges. What is to come is anybody's guess, but it is clear enough that the nation-states of Europe have been reconfigured. In part this is due to strengthening economic ties, in part due to the growing importance of a human rights culture. Both have made the boundaries of the nation-state more porous and have made policy issues, including immigration, matters of mutual legal and political action.

There was a further reconfiguration that followed: a "decentering" of war and strategic preparations. War was reconfigured, as the focus gradually shifted from state-to-state conflict toward civil wars, such as those in the former Yugoslavia or Colombia or Afghanistan or Somalia, or to transnational conflicts such as those involving Al-Qaeda. As warfare become decentered, the time-honored close relationship between a state's power and the population that it commands no longer appeared evident.

Later there was a further shift from state participants in war toward nonstate warrior networks, as the mass attacks in New York, Washington, Madrid, London, and in numerous cities in Pakistan demonstrate. These militant networks claim to be engaging in a new kind of warfare. Some of these nonstate warrior networks exploit new technologies to achieve broad and even global reach, far beyond what any comparable nonstate actors could have done only a decade or two earlier. They deploy rapid and hard-to-monitor communications and public relations via the Internet and satellite communication systems; they profit from ease of movement for operatives via increasingly accessible international air travel and from the technology available for the rapid transfer of financial resources via globalized banking and electronic transfer systems associated with economic globalization.

It must be recognized too that nonstate warrior networks have made effective use of increasing access to international migration as a strategic instrument of power. This includes the use of both legal and illegal migrations of network operatives to world regions they have identified as "enemies" that warrant violent attack. In addition, some networks (the Liberation Tigers of Tamil Eelam [Tamil Tigers] in Sri Lanka, the Palestine Liberation Organization, Al-Qaeda, and the Irish Republican Army) successfully used easy access to coethnic and/or coreligious supporters located around the world as sources for financial and material support. Finally, radical Islamic groups have taken advantage of legal visas and refugee policies to work with clerics who have migrated to Western countries, such as the United Kingdom. Some clerics have encouraged support for violent action by native-born and mostly young men who share their ethnic, national, and/or religious perspectives.

One way of understanding the origins and contours of Al-Qaeda and other groups is to see them as part of complex of multiple civil wars underway within Islam. These conflicts are being waged both between conservative Muslim states and radical minorities of Shia and Sunni Islamists, and also within and among states in the Middle East.

Now these conflicts have spilled over into the West; to central, South, and Southeast Asia; to Africa; and even to China. Strategic demography has expanded its reach from conflicts among states and perhaps among ethnic/religious groups within states, to include active debate about religious sects and movements, international migration, and global "terrorism." Indeed, the whole subject of immigration policy has come to be configured by the problem of security, understood differently in the West after 9/11.

The issues involved here have been, but should not be, exaggerated. Of the hundreds of millions of international migrants and travelers, only truly tiny factions are involved in any way in such activities. Still, it does not take large numbers to bomb commuter trains (as in Madrid and London) or attack unarmed civilians with grenades and assault rifles (as in Mumbai). It is evident that globalization has contributed to some unforeseen strategic outcomes. The expansion of international movement and communication related to the globalization of trade and investment has placed new and deadly tools in the hands of relatively small radical groups engaged in a long-term war against those they see as destroying (at least their version of) Islam, a global religion with perhaps one billion adherents. Globalization has hidden by-products, ones that inject into discussions of immigration some of the toxic language of populations that see themselves as under siege.

A quite different use of international migration as a means of asymmetric statecraft can be found in what Greenhill terms "coercive engineered migration (or migration-driven coercion)"[37]—an unconventional and nonmilitary form of coercion in which weak states and nonstate actors have repeatedly deployed the threat or reality of coerced out-migration to achieve political goals with strong states that would otherwise be unobtainable. The most common targets of such actions are liberal democracies, with their declared commitments to international human rights and their active array of domestic interest groups. Together these can be exploited to exact embarrassing "hypocrisy costs" upon any government that responds to such coerced out-migration with coercive regulation of entry. They are not alone. Even authoritarian states such as China have proved to be vulnerable to threats from North Korea of this kind: If China fails to continue to sustain the Kim regime the result would be uncontrollable flows of millions of desperate people across the common border. Greenhill identifies and analyzes more than fifty attempts at such coerced engineered migration since 1951, the year in which the United Nations Convention relating to the Status of Refugees was approved.[38] Her analysis concludes that well over half of these asymmetric initiatives succeeded in achieving at least some of their political goals.[39]

Beyond the use of international migration by nonstate warrior networks and by weak states, the high strategic importance that now attaches to technology adds yet another aspect of discussion to the implications of alternative immigration policies. It has become common for Western governments to create or expand visas tailored to highly skilled migrants, both temporary and permanent. In part this is in response to pressure from high-tech employers, in part from a belief that the road to prosperity lies in capturing and holding "the best and the brightest" of scientists and engineers from around the world—a view that some have termed "human capital mercantilism." At the urging of university leaders, related policies have been implemented to encourage admission of foreign students, many of whom seek graduate education in computer, information-technology (IT), and scientific and related fields.

From a strategic perspective, what is particularly interesting about these phenomena is that in some cases large numbers of such students and migrants come from source countries such as China, a key strategic competitor with the American or European states. The relationship between the United States and China is clearly complex. There are very large flows of trade and investment, coupled with very large US trade deficits that many attribute to currency manipulation by China. At the same time, current US trade policies receive domestic US political support from multinational firms whose profits benefit from easy access to both low-cost labor and growing markets in China. There is a somewhat murky and mixed collaboration between the United States and China with respect to strategic concerns about North Korea's nuclear weapon development. There is disagreement about human rights in China and Tibet; there are allegations of espionage activities by agents of China in the United States and vice versa; and there are active efforts to improve cultural and educational exchanges between the two countries.

Such links raise concerns among some in Western intelligence agencies about the large numbers of Chinese nationals who study and work in the United States and other Western countries, and especially in areas of science and technology relevant to strategic questions.

All we are suggesting here is that immigration is a volatile element in political and strategic thinking, one that has a very different meaning from that associated with mass immigration before the First World War. Here again, demographers ignore politics at their peril.

Continuities and Discontinuities

There are both continuities and discontinuities with the past that characterize the current waves of both globalization and migration. The most palpable discontinuity is the very rapidity of recent change itself, both within and among human societies—economic, technological, geopolitical, and demographic. The pace has been breathtaking: if not "unprecedented" throughout the whole of human history, certainly as rapid as any change that has been seen for at least a century.

A second discontinuity relates to the clarity versus the blurring of national boundaries. First, since the 1900s at least, there has been a slow but apparently relentless set of changes in the role of the sovereign state vis-à-vis transnational and nonstate actors in economic life. The transnational examples are highly visible: Perhaps the most dynamic is the so-called "multinational firm," a category that has been one of the most powerful forces driving economic globalization—"driving" both in terms of market penetration for their products and their activist role in pushing the globalization agenda politically. Increasingly such firms have become detached from their original or "national" homes. Over time it becomes less and less clear what is meant by a "multinational" firm described as "American" or "Swiss" or "British" or "Dutch": Does the firm's ascribed nationality relate to its country of incorporation? The location of its global headquarters? The location of the largest number of its employees? The largest market for its products? The country of citizenship or residence of a majority of its shareholders or lenders?

Second, what we now term "nongovernmental organizations" (NGOs) have grown exponentially. There now are literally thousands of NGOs. Most are local and bounded within a single country, but there are large multinational NGOs too, and increasingly these operate in a manner that is decoupled from the country in which they first emerged. NGOs are nonprofit organizations working to advance certain political or humanitarian agendas. Third, there are criminal networks operating in a global environment. They profit in part from modern communication and transportation technologies. Prominent examples are transnational criminal networks such as the triads based in Taiwan and China, and drug cartels originating in Columbia and Mexico but with links in many different countries. The world market in heroin and other drugs is so large that cartels can bribe senior government officials to cooperate with them, while also purchasing weaponry powerful enough to intimidate or defy national armies, as in Colombia and Mexico.

These facets of second-wave globalization separate it from the late-nineteenth-century first wave. There are some overlaps, to be sure. The Mafia was transnational before the First World War, just as are its counterparts today. But the second wave of globalization has had a different political character from the first because the boundaries of the nation state—economic as much as demographic—are increasingly porous.

In this, the second wave of globalization, there are many people who are worried about the fact that states have great difficulty controlling entry into their territories. But there are others who rejoice in that fact. Some argue, often based on religious ideas or a transcendent commitment to human rights, that relatively prosperous states have moral and hence international legal obligations to admit non-nationals who are in search of work not available in their homelands. Consider, for example, the five principles promulgated in "Strangers No Longer: Together on the Journey of Hope," a joint pastoral letter concerning migration issued in 2003 by the Catholic bishops of Mexico and the United States. The authors of this document claim that they were following "the rich tradition of church teachings with regard to migration." They asserted that five principles emerged from such teachings, which guide the Roman Catholic Church's view on migration issues. These principles are:

I. Persons have the right to find opportunities in their homeland.

    34. All persons have the right to find in their own countries the economic, political, and social opportunities to live in dignity and achieve a full life through the use of their God-given gifts. In this context, work that provides a just, living wage is a basic human need.

II. Persons have the right to migrate to support themselves and their families.

    35. The Church recognizes that all the goods of the earth belong to all people. When persons cannot find employment in their country of origin to support themselves and their families, they have a right to find work elsewhere in order to survive. Sovereign nations should provide ways to accommodate this right.

III. Sovereign nations have the right to control their borders.

    36. The Church recognizes the right of sovereign nations to control their territories but rejects such control when it is exerted merely for the purpose of acquiring additional wealth. More powerful economic nations, which have the ability to protect and feed their residents, have a stronger obligation to accommodate migration flows.

IV. Refugees and asylum seekers should be afforded protection.

    37. Those who flee wars and persecution should be protected by the global community. This requires, at a minimum, that migrants have a right to claim refugee status without incarceration and to have their claims fully considered by a competent authority.

V. The human dignity and human rights of undocumented migrants should be respected.

38. Regardless of their legal status, migrants, like all persons, possess inherent human dignity that should be respected. Often they are subject to punitive laws and harsh treatment from enforcement officers from both receiving and transit countries. Government policies that respect the basic human rights of the undocumented are necessary.

39. The Church recognizes the right of a sovereign state to control its borders in furtherance of the common good. It also recognizes the right of human persons to migrate so that they can realize their God-given rights. These teachings complement each other. While the sovereign state may impose reasonable limits on immigration, the common good is not served when the basic human rights of the individual are violated. In the current condition of the world, in which global poverty and persecution are rampant, the presumption is that persons must migrate in order to support and protect themselves and that nations who are able to receive them should do so whenever possible. It is through this lens that we assess the current migration reality between the United States and Mexico.[40]

There are other religion-based challenges to the global system of sovereign states, the most visible of which in recent years has been those calling for a restoration of the Islamic "caliphate" established by the companions of Muhammad after his death in 632. By the eighth century, the caliphate had risen to a dominant position in regions stretching across three continents, including much of what is now Spain, North Africa, the Middle East, Iran, Afghanistan, and Pakistan. A new twenty-first-century caliphate, as described by its proponents, would similarly eliminate the national boundaries that currently divide and weaken the world's Muslims. Some elements of Al-Qaeda and related organizations make similar claims. Geographically, such a caliphate would reach from Morocco in the west to Indonesia in the east of the Muslim world. It would include a population of more than 1.5 billion people.

The most visible proponents of the new caliphate, such as those associated with Al-Qaeda, deploy violence as their means to reach this goal. Others, such as Hizb ut-Tahrir (the "Party of Liberation") allegedly pursue political action toward the same goals. According to one scholar of Hizb ut-Tahrir:

> The group that most effectively employs Islam to achieve political ends is Hizb-ut Tahrir, a transnational political party founded by a Palestinian in 1952. It seeks to reestablish the caliphate, or Islamic rule, throughout the world. Like other Islamist movements, its goal is to overthrow secular Islamic governments around the world. They promote an "Islamic way of life" to bring justice and order to a chaotic world.
>
> H. T. members are engaged in open propaganda to build tension between people and their governments. They work to delegitimize governments and gradually turn people against the regimes and the security forces. When a critical mass is created outside the government, and a sufficient number of people in key positions in the military and police are on their side, the regime is peacefully overthrown.[41]

Whether or not this interpretation is credible, it ignores the fact that there are many reasons other than propaganda why such Muslim groups may attract support in corrupt and inefficient states. But what matters is not the accuracy of the assessment; what matters is the transnational character of the effort it describes, one that clearly separates our period from the first wave of globalization before the First World War.

What the two waves of globalization do share, though, is an enduring tendency for commentators on political and cultural issues to insist upon an intrinsic link between population and power. Such pronouncements relate to the destiny and future of states, but many also dwell on what their authors perceive as the threat to the continuing existence of religious, ethnic, linguistic, and other collectives through population decline defined in a variety of ways. In 1985, we surveyed such anxious formulations, and twenty-five years later we hear amplified echoes of them, but in a different global context.

In general, such rhetoric takes for granted that the extent to which power can be exercised by a given collective with its own "identity" depends on the size of its population. Hence, even as the boundaries among such identities shift, reassort, and become fuzzy, it is common to see concern expressed, sometimes in excessive ways, about any tendency of the "others" (whoever they may be) to outnumber "us." These persistent and sometimes visceral collective anxieties carry with them nightmares of demographic disappearance or displacement that we have seen before. In this context, the language of fear changes less rapidly than do the institutions and phenomena that the fearful perceive. Both waves of globalization triggered worry about anxious futures, and no one wishing to be informed about population matters can afford to ignore them.

Population Studies: Past, Present, Future

This is especially true for those who make it their business to study population questions. Only twenty-five years ago, low fertility was a sideline among those engaged professionally in the study of population. Instead, most focused upon excessively high fertility as an impediment to economic development. International migration too was a minority taste, often simply ignored by population researchers as too messy analytically to address, and at the same time a minor factor in demographic change.

Now, as we enter the second decade of the twenty-first century, it is no exaggeration to say that the postwar generation of population studies came to an end somewhere in the 1980s, although understandably few of those involved recognized what was happening at the time. Now, low fertility has become a near obsession among political elites in parts of the world, especially in Europe and parts of Asia. This is attention at the highest level to policy formulation designed both to adapt to the powerful demographic changes that are underway and to search for effective tools to nudge low and "lowest low" fertility rates up toward the replacement level. This subject is the focus of a number of the chapters in this book.

International migration now is understood as a major force in demographic change. Analytically messy it may well be, but it can no longer be ignored. Fertility and mortality measurements have been formalized for generations. Measuring migration is much more difficult and entails a wider degree of uncertainty than measuring any other demographic variable. It is impossible to provide formal demographic models about migration in the same way as demographers have done for decades with respect to life expectancy or fertility. What cannot be measured, or modeled mathematically, is no less significant than what can be measured or modeled. As long as we understand what assumptions are made in demographic studies of migration, we can learn much from them. But in this field, certainty is beyond us.

Debates about population matters continue, as they have for more than two centuries, to excite fundamental moral and ideological arguments. Issues such as abortion and gay marriage roil the politics of many states. Disagreements about the status of women resonate internationally, complicated by significant differences in women's life trajectories among the world's diverse cultures and religions.

Unlike in the period before the First World War, human rights are now a major realm of discourse; indeed, the second wave of globalization has seen an exponential expansion of the number of organizations dedicated to making human rights a reality. Claims to the exercise of such rights are invoked in active debates in the United States and elsewhere about immigration, abortion, ethnic identities, gay marriage, and other demographically connected topics, but they also apply to resistance to forced sterilization and other coercive family policies in India and China, as we shall see. In many cases these assertions of global rights collide with claims related to national sovereignty.

In the face of such turmoil, controversy, and uncertainty, it may be risky to offer a few modest predictions. These are limited and qualified in character. Some current trends are likely to continue. Recent and spreading trends toward low and "lowest low" fertility rates may now be reversing, with sometimes substantial increases appearing. Even so, it seems very unlikely that countries that have experienced very low fertility rates will soon be at or near replacement levels. Low fertility rates in some countries may rise, but we should expect further declines in others—especially in those coming most recently to low-fertility regimes of family formation.

As the lagged effects of decades of low fertility accumulate, we should not be surprised to see expressions of rising alarm among political elites and broader publics. Policy measures aimed at stimulating fertility increases are likely, though going by past experience, such policies are more likely to fail than to succeed.

We should also expect excessive rhetoric, scaremongering, and distortion, either intentional or based upon misunderstanding and confusion. The debate over the demographic future of different nations and regions will continue, and it is likely to generate more heat than light. That discussion mixes economic, political, and moral issues and language together into a highly inflammatory mixture. To prevent such disputes from turning violent is in the interest of most of us. One way to do so is to engage in sustained study of the underlying demographic phenomena about which so many people argue passionately. We cannot pretend that such phenomena are independent of the language people use to describe them, but we can be vigilant about the perennial distortion and exaggeration characterizing such debates.

Here the two waves of globalization are remarkably similar. Both provide abundant evidence of the way population and politics are bound together in an inextricable embrace. If we succeed in showing how this is so, and how it happens in a number of countries around the world, then we have realized one of our aims. Our basic premise, after all, is that demography is much too important a subject to be left to the demographers and economists alone. It is everybody's business.

European Population

Interpretations and Anxieties

The "Risk Society" and Low Fertility in Europe

We have already noted briefly what the German sociologist Ulrich Beck has termed the "risk society." Beck has pioneered an approach to the "risk society" as a way to go beyond outmoded ideas about social development in advanced industrial countries. Beck rejects both the Marxist model that capitalism is doomed to collapse and ideas associated with Max Weber about the onward relentless advance of the "iron cage" of the bureaucratic state and technology-driven production. In their place, Beck proposes a different, more open-ended set of ideas about the setting in which fertility decline to unprecedented low levels has occurred. What he offers is a sociological framework in which to set the Second Demographic Transition, while departing from some of the claims made by others about that transition.

Here in a nutshell is Beck's theory. His understanding of the past generation is captured by what he terms "reflexive modernization." By this phrase he means that modernization is not a linear phenomenon but instead one that turns in on itself in the sense that it creates unintended consequences and opens up opportunities for new forms of social life in contemporary society. These developments entail the transformation of norms and social institutions and, in particular, the transformation of family structures and sexual life. We live, he believes, in what Anthony Giddens terms a "run-away world," one in which older patterns of controlling risk—political, environmental, familial, personal—have broken down. Increased knowledge inherent in modernization leads not to greater mastery of the material world but to the sense that we face unacceptable and unpredictable risks, the ramifications of which can be substantial. We have some degree of control over those responsible for such consequences, but only after the fact. Maximizing protection against risks now is done in untraditional ways.

Beck's position rests on three premises. The first relates to increased knowledge: "The more modern a society becomes, the more knowledge it creates about its foundations, structures, dynamics and conflicts." This knowledge is what makes the process "reflexive," or filled with reflections on how to cope with the world in which we live.[1] Second, the more knowledge we have, "the more emphatically a traditionally defined constellation of action within structures is broken up" and replaced by new social forms and institutions. Third, "Knowledge forces decisions and opens up contexts for action. Individuals are released from structures, and they must redefine their context of action under conditions of insecurity" built into the process of modernization itself. We "reflect" on our modern predicament and take steps to avoid risks in our daily lives, in our families, in our work environments, and in our other social and political associations.

Beck is emphatically not a "postmodernist" critic of "modernist" notions of science and objectivity. To the contrary, Beck argues that real material crises produce real shifts in social behavior. What he offers is a dialectical approach to modernization, as a process that generates its own successes and failures. Perhaps we can put his outlook in terms of what the literary critic Svetlana Boym terms "off-modern";[2] Beck's work forces us to be alert to departures from traditional forms of coping with the risks of everyday life.

It should be evident, therefore, that for Beck and his followers modernization is not a relentless march into a technologically determined future. It is a process that produces unintended consequences and thereby departs from a closed system. The space for individual and group adaptation is greater than in orthodox Marxist or Weberian models of modernization, in which the relentless drive of capital accumulation and exploitation or the "iron cage" of bureaucracy crushes individual initiative or experimentation, however well-intentioned they may be. Beck argues that when disasters or upheavals occur today, as they do with erratic frequency, the "experts" in charge of modern systems are shown to be emperors without any clothes. And such disasters can be system failures that, though very improbable statistically, produce damage of a very significant kind when they do occur. As but three instances of such events, consider the 1986 Chernobyl nuclear disaster, or the 2010 deep-sea oil-well explosion in the Gulf of Mexico, or the 2011 meltdown of three nuclear reactors at the Fukushima Daiichi Nuclear Power Plant following the Great Eastern Japan Earthquake and tsunami. In all three, against all the odds, everything broke down—in multiple nuclear power plants and in an underwater oil field.

A parallel to economic thought may help elucidate Beck's argument. He develops a line similar to that at the heart of John Maynard Keynes's rethinking of neoclassical economics. Keynes distinguished between probability and uncertainty. The first was a statistical matter, in which the boundaries of plausible outcomes, given certain assumptions, were calculable. The second was much more disorienting: What do people do when they cannot predict the outcome of their actions? They engage in minimizing the risk associated with uncertainty.

Beck is supported by Anthony Giddens, a British sociologist, in this approach to uncertainty, especially with regard to contemporary family life. Herewith Giddens:

> Consider marriage and family, for example. Up to even a generation ago, marriage was structured by established traditions. When people got married, they knew, as it were, what they were doing. Marriage was formed to a large degree in terms of traditional expectations of gender, sexuality and so forth. Now it is a much more open system with new forms of risk. Everyone who gets married is conscious of the fact that divorce rates are high, that women demand greater equality than in the past. The very decision to get married is constitutively different from before. There has never been a

high-divorce, high-marriage society before. No one knows,
for example, what its consequences are for the future of the
family or for the health of children.[3]

Clearly this is an argument that applies to Western society but has less
purchase in an understanding of Latin America, Africa, and Asia. Yet
when we search for a framework within which to set fertility patterns in
Europe, Beck's theory of the "risk society" has some force.

To Beck, contraception and the emergence as an enduring norm
of one child or childless families are strategies of risk aversion. So is
cohabitation outside of marriage. Families in large parts of Europe are
no longer defined by marriage, which is more unstable than ever before.
Divorce is no longer exceptional, and everyone who marries knows it.
But when a couple, married or not, has children, the consequences of
breakup and the risks associated with it, especially for women and children, grow exponentially. Childbearing changes the stakes of domestic
partnership and the claims it makes on the time and resources, including emotional resources, of both partners.

From this point of view, very low fertility or childlessness is a pathway to freedom, not defined by an infinity of choices but as a strategy of
risk aversion. This is why Beck and Giddens believe that family life today
is different from that in the past. Giddens's claim is that we are in a state
of posttraditional trust, by which he means that in the past marital bonds
were supported by theological and legal provisions, provisions that have
atrophied over time. Older assumptions about the family serving, in
the words of Christopher Lasch, as a "haven in a heartless world,"[4] no
longer function. Hence cohabiting couples can dissolve their relationship whenever they choose, and so can married couples, although they
might do so less precipitously than cohabiting couples. If marriage is
unstable, so are family constellations in which grandparents and other
relatives can proliferate in recombined families. Alongside an absence
of consensus on religious values, on status or gender hierarchies, we
are at a time of uncertain gender roles and unstable male and female
identities.[5]

Both Beck and Giddens believe we live in an age of unintended
consequences, meaning disasters imbedded in the very expansion of

manufacturing and extractive industry, and now of information technology and "expertise," which are supposed to be governed by reason and science but in fact are so accident-prone that we cannot predict when the next economic, political, or climatic disaster will come. Today most people continue to be exposed to perturbations beyond their control, events that may entail disastrous results.

Beck departs from Giddens in emphasizing the chaotic nature of contemporary life. While the public face of industry and politics is that of control and order, the realities are otherwise. Everyone knows, he believes, that we are subject to the unintended consequences of processes in motion long before we were born. Early industrialization created many of its own environmental disasters. Economic development moved into a global phase, with origins in the late nineteenth century, but which accelerated in the later twentieth century. The political forms that emerged in the twentieth century were more unstable than contemporaries believed, and several times degenerated into agents of genocide. The implosion of Communism took most "experts"—in the West and East alike—by surprise. In this and many other cases, experts have been shown to be as much in the dark as we are. Hence the notion that we control our lives is less true than assumed by those who believe science, technology, or modernization are self-contained or self-correcting systems. Even though the material necessities we in the West need and use are more widely distributed than ever before, most Westerners understand that the world actually is a highly unpredictable place. We live in a "risk society."

This "risk society" faces uncertainties that are central to the process of modernization itself. The modern world's disasters are not all traditional, like cholera, famine, harvest failure due to drought, or inundation due to tropical storms. Peasants lacking "knowledge" would blame such miseries on the natural order of things or on the gods. We cannot do so, since we are the authors of the system, one of whose essential purposes is to escape from periodic encounters with unmastered climatic or material forces. Our expectations therefore are different from peasants', and when they are not met, they leave us perplexed in ways different from those who suffer from plagues beyond their control. African peasants know that disaster is always nearby. We know more, but not enough to tell us when disasters will arrive. Moreover, when disaster comes, our media amplifies it. When the media broadcasts disasters to the four corners of the globe, it turns anxiety into a contagious disease of relatively well-off populations.

This sense of disillusionment with our horizon of expectations as citizens of "modern" societies is at the heart of Beck's claim that we are living in a "risk society." With more perceived uncertainty surrounding us, the best way to manage risks is to minimize the ones we know. And two of those risks, especially for women, are marriage and childbearing. The following hypothesis, central to the argument of this book, follows from this argument: Childlessness or low fertility is a European response to the volatility of political and economic life we have faced since the 1970s and certainly since 1989.

Let us see how this framework and this hypothesis can help us distinguish the European story from the others we tell in this book. Why is Europe in the second decade of the twenty-first century different from Europe in 1980? Two unprecedented developments have given contemporary European history a revolutionary quality. The first is the collapse of the Soviet Empire in 1989 and of the Soviet Union itself in 1991. The shock of these events was both palpable and undeniable.

The second is the emergence of the European Union from the Maastricht Treaty of 1992 as a supranational federation. The consequences of this development took longer to emerge into the light of day but may have just as significant consequences as the collapse of the Soviet Union. The growth of the European Union and its regulatory, legal, and monetary policies undermines traditional nationalism and truncates state sovereignty. The creation of a common labor market has undermined traditional forms of labor relations in individual countries and has created tensions between immigrants and indigenous populations at a time of high unemployment.

The euro zone of currency stabilization worked for a time, but when the small economy of Greece went into semi-receivership in 2009, the rest of the EU had to pay the bailout costs. Ireland followed, and others—Spain, Portugal, Hungary—were at risk. Why should German citizens pay for "feckless" Greeks? The answer is: because the collapse of one currency or one economy is no longer a matter for that country's electorate alone. To be sure, the European community is run by experts who said such things could not happen; but they did happen and may very well happen again. There are indeed "black swans" in the political and economic world, just as in the natural world.[6]

In a sense, the emergence of a risk society is a response to mass disillusionment with the long-term consequences of the post-1945 settlement. On the one hand, it produced peace and unparalleled increases in real incomes in the West; on the other hand, the promise of welfare from cradle to grave now appears to have been a time-limited one. No one can be sure that today's entitlements will apply tomorrow, when citizens of France of Germany need medical care or want to live on a pension made available by the state from a fixed age, say sixty or so. If their position is uncertain, consider that of the inhabitants of Eastern Europe, whose welfare provision vanished when the Communist system collapsed suddenly. What does the future look like to them? It is filled with risks of an unquantifiable order of magnitude. These fundamental shifts in the tectonic plates under European society, eastern and western, create massive uncertainty in the minds of those well-educated and well-informed people living through them.

It is too soon to tell how Europeans will adjust to these events, but it would be foolish to ignore the way their momentum frames the demographic profile of the continent. Here political change is so sharp as to inflect economic and social life in direct ways. The risks of post-Communist society in eastern Europe are unpredictable; minimizing the consequences of such risks is a strategy that makes sense on the family level. The same is true to a lesser degree in western and southern Europe. The hold of the churches on family life and social norms is much weaker than ever before. Scandals about sexual abuse by clergy in a host of countries make matters worse and further reduce both the population of communicants and the levels of recruitment to the clergy of various denominations. What constitutes a "normal" personal life course for a man or a woman—education, army, work, marriage, children, grandchildren, retirement—is no longer a settled matter. Hence in surveying the various national trajectories we sketch in this chapter, it makes sense to measure to what extent each is the story of a risk society under pressures different from those of the past.

Postimperial Russia: The Risk Society after Communism

Let us start from the east and work westward. Perhaps the most striking examples of radical responses to insecurity and uncertainty of the kind captured by Beck's term the "risk society" may be that of the former Soviet Union.[7] The "risk hypothesis" surveyed earlier has a particular demographic meaning in the successor states of the former Soviet Union.

Here we focus on European Russia, stretching from Kaliningrad in the west, a Baltic Sea port, to the Ural Mountains in the east. Where Russia starts and stops is a difficult question, one that determines part of the answer to where Europe starts and ends. But for our purposes, we arbitrarily exclude Siberia, as well as the Baltic states, Belorussia, Ukraine, and the former Caucasian republics from the population we term "European Russia."

As we have noted, the "risk hypothesis" posits a shift of fear traditionally imbedded in natural disasters to those produced by human agency. There is little reason to exclude the catastrophic history of Stalinist Russia from the latter category, and other events reflect both political and environmental failures. The explosion at Chernobyl in 1986 was an environmental disaster of the first magnitude, but its causes were all too human.

The transition to a new political and economic order in Russia after 1991 was certainly an upheaval, although the term *order* hardly describes the aftermath of the collapse of the Soviet Union and the Soviet Empire surrounding its European Russian core. *Order* is not the word to encapsulate the creation of a market-based economy with powerful oligarchies emerging to develop and plunder Russia's huge natural energy resources and other assets set "free" by the new state.

The philosopher Isaiah Berlin used to say that whatever happened elsewhere also happened in Russia, only magnified. The best present instance of a "risk society" in the developed world is probably post-Soviet Russia, and it is there that we see evidence of phenomena evident elsewhere, though to a lesser degree.

It is important to note what is similar and what is different about the Russian case. As in the rest of Europe, Russian fertility has dropped. As in the rest of Europe, young people are entering into marriage less frequently and leaving it more frequently than ever before. But in the Russian case, a rise in mortality rates, somewhat tempered by in-migration, has yielded sharp falls in aggregate population.

Thus population decline is a reality in post-Communist Russia, and the levels of decline are greater than anywhere else in Europe. When we consider the ways politicians and demographers have surveyed this phenomenon and have tried to explain it, we find other commonali-ties with past debates. The fear of population decline is alive and well, fostered by heated images of the disappearance of Russia either numeri-cally or in its collapse as a stable state. We will later provide instances of this injection of ideological and political fearmongering, but first let us unpack these demographic changes into their components.

FERTILITY DECLINE

Until the Gorbachev period, Russian fertility rates hovered at the re-placement level of about 2.1. After 1989, the total fertility rate (TFR) fell well below 2.0. In 1999, the registered rate was at a historically low level: 1.17, though there was some increase in subsequent years. In 2007, the rate was 1.4.

For reasons related primarily to Leninist ideological commit-ments, abortion was a nearly universal practice in Soviet Russia, and it remains a robust form of family limitation in post-Communist Russia. But the termination of pregnancies is not the root cause of very low birth-rates. A much more striking change has taken place in marriage patterns ("nuptiality," in the language of demography) and family for-mation. As Eberstadt has put it, "With the collapse of Soviet rule, Russia has seen a pervasive and profound change in childbearing patterns and living arrangements"—what might be described as a "withering away" of the family itself.[8] Cohabitation outside of marriage has risen rapidly, and so has the tendency of people to divorce.

RISING MORTALITY RATES

What makes Russia's Second Demographic Transition different from that in other European countries is that it is accompanied by rising mortality rates. Despite some dampening of the trend by in-migration, the combination of very low fertility and rising mortality in Russia has yielded declining population totals from 1996 to 2009. The drop is on the order of 7 million people, or 5 percent of the 148 million registered in 1996.

There is a consensus about some causes of the rise in death rates. Feshbach has estimated that, for a host of reasons, life expectancy for males in Russia has dropped significantly. In 1999, he observed that post-Communist Russia was in the midst of a health crisis:

> Alcoholism, drug abuse, sexually transmitted diseases, malnutrition, and various chronic and infectious diseases already mean, among other things, that a third of the adult population is incapable of reproduction.
>
> The incidence of tuberculosis in Russia has skyrocketed. The number of deaths ascribed to tuberculosis in Russia in 1996 (24,877) was almost 15 percent greater than the number of new infections (usually nonfatal) that year in the United States. The Russian mortality rate for tuberculosis is 16.9 per 100,000; the U.S. rate is 0.5.[9]

Five years later, Feshbach's view was even more pessimistic. Here is a summary of his position:

> By 2050 Russia will lose at least a third of its current population. Disease, environmental hazards, and a decline in healthy newborns underlie this staggering statistic.
>
> In Russia, deaths far outnumber births. Meanwhile, only a third of Russian babies are born healthy and last year's child health census showed that some 50 to 60 percent of all Russian children suffer from a chronic illness. Current mortality rates reflect the very high share of deaths between ages 20 and 49, potentially the most productive population segment. Such a population decline has a devastating impact on the labor force, military recruitment, and family formation.[10]

And an AIDS/HIV epidemic in Russia made matters worse.[11] In 2008, the gloom had deepened further in Feshbach's interpretation. Russia, he reiterated, was "facing a public health crisis that verges on the catastrophic."[12]

Eberstadt follows Feshbach's lead in this field. His research points in particular to cardiovascular disease as the culprit leading to the health crisis. Cause-specific mortality analysis is particularly difficult to rely on, primarily due to inevitable problems of misreporting and conventional assignments of causes of death from multiple causes to one familiar (and acceptable) one. But even allowing for error in the statistics, Eberstadt does not mince his words. Russia is in the midst of "a grim downward spiral in levels of public health," producing a veritable "humanitarian catastrophe." Together with plummeting fertility, here is the source of "Russia's downward spiral," and of the emptying of towns and cities in a manner reminiscent of Pol Pot.[13] Notice how quickly demographic analysis turns into invocations of apocalypse. More on that in a moment.

RUSSIAN TWILIGHT?

To sum up: Most scholars share the view that Russia's Second Demographic Transition took place in a society with relatively low levels of per capita income and without the kind of welfare net that protects vulnerable people in European states to the west. This combination makes Russia a transitional case between the rest of Europe and North America and those states still developing to the east and south of Russia.

In a sense, seeing Russia as a "risk society" makes double sense. The cultural transformations evident in the West arise from deep changes in the way young people, and in particular women, control their fertility to keep open ways of living that were closed to their mothers and grandmothers. The risk of large families is one they do not wish to take. But their material and health risks are apparent, too. If we combine the effects of incomplete and inadequate health coverage on the one hand, and patterns of food and alcohol consumption unconducive to good health on the other, we can see that mortality contributes both to declining fertility and to declining population totals. A risk-averse response among young people to such conditions is hardly surprising.

FEAR AND IDEOLOGY

Equally unsurprising is the overheated language accompanying discussions of these matters both in Russia and elsewhere. Feshbach and Eberstadt inhabit research institutes in Washington, and though both are scholars with international reputations, they do tend to turn the volume up on their rhetoric, as it were—perhaps to be heard in the political cacophony of the capital. Consider the following nuggets in Eberstadt's study of Russian population trends. He cannot risk turning Marx on his head, in claiming, "A specter is haunting the Russian Federation today. It is not the specter of Communism but rather the specter of depopulation—a relentless, unremitting, and perhaps unstoppable depopulation. For Russia and its people, the Communist era is history. The era of depopulation, on the other hand, may only have just begun."[14] Not only is "Russia in the throes of a terrible peacetime depopulation," but this depopulation "promises to be of indefinite duration."[15] The very future of Russia as a state is in doubt. Russia, he wrote in another article, is "the sick man of Europe." "Russia is now at the brink of a steep population decline—a peacetime hemorrhage framed by a collapse of the birthrate and a catastrophic surge in the death rate. The forces that have shaped this path of depopulation and debilitation are powerful ones, and they are by now deeply rooted in Russian soil."[16] In case his message was still too measured, he wrote an article in *World Affairs. A Journal of Ideas and Debate*, entitled "Drunken Nation: Russia's Depopulation Bomb."[17]

Feshbach has put the matter in these rhetorical terms: "A declining population is robbing the military of a new generation of soldiers. Russia's economy is almost totally dependent on the price of oil."[18] For Feshbach, Russian demographic trends may be leading to decline from which recovery is simply impossible: "So much of the shrinking Russian population may soon be so ill that long-term solutions to the country's political, economic, and military problems will be inconceivable."[19]

Doom, gloom, and no way back. These are the terms in which the fear of population decline has always been expressed. Demography and ideology are braided together in a host of ways.

Not surprisingly, we find responses of a more hopeful kind among the Russian leadership itself, well aware of the political stakes at issue. In February 2010 then Prime Minister Vladimir Putin was reported to have told his cabinet: "'We have the following final data: birthrate grew by 2.9%, death rate reduced by 3%. The population's natural decline went down by 31%.'"[20] First Deputy Prime Minister Dmitry Medvedev made it clear that increasing the birthrate was a vital national priority. He supported programs "to tackle the demographic crisis," including incentive payments for second births. Posters like those depicting a young woman with three babies and reading "Love for your nation starts with love for family" are widespread.[21]

Here we remain on familiar ground. Fertility declines stir anxieties about power—national, military, as much as sexual. They also are very hard to change either by rhetoric or by policy. They reflect glacial movements in the ways in which people organize their private, sexual, and family lives. And though there are moments when long-term trends are inflected, the best way to approach Russian demography today is to set it in a long-term context. Just as in the study of the First Demographic Transition, demographic trends in European Russia are indeed European.[22] It is clear too that the Second Demographic Transition has been underway for at least fifty years, and that mortality regimes deepen trends whose primary origins lie in reproductive behavior. It may be possible for Russia to lower its mortality rates due to alcohol-related disease, but it is probably unlikely that its recent pronatalist policies will yield a sharp or immediate rebound in the birthrate. Policy initiatives rarely work this way.

Our conclusion is that the Second Demographic Transition is located in the minds of men and women, young men and women in particular, who face the instability and uncertainty of the "risk society" in which they live, and plan their intimate lives accordingly. In this sense, Russia has joined the "risk society" in Europe and is there to stay. The risks may vary, but the strategies of survival are the same.

From United Germany to German Twilight?

UNITED GERMANY

Whenever population issues arise in Germany, the discursive landscape is full of trip wires and minefields. On 12 October 2010, Horst Seehofer, the premier of Bavaria, "said in an interview with a German magazine that Turkish and Arab migrants were no longer needed in the country."[23] Said in Italy or Britain, the statement would cause a flurry of comment on the inwardness of the political right; said in Germany, the same comment evokes specters of Adolf Hitler and Auschwitz.

That such rhetorical mines blow up in Germany today is hardly surprising. The "Jewish problem" has few of the contours it had in the 1930s; indeed there is a strong current of interest in, respect for, and appreciation of Jewish culture in contemporary Germany. But the treatment of other non-Christian populations in Germany brings back the bad old days and suggests that there has been not a decline in prejudice but a shift in its targets.

The discomfort that seems inevitable in all such discussions is not restricted to political leaders. Thilo Sarrazin, then on the board of the Bundesbank, the central bank of Germany, triggered a storm of protest for telling *Welt am Sonntag* that "all Jews share a certain gene, all Basques have certain genes that make them different from other people."[24]

He added to the storm with excerpts from his book *Germany Abolishes Itself: How We Are Risking the Future of Our Nation*. In it he said, "I don't want the country of my grandchildren and great-grandchildren to be largely Muslim, or that Turkish or Arabic will be spoken in large areas, that women will wear head scarves and the daily rhythm is set by the call of the muezzin. . . . If I want to experience that, I can just take a vacation in the Orient."[25]

Sarrazin was expelled from the Social Democratic Party, censured by the German chancellor from the Christian Democratic Union, and resigned from the board of the Bundesbank. His book is selling briskly according to press reports.[26] Once again, there are parallels when mandarins make excessive and provocative statements in other countries, but in Germany such remarks evoke an unmastered past.[27]

On 17 October 2010, the German chancellor Angela Merkel addressed the youth section of her Christian Democratic Union Party in Potsdam, just outside of Berlin. She told her audience that multiculturalism had "utterly failed. . . . The idea of people from different cultural backgrounds living happily 'side by side' did not work." It was up to "immigrants to do more to integrate into German society." By not learning German, they were unable to exploit opportunities in the labor market and constituted a major social problem within Germany itself.[28]

Four days earlier, the *New York Times* reported a survey that showed that one-third of the German population wanted to repatriate foreigners, and 10 percent wanted a führer to lead them out of the current political morass.[29] The echoes are deafening and inevitably put the German case in a different framework from that of other European nations. History matters in Germany as elsewhere, but perhaps it matters more in Germany.

There is no better case anywhere of the significant political element in contemporary demographic history than in Germany. It is not only the constant over-the-shoulder look at the Nazi past, but also the upheaval associated with unification after the collapse of the Berlin Wall and the Communist system in East Germany.

DEMOGRAPHIC TRENDS SINCE 1990

The end of the Soviet Empire and its client states came quickly. It shocked those who were supposed to be experts in the politics of the Communist world, perhaps almost as much as it shocked those who lived on the eastern side of the divisions between East and West Berlin and between East and West Germany.

In the twenty years that have passed, there has been a radical change in the population balance between the two former German states.[30] Between 1989 and 1996, 1 million of about 16 million residents left the territory of East Germany, and the overwhelming majority resettled in what had been West Germany. In the years 1989 to 1993, those in extradomestic employment in the former East Germany dropped by

3.5 million. Women workers were hardest hit by the transition to capitalism. Productivity levels in East Germany had been much lower than in West Germany before the fall of the Communist system, and it took time before the two parts of the new unified economy meshed. Capital investment in communications and transportation moved ahead rapidly, but the environmental disaster that had been created in East Germany took longer to rectify.

Here was a fascinating instance, anticipated by Ulrich Beck, of a "risk society" in turmoil. Displacement was in part a matter of escape, after decades of restrictions on travel and on work abroad. Now West Germany was no longer "abroad," and the higher pay and better conditions of work there attracted East German workers by the thousands, especially those in their teens, twenties, and thirties.

Yet it was not just the wreckage of Communism and the paucity of well-paying jobs that mattered. It was also the collapse of a social welfare system in East Germany that had supported working mothers relatively well. These multiple upheavals lay behind a significant drop in marriage, the birthrate, and in total fertility in the space of two generations, between the 1970s and today.

German developments after 1990 must be placed against the background of earlier fertility decline. Within Europe, Germany (East and West combined) was the first to register total fertility rates of below 1.5. It reached 1.3 in 1985, and only thereafter did the rest of central, Eastern, and southern Europe follow suit.[31] The crude birthrate in Germany in 1998 was 9.57 per 1,000; this figure was about 10 percent below the average for the twenty-five European Union countries in that year. But a decade later, the German birthrate had declined still further to 7.88 per 1,000. That put the German birthrate 27 percent below the European Union average.[32]

Confirmation that German fertility in 2008 is among Europe's lowest may be found in data on total fertility rates, which are more sensitive indicators than crude birthrates. In 1998, the TFR for Germany stood at 1.38; a decade later, the figure was almost identical. The German figure is well below that for the European Union and just slightly above the Italian rate of 1.37 registered in 2007. German fertility is at the lower end of the range of European fertility, and despite minor annual fluctuations, it seems to be stably located there.

Even with in-migration and declining mortality rates, German population totals have declined both absolutely and in relation to all other European Union nations. Of the twenty-seven member states of the European Union in 2007, Germany was the only large country to register some active population decline. (Other smaller countries, all former Warsaw Pact states in eastern Europe, did so as well, including Bulgaria, Hungary, and the three Baltic states of Latvia, Lithuania, and Estonia.)[33] In all cases the declines were small relative to the overall population—over the decade 2001–2011, the total decline in Germany amounted to 0.8 percent of the German population of more than 80 million.[34] Virtually all of this reduction is accounted for by natural increase, or the difference between births and deaths. Net in-migration was a countervailing positive, but not quite large enough to compensate for very low fertility rates in Germany.[35] Although the percentage decline was small, its symbolic importance was substantial since it was larger in absolute terms than that in any other EU state.[36] As in the case of Russia, population decline is a reality in Germany, though as we shall see, its significance may be exaggerated for a range of political and ideological reasons.

Another element of demographic debate in Germany relates to changes in fertility, family structures, and childrearing, which the data show are governed today by norms different from those evident in mid-twentieth-century Germany. While German women are giving birth less frequently than ever before, more of their births are occurring outside of marriage than ever before.[37] For example, over the period 1997–2009, the proportion of live births to couples outside of marriage in Germany rose from about 18 percent to 32 percent, compared to a rise from 25 to 35 percent in the European Union.

Hence, discussions of German population questions take place against the backdrop of major changes in the life course of women in particular. Fewer are marrying than ever before, and whatever their marital status, couples are having fewer children than ever before. There is no reason to believe that the current situation will continue indefinitely, but equally there is no reason to think that it will change dramatically.

There are studies positing a clustering of births among women who defer their childbearing until they are in their late thirties and early forties, but most observers still believe that the present demographic regime is here to last.[38] While levels of below-replacement fertility in Europe fluctuate, there is no indication that they will return to the notional 2.1 replacement level associated with stable or growing numbers.

Why? From Economic and Welfare Determinism to the "Risk Society"

In the 1980s, West Germany led the way into the new below-replacement regime in Europe. Although there have been many detailed studies of German legal and administrative approaches to family policy, as well as sophisticated examinations of the German labor market,[39] there is no clear consensus on why so many countries have followed Germany's lead.

Many observers follow the old maxim that massive social and economic changes over the past century lay behind below-replacement fertility. In the 1930s, there was considerable discussion of the possibility of what then was termed "race suicide," understood as the persistence of below-replacement fertility to the point that the great European powers would lose their hold on world power, while social elites would give way to their more-fertile social inferiors. The Second World War and its aftermath allayed these fears, at least for a time.[40] The spectacular increase in per capita income since the 1950s was matched by increasing educational provision roughly equalizing the access that men and women have to the information revolution, driving job expansion and patterns of discretionary consumption levels alike. Three-quarters of the population in the developed world live in cities; life expectation at birth has reached unprecedented levels, nearing and sometimes exceeding eighty. Consequently, women entered the urban, extradomestic labor force at higher rates and stayed there longer than ever before. Planning pregnancies became an essential, indeed an unavoidable, part of the female life cycle, no longer constrained in a general sense by the force of religious institutions or beliefs. As early as 1979, Ryder suggested that the discriminatory treatment of women constrained their childbearing patterns."[41] In other words, the more freedom women felt they had outside of the home, the less likely they were to have two or more children. Childlessness or smaller families were products of liberation, Caldwell wrote similarly in 1982.[42] The French demographer Philippe Ariès reached the same conclusion about Europe virtually at the same time. The child is no longer the "essential variable" in family or in personal life, he suggested.[43]

Problems remain, though, in this interpretation. This "failure in social reproduction," in Caldwell and Schindlmayr's phrase,[44] is so general that each national story, or indeed each regional or local story, gets folded into it. What makes German fertility decline happen is never clear, except that like lemmings, we are all following the same subterranean trends. And to a degree, this interpretation may be right.

Both West Germany, with its booming economy and high social provision and productivity levels in the 1980s, and less-prosperous East Germany led the way toward below-replacement fertility. But then came the puzzle that the next to follow were Italy, Spain, and Greece, where patterns of female subordination were much more in evidence and where, in the case of Spain and Greece, per capita income levels were much lower than in Germany. Demographers tried a "south–north" division, where "northern" rich countries might still adopt a replacement or near-replacement fertility regime. But this approach did not work either, and was further embarrassed by the drop in Eastern European fertility levels in societies without the affluence of Western Europe.[45]

The shared feature of most of these failed hypotheses was that each adopted a form of economic determinism. Rational-choice theory posited that women maximized their earnings potentials by dropping out of the childbearing business. Economic instability in regimes of high salaries made men and women adopt risk-averse personal profiles, especially when pension systems began to creak at the financial seams. Preparing for a rainy day tomorrow meant avoiding the costly matter of raising children today.

These interpretations must be qualified, since they do not allow for the possibility that women might "catch up" on family formation later in their fertile years, thereby creating a gap between low period-fertility rates and higher cohort-fertility rates. (See appendix B.) Most commentators genuflect in the direction of this distinction, but still go on to make inferences primarily from low, or very low, period rates. Caution is in order here, as always in demographic projections and interpretations. Let us consider this matter in a bit more detail.

Part of the confusion arises from the way fertility rates are calculated in demography. The total fertility rate that is commonly used to summarize fertility behavior for a given time period (a year, a five-year period, and so on) is a "synthetic" rate. It sums up the fertility behaviors in that time period of women in all age groups. By doing so it usefully controls for the distortion that can result if one population has a higher density of young-adult women than others. Yet in so doing, this "period TFR" injects its own source of distortion if it is calculated for years in which substantial numbers of women of reproductive age are deferring their childbearing. Imagine a cohort of women aged twenty to twenty-four (the peak years of biological capacity to reproduce) who collectively delay their childbearing for a period of years but then produce the same ultimate family size. In this case the period TFR during this period of fertility delay would be distorted downward, but the ultimate completed family size (a measure of cohort fertility) for these cohorts of women would not have declined. The period of the past few decades has indeed been one of such fertility deferral, especially in Mediterranean countries such as Italy, Greece, Spain, and others.[46]

Welfare provision is another variable that has been used to account for national differences within European fertility patterns. Gauthier advanced an institutional argument to account for different levels of fertility in Europe. Social-democratic states like Sweden were at the top of the "league table," offering "universal" welfare provision. Conservative states in central and western Europe with more limited provision followed. Then came southern European countries, with little guaranteed social provision. At the tail end were what she termed "Liberal" countries like Britain and Switzerland, targeting needy families with patchy child-care provision.[47] The problem remains that there are too many national anomalies to sustain the argument. While social provision matters, it does not "predict" national differences in total fertility rates.

Instead of focusing on labor-market or welfare determinants of fertility levels, Beck's theory of the "risk society" draws upon them and goes beyond them. It offers a way out of deterministic models, or accounts that specify an "individualist" society in Germany and a "familial" one in Italy,[48] in both of which below-replacement fertility levels prevail.

The "risk society" means something very particular in Germany. Nowhere else in late-twentieth-century Europe did two independent states speaking the same language but following a different political system merge into one. The costs were staggering, but so were the benefits, especially to those in the former East Germany moving west in search of better prospects and freer lives. But unification came at virtually the same time as the collapse of both the Soviet Empire and the former Yugoslavia. From both of these developments, there emerged very large and unpredicted migratory flows that converged on Germany. Older communities of guest workers from Turkey and other countries now saw their position as less stable than before, since the host country in which they had chosen to settle now had its hands full with other groups of refugees and asylum seekers.[49]

Add to this complex ethnic pattern the emergence after 2001 of radical Islam as a perceived threat to the West, and it becomes apparent that the two decades following German unification have been particularly turbulent, especially given the catastrophes of its longer-term past, against which recent trends must be set. Germany does not have a very good track record of dealing with non-German-speaking populations living in its midst; but neither does any other major European country, with the possible exception of France. What Germany has is a criminal past that refuses to go away, criminal in the presence within Germany of the descendants of Nazis and of East German "Stasi" agents alike. At the same time, Germany has become a liberal democracy without significant trace of its militaristic past. When Britain and the United States decided to overthrow Saddam Hussein in 2003, the German population, left and right, was not with them.

The key point is that the German state suffers from particular fault lines on questions of population in general and on ethnicity and race in particular. Within the European Union, only in Germany did citizenship rest almost exclusively on blood lines (*jus sanguinis*) rather than birth on German soil (*jus soli*), until a 1999 law made it possible for some residents to obtain German citizenship if they renounce their own. This legal history—alongside the totalitarian past—gives the assimilation of foreign-born residents into German society a different coloration, as it were.

Modern Germany is a "risk society," in the sense Beck uses this term, in that it is a relatively young state with a past that defines intolerance and persecution as the norm. Anyone spending any extended period in Germany will see how far the society has come since the 1950s, but the past is not a foreign country there: It is just below your feet.[50]

It would be surprising indeed if discussions of today's population problems, related to below-replacement fertility and immigration, did not refer even indirectly to this tragic past. In another fifty years, two full centuries after the first German unification in 1871, perhaps we can ignore the weight of the past in surveys of German social, cultural, and demographic life. But today that is not an option.

Instead we hear the echoes of older upheavals in German history in the language of leading figures referring to the existence of a "Jewish gene" or complaining that there are too many foreigners in the country. Tolerance is a relatively new pillar of the German political and social order, and as in every other country it easily gives way to fear. Note the precise wording of the book that caused such a stir when Thilo Sarrazin published it: *Germany Abolishes Itself: How We Are Risking the Future of Our Nation.* Words such as *risk, future, nation,* and *abolish* (in the sense of self-destruction) are not value-free in anybody's vocabulary about the German past. The reactions evoked by Sarrazin's book showed that he had exposed some troubling continuities between Germany's totalitarian past and her democratic present.

For our purposes, the key issue is that population matters in general, and fertility decisions in particular, can never be reduced to reflections of any one facet of social life. Economic determinism is as fruitless as political determinism, and yet we ignore both economic change and political change at our peril in attempting to understand recent demographic history.

Here is where Beck's work on the "risk society" comes in handy. Written in the 1980s at precisely the moment that German fertility became palpably below replacement, Beck challenged the notion that industrialization and affluence reduce the risks in which modern individuals and groups are placed. The Chernobyl disaster occurred in 1986, the same year *Risk Society* was published in German. Ecological politics have taken off since then, drawing supporters from those disabused from early beliefs in the reliably predictive powers of science and technology. If the structures that rule our lives are less well equipped than they pretend to provide us with safe environments in which to live, and if such dangers are more evidently transnational in character, then relying on the welfare state, or employment contracts, or trade unions, or even the family is no longer a safe proposition. Living in the "risk society" means escaping from older conventions and social institutions, one of which is the two- or three-child family. Below-replacement fertility, in Beck's framework, is the demographic face of the "risk society."

To be sure, there were earlier forms of risk-averse fertility decline. In the 1930s, the world economic crisis made it difficult for couples in many European countries to afford large families, and some people were averse to bringing children into a world seemingly hell-bent on returning to war. Beck does not cite such earlier cases, probably since there is little evidence that social conventions changed during times of economic crisis. His "risk society" is the one created by post-1945 economic and educational expansion.

To be sure, this interpretation cannot be "disconfirmed," in the way experimental scientists understand the term. But since all other metatheories appear to be weak when applied to demographic developments, we have little to lose by seeing how this approach might help illuminate recent demographic history in Germany, as elsewhere.

Club Med

The European Mediterranean region provides additional evidence that economic determinism is a poor option to account for recent demographic developments. Again, let us survey current trends before examining the claim that these are "risk societies."

The decline in fertility we have observed in eastern and central Europe was matched by similar developments in Mediterranean Europe. For purposes of comparison, we limit our discussion to three Mediterranean countries, while recognizing that there are other patterns in the region and there are significant differences among the three states we consider—Italy, Spain, and Greece.

Italy

In 1990, the Italian TFR stood at 1.33. In 1997, total fertility rates in Italy had declined still further. At 1.21, this rate was among the lowest in the world, and it spanned a range of regional patterns, some of which—for instance, in Tuscany—were lower still. Ten years later, in 2007, the Italian TFR had risen to 1.37, but once more it was a composite of very, very low rates and those hovering around the European average. Clearly, despite recent fluctuations, these rates have reached historically unprecedented levels, substantially below replacement levels.

Spain

In 1990, the Spanish TFR stood at 1.36; seven years later, the rate was down to 1.21. Ten years later, the TFR had recovered, and had reached 1.40, surpassing the 1990 level. As in the case of Italy, this upward movement in fertility was significant but still left Spain, like Italy, below the arbitrary level of 1.50 used by some demographers to refer to very low fertility.[51]

Greece

In 1990, the Greek TFR stood at 1.40, slightly above that of Italy and Spain. Seven years later, in 1997, total fertility rates in Greece had dropped further to 1.28, just above the Italian level, but still well below the average for the European Union as a whole. A decade later, the TFR had reached 1.41, that is, Greek fertility had returned to the 1990 level. Like Spain and Italy, Greece remains among those countries hovering around what may be termed the Mediterranean norm of very low levels arbitrarily located below the 1.5 mark.

The "Risk Society" in the Mediterranean

How do we account for this extraordinary pattern of historically unprecedented very low fertility in this region of southern Europe? It is
not possible to provide any one set of explanations that will accommodate developments in these diverse societies. In this region especially,
we need to return to the distinction made earlier between period and
cohort rates and allow for the possibility of deferment of both marriage
and childbearing as significant strategies of family formation. Even
when we do so though, it is apparent that there have been fundamental
transformations in the political and cultural lives of all three countries.

We need to acknowledge the force of economic factors in inform-
ing fertility decisions throughout Europe but also to see that deterministic economic accounts are incomplete or inadequate in accounting
for regional contrasts.[52] Until the 1970s, fertility rates in this region had
persistently been higher than in northern Europe. Received wisdom had
it that the sources of higher fertility in Mediterranean Europe lay in the
enduring strength of the churches, Catholic or Orthodox, and in the
persistently patriarchal organization of social life. Both helped account
for relatively low rates of extradomestic female employment and consequently higher rates of marriage at younger ages and higher fertility
rates.

By 1990, however, analysts had to think again, because southern
Europe had lower fertility rates than did Protestant northern Europe.
This was true despite the fact that in the north there continued to be
higher rates of extradomestic employment, longer traditions of secularization, and a distancing from religious practices and values than in the
south. Either the modernization model of fertility was flawed or there
had been a cultural revolution in the south.

Paradoxically, both of these possibilities actually were true. Italian
fertility declined sharply despite the fact that her rates of female extradomestic labor-force participation was (and still is) lower than in northern Europe. In the mid-1990s, 64 percent of women in the north of Italy
worked outside the home, whereas only 36 percent did in the south. And
yet the massive decline in fertility occurred primarily in the south of the

country. The same paradox applies to data on gender norms, which in-dicate stable fertility in the more egalitarian north, and rapid decline in fertility in the less-egalitarian south of the country.[53] Similarly puzzling is the rapidity of fertility decline in these southern regions of Italy, with the highest proportion of marriages conducted by the Roman Catho-lic Church. Secularization, measured indirectly by civil marriage, was not the apparent source of changing fertility behavior here.[54] In light of major variations among Italian regions the presence or absence of par-ticular forms of child-friendly social policies or communal norms do not seem to produce fertility outcomes in expected ways. Social policy affects but does not govern patterns of family formation in Italy as else-where in Europe.[55]

In the most sophisticated statistical study to date, Kertzer and his colleagues have shown the need to go beyond either the conventional labor-force participation model or the Second Demographic Transi-tion model of fertility decline. By using longitudinal studies based on individual records, they have shown that while it would be foolish to ignore these labor market or secularization elements in the history of fertility decline, it would be even more foolish to limit our attention to them.[56]

Let us see how this pluralistic approach could be helpful in unpack-ing similar contradictory elements in the recent demographic history of two other Mediterranean countries with similarly unprecedented levels of low fertility. The concept of risk certainly applied to political dissi-dents under the forty-year rule of Francisco Franco, but severe divisions within Spanish society persisted after the rapid liberalization of Spain during and after the period of the transition to democracy. A military coup by disgruntled colonels in 1982 captured virtually the whole of the Spanish parliament, and it was only with great skill on the part of King Juan Carlos and a few other politicians who were not in the parliament building when it was seized that a bloodbath was averted. The wounds of the 1930s Spanish Civil War had been covered over by a blanket am-nesty, but those wounds hardly had healed, and left blood enemies living side by side in hundreds of villages and neighborhoods. The new urban Spain thrived with European money and stable democratic institutions, and culturally most people moved irreversibly outside of the orbit of the Roman Catholic Church. The arts flourished, and so did their defiance of conservative traditions and sanctions.

Spanish economic prosperity was real but relatively short-lived. Here the pattern of rapid growth followed by a failure of expectations for further growth recurred, though the troubles emerged most forcefully not in the 1970s, at the time of the transition to democracy, but at and after the turn of the twenty-first century.

The story of Greece is parallel, but the timing is different. The burial of military domination of the political order happened at about the same time as it did in Spain, but the rate of economic growth registered in Spain was not matched in Greece. And after the turn of the century, a series of severe fiscal and banking crises threatened to take down not only the Greek economy but that of the European Union as well. The European Union provided the same stabilization of the political order in Greece as in Spain, but the Greek economic and social order remained at least as precarious as it had been in the old days of dictatorship. In these two cases, both liberal successor states to dictatorial regimes, market economies rested on unstable foundations. The story of such unstable European economies has since been repeated time and again, in Greece, in Iceland, and in Ireland. Who's next? is the question that everyone asks sooner or later.

The links between such fault lines in the economic and social structure of a number of European states may be obscured by their relative prosperity, especially when placed alongside the efforts of millions of Asian and African migrants who take all kinds of risks to get to Europe. And yet for the indigenous population, the presence of such migrants is a further destabilizing and occasionally radicalizing process, disinterring ugly strata of European prejudice. Such prejudices may represent what in the later nineteenth century was termed the "socialism of the fools,"[57] an irrational way of dealing with risk by blaming an out-group for the problems in-groups cannot resolve. But whatever their character or origins, reactions to substantial extra-European immigration, especially of Muslim men and women, have turned Europe into a "risk society" in new and ominous ways.

Rising Fertility, above 1.5, in Northwestern Europe

In 2009, the highest birthrates in Europe were registered by France, the United Kingdom, Ireland, and Sweden. Fifty years earlier, these countries all were experiencing substantial natural increase, but over time they recorded total fertility rates below the replacement level of 2.1. By the turn of the century, their fertility levels were all above the notional 1.5 mark arbitrarily fixed as indicating the "very low" fertility observed in central, eastern and southern Europe. By 2008 the French and Irish rates approached the 2.0 level, with Sweden and the United Kingdom not far behind, at roughly 1.9. Thus, in both traditionally Catholic populations in France and Ireland and Protestant populations in Sweden and the United Kingdom, there was a common pattern of increasing fertility, such that (for the moment at least) we can clearly separate Europe into two fertility regimes: one in the northwest, where fertility is close to replacement levels, and another one in southern, central and eastern Europe, where TFRs are strikingly lower—and in some cases lower than ever before.

Why the regional difference? One explanation is political stability. The apparent end of eighty years of violent conflict over the division of Ireland may have made a difference. But by and large, the four countries under review here underwent a decade of prosperity in the 1990s and, especially in the Irish case, benefited substantially from the robust economic growth and large subsidies of the European Union. The emergence of a common labor market in Europe was an added benefit, though it meant that there were more foreign-born workers in these countries than ever before. We shall return to this point later.

Another, more testable, hypothesis is that higher fertility rates than elsewhere in Europe reflected the development of more-robust and inclusive forms of family policy in this region, making it easier for women to combine childbearing with careers throughout their thirties and forties. And yet there are major differences between the British approach, favoring families in need, and the more-general approach in France, Ireland, and Sweden of helping most families defray the costs of childbearing and childrearing.[58] It is sometimes not understood that

France and Sweden pioneered such social policies in the hope of raising the birthrate at the end of the nineteenth century and after.[59] Most other countries in northwestern Europe firmly institutionalized pronatalist policies during the interwar depression and in the aftermath of the Second World War.[60] Daly and Clavero note that a third phase of family policies including universal preschooling and other subsidies emerged in the 1990s, and that such policies may have been effective in stimulating the upward movement of total fertility rates in the northwestern quadrant of Europe.[61]

There were four elements in this contemporary basket of family-support policies. The first is direct care, meaning many kinds of public care and preschooling activities made available without reference to the marital status or income level of the mother. The second is the separation of children's policy (meaning nurturing the child) from family policy (meaning protecting the family as a social and economic unit), in the form of the Irish National Children's Strategy. The third is the active effort to reconcile work and family lives, by helping parents see that they have choices when they enter their childbearing histories; this in part is a push for gender equality and the encouragement of women to see that they are not trapped by childbearing into a life of poverty or a home-centered daily life. Work outside the home is taken as a positive value, in addition to its income-generating function. The fourth is helping parents to be better at parenting through education and counseling, and the provision of childcare or preschool education as part of the normal pathway of children in their early years.[62]

In all cases, the challenge of social policy, as Daly and Clavero remark, is "to make social provision for a society in which women and children can no longer rely on a long-term basis on men and families to provide for them."[63] Adaptation to new family forms and "remarried couple family" structures is the hallmark of such programs, which recognize that parents and children face new risks in relatively new family regimes in which cohabitation and changing family forms rather than conventional marriage describe the framework of family life.

Conclusion: Risks, Present and Future

In sum, the current pattern of fertility in Europe is varied but markedly different from that of the past. One region, in the northwest quadrant of Europe, has registered near-replacement levels of fertility; all others have markedly lower fertility rates. It is clear that no one explanatory model can accommodate this notably varied pattern, even within the confines of Europe.

While there is still some force in the labor-market or secularization models of fertility decline, we need to be flexible enough to consider additional possibilities. One that warrants consideration is the "risk hypothesis," in which fertility decisions are understood as relating as much to status and material insecurity as to changing work patterns or the loss of belief in religious precepts or practices. The "risk hypothesis" of Beck and others has still to be tested formally, but at the outset it might to be useful to speculate about some of the ways in which in contemporary life risk is an element that demographers and other analysts ignore at their peril.

There were risks both old and new in the 1990s, when the pace quickened and the slope of Europe's fertility decline increased in a number of different countries. There are both cohort effects and period effects we need to consider. The general alternation of a period of recovery and massive economic growth in the period 1945–1975—what the French term *les trentes glorieuses*—with a subsequent period of deep economic instability in the 1970s and 1980s, had a greater bearing on Western than on Eastern Europe. But in countries of the West, what Gary Runciman has termed "relative deprivation" may have been a very powerful incentive to limit marital fertility. Relative deprivation posits the potentially disruptive effects not of an absolute decline in incomes, real or monetary, but a relative decline in the trajectory that cohorts in the reproductive ages anticipated—say, on the basis of the economic climate in the 1950s and 1960s—in the more inclement economic climate of the 1970s and 1980s. Individuals might even be better off during the downturn of these latter decades than they had been in the 1950s or 1960s, but through the lens of relative deprivation they would not have achieved the *anticipated* increases in disposable income or job security to which they believed they were entitled, based on the buoyant experience of the previous twenty years.

One powerful way of dealing with relative deprivation is by fertility limitation. Those who feel they are living in a "risk society" would respond to such perceived deprivation by taking a more cautious attitude to family formation at that time. Later, when economic growth returned to robust levels in the 1990s, especially in northwestern Europe, fertility levels would rise.

Not so in Eastern Europe. Here the "risk hypothesis" would have different interpretations. The last years of the Communist system, and the upheavals that followed the collapse of the Eastern Bloc in 1989 and the Soviet Union in 1991, led understandably to declining expectations as to the support families would be likely to have in their childbearing and child-raising years. The painful transition to a market economy created massive inequalities of wealth, and in some cases corruption on a grand scale. To be sure, freedom of movement occurred, and so did freedom of access to Western media, ideas, dress, music, and so on. The mix of Westernization of the former Communist world and global communications networks accessible to all probably brought about normative changes, the full nature of which we still do not know. The "risk hypothesis" is one way to configure these new sets of social assumptions. That is, childbearing and family life under such radically unstable conditions present challenges—especially to women—that cause more and more people to opt out of what had been the conventional forms of marital life of their parents and grandparents. Reducing family size to one child, or transforming cohabitation into a sexual but childless union, may be interpreted as a rational response to the massive risks of everyday life in the new order in eastern Europe.

A "risk hypothesis" about fertility decline need not ignore the conventional measures of labor-force participation rates or secularization. In some cases, they do seem to apply. But there are other ways in which risk is experienced, and the knowledge that such risks exist and are all around us is shared more rapidly through the mass media and the Internet than ever before. Ecological risks are not necessarily worse than they had been in the 1970s, but the horrors of the Chernobyl and Fukushima nuclear meltdowns or the Bhopal chemical leak or the BP oil-well disaster are no longer seen in many quarters as so wildly improbable as not to be taken seriously.

As Beck predicted, the rule of experts is a rule of those who sometimes have no clothes. That was blatantly clear in the case of Soviet apparatchiks, but skeptics might ask what the real difference is between their smug indifference to the sufferings of others and the attitude of the mortgage and investment bankers who lost tens of billions of dollars in the subprime mortgage disaster and wound up being rescued by the governments representing the people they defrauded. In most cases, both sets of crooks got away with their crimes. Such an analogy must be tempered by recognizing the difference between tolerating loss of life and loss of savings and homes, but the key point here is the embarrassment to the prestige of experts, who had untrammeled authority and yet less understanding than they claimed.

In a world at times seemingly out of control, risk-averse behavior is a rational response. The central point here is that men and women, and perhaps women more than men, risk more by engaging in parenting two or three children than did their parents or grandparents, the fathers and mothers of the two generations born after the Second World War. Those born in the 1970s, who are now entering the latter part of their childbearing years, have been socialized and entered into adulthood at a time when old certainties—about employment, careers, pensions, retirement, savings, homeownership, and so on—no longer hold with the force they seemed to retain before 1970. How many Americans can remember low-cost energy? How many British people remember when university education was financed entirely by the government? There are equivalents in every European country. The latter part of the twentieth century and the beginning of the twenty-first century have become periods of adjustment to a world different from that which many had come to expect.

This is the core of Beck's "reflexive" sociology. Instead of seeing bureaucratization or modernization however defined as inexorable trends, his claim is that they have produced traps and flaws along the way to the future that not only create risk but that ruin our faith in the high priests of modernization—be they bureaucrats, economists, scientists, engineers, or other experts. Uncertainty is a much more unsettling condition in which to live than can be understood by reference to statistical probabilities and improbabilities. Statistics can tell us what, under certain conditions, is likely to happen. What do people do when statistics do not help? One answer is to create the most risk-averse environment they can shape. And one such environment is the one-child or no-child family.

This framework of analysis has room in it for the other labor-market or Second Demographic Transition explanations demographers and sociologists have devised to account for very low fertility in Europe. New and creative career paths have opened up for many women, but contradictions still persist. All too many women live in cultures celebrating gender equality while penalizing women for their sex in the establishment of pay scales for similar jobs. The churches have lost their hold on their parishioners in many respects, but a substantial number of people who restrict their fertility radically still marry in churches, and many stay on as communicants. Older collectives, like trade unions, have either collapsed or faded away, but new forms of communitarianism have emerged alongside older collectivities in social and cultural life, from sporting clubs to Internet-based social networks to ethnic societies catering to millions of workers migrating to Europe or within Europe itself.

This brief survey of some facets of fertility decline in contemporary Europe cannot do more than suggest hypotheses and patterns that need further investigation. But keeping an open mind to the "risk hypothesis" may be the best way to avoid either economic determinism, which has failed in most cases to predict or explain fertility behavior, or in following slavishly Weber's arguments about the onward and relentless march of bureaucratization. Risk is a condition we all know in our lives, and its bearing on patterns of family formation may be greater than scholars have acknowledged in the past.

There are two additional reasons to privilege risk in our interpretation of changing demographic trends. The first is that even in countries where fertility levels have risen to near the 2.0 level, anxiety about immigrants and immigration has risen sharply over the last decade. This may be an element linking the higher fertility in northwest Europe with the lower fertility regimes in the rest of the continent, a phenomenon highlighted by worry over Muslim Europeans, which we analyze in the next chapter.

A second set of concerns focus on environmental risks. These are transnational in character, and seen as such. We have already referred to the 1986 Chernobyl meltdown, which sent a cloud of radiation across northern Europe through Poland, Germany, and Sweden. Who knows how far the pollution of the water supply of the Ukraine went, but the Black Sea links the Ukraine with the whole of the eastern Mediterranean, as well as Bulgaria, Russia, Romania, Turkey, and Greece. A catastrophe for one is, in a way, a catastrophe for all. The rundown of coal-powered and nuclear power plants in Eastern Europe in the Communist era required massive investment in new technologies, which may have reduced levels of pollution but still left much of the older technologies intact.

In light of current (2013) uncertainties about the viability of the euro, it would be foolish for western and central Europeans to feel smug about the future the inhabitants of the European Union face. The experiment of European integration continues, but anyone with eyes to see can trace the fault lines in it, and there remain powerful political forces of resistance in each of its member states. Some, like Norway, have shown that independence from the European experiment has its virtues, but that country's energy resources and the political astuteness demonstrated by its leadership in managing them put such a choice beyond most other European states. It is anyone's guess as to the future of Europe, but whatever it may be it will be far from the idyll envisioned by the founders of the European movement.

Europe is not an integrated continent, and we have emphasized the variety of demographic profiles in this chapter. But on the whole, the story of post-twentieth-century Europe is one in which an early phase of fertility decline, with cultural as much as economic origins, has been superseded by a new phase, bringing fertility levels to the lowest levels ever recorded. Europe still leads the way in fertility decline, just as it did more than a century ago. Today, what is different is that most other world regions are following suit.

Islam in Europe

One of the most controversial elements in contemporary European politics concerns the place of Muslims within European society and the effect of Muslim immigration on the future of Europe. Much of this debate revolves around the concept of Islamophobia. On 20 January 2011, Baroness Warsi, the cochair of the Conservative Party in Britain, attacked prejudice against Muslims as what she termed "Islamophobia."[1] This speech was reported throughout the popular press. Clearly the term Islamophobia is in common usage, but it has been deployed in a host of ways.

The term may be a useful one, but only when carefully defined. On the one hand, it helps to describe some European fears of Islam in general and of Muslim immigrants in particular and to compare these fears with earlier patterns of racial and religious prejudice. But the term has its limits, in that it tends to conflate considered criticism of Islamic practices, customs, and political activity with exaggerated fears and prejudices. Its use in this way is a disservice to those who offer considered and informed criticism of Islam, painting them all as purveyors of prejudice. For this reason we begin by examining the uses and abuses of the term Islamophobia and then offer some thoughts on a way out of the disputes triggered by the term by suggesting a human-rights framework as the appropriate one on which to base our understanding of discussions of the Muslim presence in Europe.

Fear of Islam: The Emergence of Islamophobia

First let us consider how the term Islamophobia entered the public domain and offer some information about the intention of those who first used it. In November 1997 the Runnymede Trust, a British charity and publicly funded think tank focused on problems of discrimination in an ethnically diverse society, published a report entitled *Islamophobia: A Challenge for Us All.*[2] This report was a follow-up to an earlier report prepared by the Trust on anti-Semitism, seeking to understand the parallels, if any, between anti-Muslim and anti-Semitic attitudes.[3] The Runnymede Trust report was drawn up by a group of activists, community workers, clergymen, and social scientists selected by the Runnymede Trust itself.[4] As may be seen by an inspection of its membership, the group appeared to include a large majority with strong prior commitments to Islam, to other organized religions, or to interfaith relations, along with two trustees of the Runnymede Trust itself. Its membership was seemingly lacking in uncommitted experts on relevant issues such as public opinion, political and social movements, and labor markets, which may have limited the report's influence among opinion leaders and public opinion.

Although the 1997 report did receive public support in the media from British Home Secretary Jack Straw, the report's sixty recommendations were largely ignored by the new Labour government. A follow-up report reopened discussion of the subject in 2004.[5] Despite the paucity of legislative follow-through, publicity mattered. These reports and the discussions surrounding them helped introduce the term Islamophobia into the vocabulary widely used in the media to discuss negative stereotypical reactions to the presence of Muslims in British and in other Western societies.

The Runnymede Trust group produced the following checklist of elements that in their view tended to form a frame of mind they termed Islamophobia:

1. Islam seen as a single monolithic bloc, static and unresponsive to new realities.
2. Islam seen as separate and other—(a) not having any aims or values in common with other cultures, (b) not affected by them, (c) not influencing them.
3. Islam seen as inferior to the West—barbaric, irrational, primitive, sexist.
4. Islam seen as violent, aggressive, threatening, supportive of terrorism, engaged in "a clash of civilizations."
5. Islam seen as a political ideology, used for political or military advantage.
6. Criticisms made by Islam of "the West" rejected out of hand.
7. Hostility towards Islam used to justify discriminatory practices towards Muslims and exclusion of Muslims from mainstream society.
8. Anti-Muslim hostility accepted as natural and "normal."

In sum, the Runnymede Trust group defined Islamophobia as "an outlook or world-view involving an unfounded dread and dislike of Muslims, which results in practices of exclusion and discrimination."[6]

DOUBTS AND DIFFICULTIES

The Runnymede Trust reports quickly became subjects of controversy. Their choice of the Islamophobia terminology was part of the reason for this. The use of a concept that includes the Greek root *phobia* carried with it the term's meaning of "fear that is either irrational or excessive." Indeed the term *phobia* is a central one in the practice of modern psychiatry, described by the American Psychiatric Association as follows:

"'Fear' is the normal response to a genuine danger. With phobias, the fear is either irrational or excessive. It is an abnormally fearful response to a danger that is imagined or is irrationally exaggerated. People can develop phobic reactions to animals (e.g., spiders), activities (e.g., flying), or social situations (e.g., eating in public or simply being in a public environment). Phobias affect people of all ages, from all walks of life, and in every part of the world."[7]

Whether intended or not, application of the term Islamophobic to critics of Islam is a way of labeling the criticism as unbalanced or disturbed. It is extremely difficult to identify the boundary between "irrational or excessive" feelings about Islam and strongly held objections to elements of Islamic belief or practice. Those who found elements of Muslim cultural practices offensive felt shackled by the term, which in their view turned legitimate and responsible criticism of practices such as female circumcision and full-face veiling of women into rhetorical hate crimes. To brand all critics of certain Muslim ideas or behaviors as "Islamophobes" seemed to fall into the same trap as did some critics of policies of the Israeli state who found themselves branded as "anti-Semites."

As we shall see later, some objected to the term on the grounds that it actually was reasonable to fear and distrust Muslims, since it was real Islamist extremists and not imagined stereotypes who were perpetrating terrorist crimes on European soil. And yet, despite such protests, since 1997, the term Islamophobia has gained purchase.

In part this is because the neologism Islamophobia was well-framed to be a pithy and memorable cousin to *xenophobia*. There is, perhaps inevitably, dispute about its origins. The first recorded use of Islamophobia is attributed in one source to a leading Austrian-American Arabist named Gustave Edmund von Grunebaum, who coined the word in 1976 to refer to those who refuse to interpret the Koran literally.[8] However another source attributes the origin of the word to French Muslim artists and writers Étienne Dinet and Sliman Ben Ibrahim, writing in the years just before and after the end of World War I. The same author notes that while the meaning of the word was later influenced by 1985 writings of the late Edward Said, the Palestinian-American postcolonialism theorist and longtime member of the Palestinian National Council, "what secured its status in the present usage was its adoption by the Runnymede Trust Commission on British Muslims and Islamophobia, in its title and terms of reference, in 1996, and, especially, in its Report, the following year."[9]

Whatever its origins may be, the term gained traction in part because it does reflect a recrudescence of fear and distrust of Muslims and things Muslim in Europe. In 2004, UN Secretary General Kofi Annan addressed a United Nations conference on Islamophobia and specifically used the term. When "the world is compelled to coin a new term to take account of increasingly widespread bigotry," he said, "that is a sad and troubling development. Such is the case with Islamophobia."[10]

By 2010, lead stories with the word Islamophobia and Islamophobic in large fonts were gracing the covers of international mass media, such as *Time* magazine.[11] Islamophobia thus became an umbrella term, with meanings along a spectrum of negative reactions ranging from fear of Muslims to dislike, distaste, and even at times hatred of Islam or of those who practice it. Like xenophobia and anti-Semitism, the term Islamophobia is a house of many mansions, ranging from a rejection of the unfamiliar or the exotic, to fear of a takeover by strangers or, more threateningly, by those deemed to be loyal to a foreign entity and/or incapable of integrating into older communities. Behaviors included in the term extend from discrimination in housing or employment to violent acts against Muslims or symbols of Muslim life, such as mosques, minarets, or cemeteries, but they are by no means confined to physical aggression. Fear of Muslims sometimes is matched by hatred of them, but it need not degenerate into rhetorical or physical abuse of individual people. Those who are truly Islamophobic, like those who are anti-Semitic, can keep their distaste to themselves, or they can translate it into action.

It makes no sense, however, to consider Islamophobia as a form of *racial* hatred. The multiracial character of Islam is evident to all observers. Much more common is the use of the term Islamophobia to cover negative stereotypes applying not to all Muslims but primarily to Arabs and especially to those from some of the more-fundamentalist Persian Gulf states.

The problem here is that fundamentalist Islam extends to other parts of the Muslim world. The wars in Iran and Afghanistan present shocking images of Muslims engaged in violence and terrorism, starting in the 1990s and continuing through 9/11 and beyond. These images do what all stereotypes do: simplify and reduce a social group to a lowest common denominator, in this case, terrorism and cruelty. The fact that these attitudes are profound distortions of the nature of Islam or of most Muslim life is neither here nor there. The ugly face of terrorism is what many Europeans conjure up when they are asked what they think of Islam. Islamophobia, then, is rarely fear of Islam or of all Muslims, but rather it is a negative reaction to stereotypes of Muslims, derived from the protracted Israeli-Palestinian conflict, from terrorist attacks in New York, London, and Madrid, and from the wars in Iraq and Afghanistan.

In short, Islamophobia is a language of fear, which changes over time as the contours of international conflict change. It is about Muslims in war zones and in terrorist cells, there and here. It emerges when non-Muslims feel troubled by the presence of Muslims among them and turn those anxieties into fear and distrust. Considered criticism of Muslim practices or politics is not in itself Islamophobic, as some allege, but in the past two decades there has been in some cases a slide from considered criticism to repugnance and even to fear, hatred, and violence.

It is unclear whether the term Islamophobia has any power to distinguish between those who examine Islam critically but fairly and those who fear or detest it unfairly or irrationally. When Salman Rushdie's novel *The Satanic Verses* was burned by British Muslims in Yorkshire, as "blasphemy," and Rushdie himself was targeted for assassination, were those who defended Rushdie's right to free speech Islamophobes? The term itself both clarified and obscured reaction to Islam and thus cannot be used as if it had clear analytical powers.

It is easy enough to see the difference between rational discussions of Islam in Europe and the use of emotive stereotypes of Muslims as inherently different and dangerous. All we need to do is to survey briefly a series of public controversies in several European countries over the past decade. In each case, four central questions can be raised:

- Do Muslim practices and values clash with Western practices and values?
- Can Muslims assimilate within European society? If so, do they want to assimilate?
- If Muslims do not assimilate, does their growing presence in Europe constitute a matter for alarm and resistance?

- Does the growth of Islam and the Islamic population, at a time of declining fertility in Europe, constitute a form of demographic conquest?

The first and second questions elicit a range of answers from the considered to the ignorant. The third and fourth, when answered in the affirmative, occasionally arrive at Islamophobia, although there are those whose concern about Islam is logical and considered rather than pathological. There are gradations of Islamophobia, and some of the milder forms merge easily with nativist or conservative political currents. Each case is different, showing the danger of adopting any one term or category to interpret current European trends.

"The Veil" in France

On 15 March 2004, French President Jacques Chirac signed into law an amendment to the French code of education, enforcing a ban on wearing symbols or clothing expressing religious affiliations within the grounds of state secondary schools.[12] That ban affected roughly six hundred young Muslim women who chose to wear headscarves in school. In applying the rule, French administrators negotiated with Muslim families and persuaded most of them to abide by it. But some young women, supported by their families, refused. They were expelled and continued their education by correspondence.[13]

Six years later, a related debate ensued, this time with respect not to headscarves but instead to the "veils" or other garments that hide women's faces and are worn by some Muslim women as a sign of modesty in public, though not in their homes. A parliamentary panel considered banning such face-covering garments anywhere in public, following the lead of President Nicolas Sarkozy, who in June 2009 said such dress was "not welcome" in France.[14]

The draft bill contained the following clause: "No one may, in spaces open to the public and on public streets, wear a garment or an accessory that has the effect of hiding the face." After surveying public reaction to the bill, Sarkozy initially appeared to back off, and indeed in January 2010 he said such a ban might be "unworkable": "The full veil is not welcome in France because it is contrary to our values and contrary to the ideals we have of a woman's dignity," he said. "But it is vital to conduct ourselves in a way that no-one feels stigmatized. We must find a solution which enables us to win the widest support."[15]

Public and political support for such a provision, however, proved to be strong, and it was approved by overwhelming majorities in the National Assembly in July 2010 and in the Senate in September 2010. Opponents of the proposed new law had hoped that the Constitutional Council would reject it as inconsistent with French constitutional protections, but in October 2010 the council approved the law with only one small change—that it could not be applied in public places of religious worship.[16] Opponents of the French legislation expressed their intent to file a challenge to its provisions before the European Court of Human Rights in Strasbourg, which, if successful, might raise serious issues of conflict between the court and the French state.

The law provided for a six-month period of public education, during which women wearing a full-face veil in public were to be advised that they would face arrest and a fine if they continued to do so. The fine would be 150 euros and/or a requirement that they take a course in French citizenship. Anyone found by the courts to be forcing a woman to wear a full-face veil in public would be subject to a fine of up to 30,000 euros and up to one year in jail.

To some degree the cacophony of views on this subject is driven by linguistic ambiguities, differences, and confusions. In some but not all Islamic societies there are multiple but very different types of coverings worn by females, some or all of which are sometimes referred to confusingly under the single English term *veil*. Most English usage of *veil* does not include the headscarf or *hijāb*, which derives from the Arabic term for "modesty" and usually covers a woman's head and neck but not normally her face. On the other hand the *niqāb*, a facial covering that leaves only the eyes of the woman visible, is usually termed a *veil*. It is most typically found in a minority of Arab cultures, especially those in the conservative Gulf states, and in some cases women also wear a separate covering for the eyes, in which case their veil becomes a full-face covering. The *veil* usage almost always includes the burka or *burqa'*, a garment largely confined to parts of Afghanistan, which covers the entire face and entire body of the woman, providing only a mesh screen for her to see through.[17]

Outside of the Islamic world these differences in meaning and connotation are often simply ignored in media and other discussions. If debates in English or French about the veil or *le voile* make inconsistent distinctions between the wearing of a casual headscarf and a total head-to-toe covering, it is no wonder that confusion is endemic.

Finally, in English the word *veil* also carries other meanings. The term applies to see-through netting or gauze that can be attached to a woman's hat or clothing, whether as a fashion component or as in the "wedding veil." The same word even is used in English to refer to the part of a Catholic nun's headdress that frames but does not cover the face and falls over the shoulders; indeed a woman who chooses to become a nun is often described as having "taken the veil."

In French, the equivalent word *le voile* carries with it some quite different connotations. A cloth covering of the hair, head, *or* the face is referred to in French as *le voile*. This connotation includes the wearing of a headscarf, which in English is not commonly denoted by the word *veil*. In its feminine form, *la voile* refers to the sail of a sailboat, a meaning that does not attach at all to the English word *veil*. Meanwhile, those who wish to be more precise distinguish the headscarf (*hijāb*) from full-face forms of *le voile*, such as the *burqa'* or the *niqāb*. It is clear that we have entered a murky area of linguistic and cultural differences.

In France, the idea of a facially veiled presence on the public streets ran counter to long-cherished claims to equality and fraternity as pillars of French public life. If women's faces were veiled, how could they be deemed equal to men whose faces were there for all to see? In France the police have the right to examine identity cards, but do they have the right to scrutinize faces? Most people think so, and so does a majority of the French parliament. Not all those opposed to the full-face veil are Islamophobes, though some may be so.

It also is important to note that there is some support within the French Muslim community for a ban on the full-facial veil, the *niqāb*, or the fully-body cover for women, the *burqa'*. A Tunisian-born Parisian imam, Hassen Chalghoumi, finds no support for these practices within the Koran and considers them symbols of inequality, not of modesty. The full-face veil such as the *niqāb* or the *burqa'* "cuts off Muslims from France and frightens many. A man who knows nothing about religion and sees a woman hidden from head to toe, what is he going to understand from that religion? The *burqa'* is a sign of extremism, and it's normal that the state is fighting against that." Chalghoumi goes on to reject the argument that women wearing the full-face veil were expressing their religious freedom: "If some 'acts of freedom' stir hatred, it's not good. And will it show the good side of Islam? I don't think so. One has to respect the feelings of others. The French have not accepted the hijab, . . . How do you expect them to accept the niqab? . . . You see the problem? . . . People think Islam is a dark, closed religion, that women are imprisoned and men think only about sex. What an image! This is the perception I refuse!"[18] Chalghoumi's is a minority voice, and he has faced death threats for speaking out on this subject.[19] He has also encouraged dialogue between Muslims and Jews, another unpopular stance in some fundamentalist Muslim circles. It should be noted in addition that Chalghoumi's cultural background is Tunisian, where any version of the full-face veil is quite uncommon, and not Gulf Arab, where it is common. His opinions illustrate the variety of views among Muslims on the practice of veiling, which parallel a wide array of thinking among non-Muslims too.

These two French political controversies—about the headscarf in French public schools and the full-face veil in public settings—show in different ways the rough outline of a series of European debates about the compatibility of Islamic practices with full citizenship in twenty-first-century Europe. The headscarf incident focused on a central pillar of French Republic political practice: the creation of a privileged space in the schools for the formation of the future citizens of the French state. Here the ban on headscarves had a specific set of boundaries attached to it. Dress or symbols expressing religious affiliation in what were deemed significant ways were excluded from the schools. Small Christian crosses were inoffensive and could be tolerated. But large crosses were demonstrative and unacceptable. So too, argued the French parliament and French educational officials, was the headscarf.

Let us leave aside the arbitrariness of the distinction between small and large symbols and focus on the principle involved. Here the clash between religious expression and secular institutions has a very long history. It is not only that church and state—in effect the Roman Catholic Church and the French Republic—have been at daggers drawn since the French Revolution itself, and that a vivid line was drawn separating church and state again in 1905; it was also that since the 1870s, the school system has served as the central set of institutions through which the republic reproduces itself by educating the young in what it means to be a *citoyen* of France, a central concept going back to the French Revolution.

Thus the questioning of religious garb or symbols in that particular setting is imbedded deeply within the history of France. Consequently, the fuss over the headscarf in schools abated not long after the 2004 legislation was passed. Feminists continued to struggle over this issue, some choosing the right of young women to express themselves without constraint, while others saw the force of accepting Republican norms.[20]

The 2010 legislation banning the full covering of the face in public proved to be even more controversial. [21] It makes unlawful the wearing of full-face coverings in public spaces, as distinct from the privileged institutional space of the schoolyard and classroom, where the headscarf is also prohibited. Although it has attracted overwhelming support in the French parliament and in public opinion, it continues to be opposed by those who see France as a country of massive immigration from Africa (especially the Muslim Maghreb) and Asia, and which has long prided itself on its openness to people of any religion or color to join the republic. From this admittedly minority French perspective, this legislation bans in most public settings forms of dress associated with one particular version of one particular religion—Islam.

While many Muslims saw both bans as Islamophobic, we argue that they are nothing of the kind. The fact that the secular Turkish state enforces a similar ban on the headscarf in schools in a country 98 percent of whose citizens are Muslims reinforces the point. The second ban is different, a rejection of one form of dress associated with a minority of Muslims. Critics argue that this is something that would hardly be tolerated if it applied to Sikh turbans or Hasidic Jewish dress or Amish dress or nuns' habits. Yet the masking of a woman's face carries different connotations than do the denominational dress of Sikhs, Hasidic Jews, or Amish.

It is, first, the gendered character of the practice that opens it to a range of criticism, which rarely constitutes the prejudice conveyed by the term Islamophobia. In addition, the full masking of a woman's face seems to be qualitatively different from mere "dress," for example, wearing a turban, a black suit and fur hat, a robe, or long/short hair. The reasons for this response are no doubt deeply psychological, con-founded with the mask's image of secretiveness, of cutting off from oth-ers, or secretly observing others without any possibility of reciprocal human interaction. Indeed, one common symbol of drama is that of the dual comedic and tragic masks, originating from the practice in an-cient Greece in which all actors wore masks on the stage. While masking through makeup or plastic surgery are time-honored practices that do not convey any threat, they are conventional or self-protective practices with little menace attached to them.

In addition to such psychological and cultural considerations, there are specific problems of a more-contemporary kind introduced when we consider masking the face, especially at a time of sustained security alerts and terrorist threats. In airports today head cover of any kind must be removed by most people to complete security clear-ance, though security officials are allowed to exercise discretion in this regard.

It is apparent that there are powerful symbols and cultural clashes at play here. To some, full-facial veiling conveys the notion of modesty. To others it indicates hiddenness, separation, or secrecy. Some critics may harbor Islamophobia, but their criticism of the Muslim veil does not in and of itself indicate any prejudice at all. The face-to-face politics of a western European republic such as France embraces such cultural practices only with difficulty.

Of most importance, according to some of those who support the new French legislation, the full covering of women's bodies including their faces represents deep degradation of women. It may be not the practice so much as its gendered character and associations of inferior-ity or uncontrollable sexual attraction that invites so much criticism and opposition. And since equality is a principle of republican life, those who deny equality for women in public cannot share in the life of the republic. Hence, the full-facial covering of women, seen by a subset of Muslims as a form of piety, is repugnant to those who stand by the principle of gender equality in particular and equality in general. Consequently, they argue, those who dress in this particular manner, involving full coverage of the face—clearly a small but visible minority of Muslims—cannot assimilate into French or European life. They are outsiders and must remain so.

Are there elements of Islamophobia in this argument? After all, the objection does not apply to any other religious group dressing in particular ways on the streets of France. Yet the same could be said of conventional Western prohibitions on child marriage and polygamy, since these apply to only particular parts of specific religious traditions (Muslims, some Mormons, some traditional African religions). The French ban on full-face coverings in public would apply to any other group that might someday embrace such a practice as its dress code. Since there is no such group at the moment, the effect of the ban is to single out for special opprobrium certain Muslims wearing certain dress they choose to wear for religious or cultural reasons. Such people cannot be French; they are "other" and must take the consequences.

Those who object to the conclusion that banning full-face covering is prejudicial argue that this prohibition refers to all populations, whatever their religious beliefs. When the difference objected to is one that involves long-standing norms applying to all people, then it hardly makes sense to refer to the objection as Islamophobic. The prohibition against child marriage also applies to Muslims, but not only to them. Female genital mutilation is practiced among some Muslim and non-Muslim African populations, but that does not justify tolerating it in Europe or elsewhere. There are norms of human dignity that apply explicitly within European society that transcend cultural difference. We turn to these in the conclusion later.

Murder in Holland

In 2004, a few months after the passage of the law prohibiting the wearing of headscarves in French schools, a second incident highlighted the difficulty many Europeans had in squaring Muslim practices with European customs and beliefs. On 2 November 2004, the Dutch writer and filmmaker Theodoor van Gogh, the great-grandson of the artist Vincent van Gogh's brother Theo, was murdered in Amsterdam. The self-confessed killer was Mohammed Bouyeri, a Muslim born in Amsterdam of Dutch-Moroccan descent. Bouyeri shot van Gogh eight times, cut his throat, and left a dagger in his chest. A five-page note was attached to one of the daggers, threatening Western governments and van Gogh's collaborator Ayaan Hirsi Ali, the Somali- and Muslim-born Dutch feminist, writer, and former member of parliament.

Theodoor van Gogh had been no stranger to controversy. He was an equal-opportunity critic of religion. He complained about the Jewish obsession with Auschwitz and on one occasion replied to a Jewish critic that he suspected she had had erotic dreams about having sex with Dr. Josef Mengele. Here is free speech red in tooth and claw, but it attracted relatively little attention until van Gogh and Hirsi Ali turned their attention to Islam and made a film together about the cruelty inflicted on women in Muslim countries. As a well-known agent provocateur, annoying people was van Gogh's métier, but in this case annoyance turned into assassination.[22]

Bouyeri admitted the killing and pronounced his motive: outrage over the portrayal of women in Islam in the film van Gogh made together with Hirsi Ali. Entitled *Submission*, the film focused on violence against women in Islamic nations. Barely clad women on their knees tell stories of their oppression, and verses from the Koran in Arabic script are projected onto women's bodies, presenting a strong indictment of Islamic misogyny. A few weeks before the crime, an Islamic preacher referred to van Gogh as a "criminal bastard" who deserved to contract an incurable disease.[23]

Some Muslim activists were arrested in the wake of the crime, and a series of violent incidents took place, some attributed to Muslims and others evidently against them. The repercussions were lingering. The right-wing Dutch politician Geert Wilders started a campaign to declare a five-year halt to non-European immigration to the country. "The Netherlands," he said, "has been too tolerant [to] intolerant people for too long. We should not import a retarded political Islamic society to our country."[24] Wilders's pronouncements apparently hit a resonant chord, because in the parliamentary elections of June 2010 his PVV Party

(Party for Freedom) increased its parliamentary representation from 9 to 24 seats (out of 150) by winning over 15 percent of the vote. Following this electoral success, Wilders agreed to provide parliamentary support for a governing coalition between the larger VVD (People's Party for Freedom) and CDA (Christian Democratic Appeal) parties, but not to join the coalition government per se.

Here again, we see in another form the mix of responses to Islam in western Europe. Some felt, after van Gogh's murder, that Muslim values were incompatible with the open tolerance of difference that is central to European culture in general and Dutch culture in particular. Such an argument does not constitute Islamophobia, though it does tend to treat Islam or Muslim values as a monolith. There was a very short distance, though, between the critique of Muslim intolerance of the rights of artists and writers to express their views on Islam and on the rights of women in Islam, and the stereotyping of Islam as simply "retarded," primitive or barbaric. The gap between reasonable criticism and prejudice was a narrow and narrowing one. The slide from one to the other was all too easy and predictable.[25]

Danish Cartoons

Very similar issues were brought to a head by an incident in Denmark the following year.[26] On 30 September 2005, the conservative newspaper the *Jyllands-Posten* published twelve cartoons its editors had commissioned depicting the Prophet Muhammad, saying that they published these images as a contribution to the debate surrounding Islam and self-censorship. One cartoon in particular, drawn by artist Kurt Westergaard, portrayed the Prophet with a bomb in his turban with its fuse lit. In a stroke, the newspaper both attracted considerable attention and provoked strong reactions from the public. There is hardly anything remarkable in that; after all, it is what newspapers do in the West, for reasons usually more pecuniary than principled.

The editors of the newspaper succeeded beyond their dreams. Their position was that there was no justification to follow a silent but powerful ban on discussing Islam and terror; why should one religion be treated with kid gloves while all others were pilloried with impunity?

This is, after all, the same question Salman Rushdie had posed in his *Satanic Verses*, published in 1988. In it there is a satirical portrayal of the Prophet Muhammad mistaking the whisperings of the devil in his ear for the words of God. As we noted in our book *A Question of Numbers*, the outcome was a fatwa, or legal decree, issued initially by the Grand Ayatollah Khomeini, the supreme leader of the Islamic Republic of Iran, and still in effect two decades later.[27]

In the same way, the Danish newspaper's cartoons provoked Muslim anger and hostility, just as Hirsi Ali and van Gogh had done in the Netherlands. To add fuel to the fire, these images of Muhammad were reprinted in fifty countries.

Initially the Danish government ignored the whole affair, but then a small number of Danish Muslims decided to go on a tour of Islamic countries to drum up support for strong international representations to the Danish government and its ambassadors expressing Muslim anger and threatening a boycott of Danish exports. Demonstrations against Denmark, the newspaper, and the cartoonist ensued in multiple countries, in some cases turning violent. In response, the Danish government swung into action, expressing regret over any perceived humiliation of Muslims in the publication of such cartoons, while explaining that it was within the normal boundaries of free speech in Denmark for newspapers to publish such images.

The aftershocks of the crisis continued long afterward. In January 2010 the cartoonist Westergaard was attacked in his home by an ax-wielding Somali man. The artist had already been warned of threats to his life, and he and his grandson retreated to a safe room that the Danish police had recommended he have constructed, from which he called the police for help. The police arrived in time to shoot and wound the intruder before he could penetrate the safe room with his ax.[28]

The compatibility of a culture of rough-and-tumble exchange in the European daily press with the sensitivities of devout Muslims living within European society was once more called into question. Here we can see the shift from reasoned consideration of this real predicament to emotional and self-proclaimed provocation; the slide from the first to the second describes the all-too-rapid degeneration of responsible public comment into what some would call Islamophobia.

The cartoons occupy the middle space between reason and prejudice. That is what caricature does. It visualizes and drastically simplifies issues and problems that require subtlety and caution to understand. One could read these cartoons as harmless examples of the art of exaggeration so common to cartoon caricatures. One could also read them as intolerable insults directed at Islam. Both are possible readings, and it is their ambiguity—like caricatures of Jews with big noses or African-origin people with thick lips and curly hair—that makes them potentially dangerous.

The reason why the free speech defense is not entirely persuasive to all is that they believe there must be limits to what can be said in polite company about other religious groups, reflecting secular sensitivity to religious groups that was lacking in the Muhammad cartoons case. Denying the Holocaust—a criminal offense in Germany and Austria—is repugnant in part because it entails further injuring Jewish people still recovering from the crime. And yet few would doubt that this prohibition represents an infringement upon individuals' freedom of speech. It provides a good example of the difficult trade-offs that contesting claims about fundamental human rights (for example, speech, religious beliefs, political commitments) frequently impose. We shall return to this point later.

Imagine for a moment cartoons of Catholic priests engaged in inducing abortions or abusing altar boys. Such hypothetical cartoons might provoke similar outrage among a sensitive minority of Catholics. While it might be argued that the church's sexual abuse scandals touch less upon international affairs than do many aspects involving Jews and Arabs, it is evident that with respect to abortion the Holy See and other church leaders have long been actively engaged in promoting its dogma through both domestic politics and international diplomacy.

Consider a cartoonist who presented the biblical King David or the medieval Jewish philosopher Maimonides as a pedophile; many people would just shrug, but there are Jewish groups who would react—and react strongly. During a speaking engagement at Yale University in 2010, the chairman of a United Nations report assessing possible Israeli war crimes in the 2009 war in Gaza was protected by a police guard, and police dogs were present in case needed for crowd control. During the meeting he was vilified in public as an anti-Semite, a follower of the persecutors of Captain Dreyfus and of the authors of the infamous czarist literary forgery known as *The Protocols of the Elders of Zion*. A reasoned critique of the actions of Israeli soldiers in their military operation in Gaza slid rapidly in the minds of some Jewish activists into what they alleged was his hatred of Jews as Jews. Indeed, death threats are a common experience among Jews who take visible stands on peace in the Middle East; to their enemies, they are "self-hating Jews" who need to be chastised or punished. The prominent Israeli political scientist Zeev Sternhell was injured by a letter bomb sent to him in Jerusalem by a settler on the West Bank, not only to injure him for his political statements against the continued occupation of the West Bank but also, in Voltaire's famous quotation often invoked regarding political persecution, *pour encourager les autres.*[29]

The same slide from responding to political differences rationally to reacting to them with violence or the threat of violence describes the shift from considering a spirited or visually provocative critique of radical Islam as bad taste into taking it as an attack on Islam and responding violently to it. There were demonstrations in Syria, Lebanon, and Pakistan to protest the publication of the Danish cartoons. Some led to violence: Three people, including an eight-year-old boy, died in riots in Peshawar, Pakistan;[30] more grist for the mill of those who see not only individual Muslims but Islam itself as irrational, violent, and intolerant. Those aggrieved who turn to violence tend to generate precisely the prejudices they were and are so quick to detect and indict. The case of the Danish cartoons shows both the uses and abuses of the term Islamophobia. "Handle with care" should be written on all versions of it.

Minarets in Switzerland

European reactions to the conflict over what could be said about Islam took a new turn in 2010, this time in Switzerland—the base of numerous international human rights organizations. In this incident, the prior cases of Muslim "intolerance" were part of the background. In the foreground was the symbolic space in which Muslims announced their presence within European society. It was not the mosque per se, but the minaret, the site of the call to prayer. Its long, slender spire announced in a highly visual manner that Islam was in Europe and that the faithful were there to stay.

As in Denmark, domestic politics precipitated an international incident provoked by Christoph Blocher, a wealthy industrialist turned Swiss politician. He served as minister of justice and police in the Swiss Federal Council from 2004 to 2007. As of this writing (2013), he is vice-president of the Swiss People's Party, which proclaims itself as right-wing, free market, anti-EU, and an opponent of further immigration to Switzerland.

Blocher is a controversial figure, a provocative right-winger in the line of Jean-Marie Le Pen in France and the late Jörg Haider in Austria. The Swiss artist Thomas Hirschhorn was said to have urinated on Blocher's photograph during a performance in December 2004. In 2006 Blocher called two Albanians seeking political asylum "criminals," then denied he used the word to describe men who had not been convicted of any crime. Later he admitted he had lied, eliciting an unprecedented reprimand from a federal commission for having made false statements as minister of justice. He was dogged by allegations of corruption and failed in his bid for reelection to the Federal Council in late 2007. His Swiss People's Party used posters in its anti-immigration efforts, the most famous of which showed three white sheep kicking a black sheep off a Swiss flag, with the caption "For More Security."[31]

In 2009, Blocher revived his stalled political career by masterminding a public referendum on minarets in Switzerland. "The minarets interrupt the Christian horizon," he opined, and in Switzerland that is dangerous since the landscape is "the trademark of our culture." Blocher succeeded in tapping worry and anger over Islamic terrorism by conjuring up a material target of their fears—the minaret. He failed to note that in Switzerland there are many mosques, but only four minarets. The number in France is twelve.[32]

Blocher and his allies were determined to ensure that there would be no additional minarets in Switzerland. Mechanisms for direct democracy, such as public referenda, are a long-standing Swiss form for the expression of national sentiment on issues of public concern. Between January and July of 2008, Blocher and his political allies collected over one hundred thousand signatures, a sufficient number to force a referendum on the single question as to whether there ought to be a ban on the future construction of minarets. Arguing that minarets are symbols of political and religious claims to power, the sponsors of the referendum asked Swiss voters not to prohibit mosques but to ban the future building of minarets.[33] Under Swiss law, a yes vote would gain constitutional sanction, requiring the Swiss parliament to pass a law giving force to the people's will.

Most of the Swiss elite—political, religious, media, economic, and educational—opposed the referendum in strong terms. To pass, it was required to achieve a "double majority"—not only support from a majority of citizen voters but also from the voters in a majority of the nation's twenty-three cantons. To the surprise (and alarm) of many observers, the referendum easily exceeded these requirements, receiving support from more than 57 percent of voters and 85 percent of Swiss cantons.

One of the political posters supporting the ban shows black towers, minarets. While these towers clearly have balconies, to some commentators who opposed the referendum they appeared to be the shape of ballistic missiles, protruding threateningly out of a Swiss flag and with the motif dominated by a fully veiled female profile garbed in black.[34]

As framed, the ban on new minarets did not affect either the construction of new mosques already under way or the four existing minarets in Switzerland. John Esposito, director of the Georgetown University Center for Muslim-Christian Understanding, suggested that the vote expressed fears of militant Islam, symbolized by minarets. The antiminaret position, he said, drew on fears that mosques breed fundamentalism and that fundamentalists feed terrorism.[35] The ruling Federal Council noted that it takes such fears seriously. "However, the Federal Council takes the view that a ban on the construction of new minarets is not a feasible means of countering extremist tendencies."[36]

The outcome of the Swiss referendum may also reflect a gap between elite and popular opinion on matters of national identity as a whole. Indeed, such a gap may be a phenomenon common to other countries as well and may be ignored by political leaders at their peril.[37] The Swiss People's Party has gained support among Swiss who are opposed to the encroachment of the European Union on traditional Swiss neutrality and independence. When the new European constitution was put to a referendum on 2005, it was voted down in several European countries. The Swiss popular vote on future minaret construction reflects many currents of opinion, only some of which touch on questions of the compatibility of Muslim practices in European society. The key point, though, is that there is a substantial gap between the views held by many of those in office and the proverbial "man in the street" on such matters. The Swiss vote may have been a warning signal by ordinary men and women to their leaders that if they ignore their views, they will have to answer for it.

The Swiss vote to ban new minarets, therefore, reflected many currents of thought. But among those supporting the ban were people unhappy with a highly visible architectural structure announcing that Islam is part of the landscape. That is what the Swiss People's Party leader said. His views matter, though perhaps not as much as he may think. In this case too we see the binary character of public rhetoric on Islam in Europe. There is a reasoned discourse alongside an emotive and fear-ridden discourse. Elite opinion and popular sentiment frequently move in different directions. The same has been true with respect to the death penalty over decades in Europe: Popular support for it is suppressed by elite rejection. The vote against more minarets in Switzerland was symbolic politics of a high order, but it is consistent with both reasoned and irrational responses to Islam. Switzerland is by no means the only country in which such a mixed brew of reason and prejudice may be found. Those who doubt this claim should look in the mirror.

Between Considered Debate and Islamophobia

Based on the foregoing considerations, the rule of thumb we adopt is that the term Islamophobia is a fair characterization of only a small proportion of comment about Muslims in Europe today. *What* precise proportion is impossible to say, but it is wrong to bracket together critics of some Islamic practices with hatemongers and racists.

And yet the fact that there is indeed some Islamophobic sentiment in Europe is a cause for concern. One question that arises in this context is whether Islamophobia is a substitute for anti-communism as a rallying call for the political right. Perhaps so, though there is a more negative character to the Islamophobic appeal than in anti-communism. Islamophobia tends to coincide with hostility to the European Union, seen as too weak or too divided to defend the interests of citizens of countries still proud of their national and historically Christian traditions.

The timescale for further developments in this controversy is unforeseeable. One possible step is for the Swiss Green Party to challenge the minarets referendum outcome before the European Court of Human Rights in Strasbourg. Such a challenge would likely further antagonize nationalists in several countries, since it highlights the truncation of national sovereignty imbedded in the European project. Would the Swiss government defend the referendum as a legitimate expression of the sovereignty of the Swiss people and state? Or would it decline to do so, as being in conflict with its own views on Swiss human rights practice? Would it join as a supporter of such a challenge against a referendum passed by a substantial majority of its own voters? If the European Court of Human Rights were to declare that this Swiss constitutional amendment violates the European Convention on Human Rights, to which Switzerland is a signatory, how would the Swiss government respond? No one knows the answer to these or similar questions.

What Islamophobia represents, therefore, is a new form of the old tradition of European distaste, discomfort, and fear of the other. This mix of angry and mean sentiments has both religious and racial undertones, to be sure, which create obstacles for Europeans of sub-Saharan African descent in the housing and labor markets. It is important to note that these views are decidedly marginal, but that does not mean they will not grow in coming years.

The second question that arises is whether Islamophobia is a new form of European anti-Semitism, taking the term *Semite* to apply to Arab and Jew alike. Since most Muslims are not Arabs, we enter here into another linguistic quagmire: How can *anti-Semitism* apply to Muslims from Indonesia or Nigeria?

But even if we admit the objections to using the term *anti-Semitism* as a parallel to anti-Islamic sentiment, there are still disturbing historical similarities to note. Many of the features of pre-1945 anti-Semitism are indeed mirrored in today's Islamophobia. European anti-Semites argued that Jews were unable and unwilling to assimilate, that they had loyalties not to the nation in which they lived but to the Jewish people, and after 1948 to the state of Israel. Europe was a Christian continent, and Jews had no part in it. These are well-known clichés, and we can hear their echoes in some extreme forms of today's debates on Muslims in Europe.

There are two major differences, though, between the two cases. The first is a difference in scale, and the second is a difference in international context. The size of the Muslim population currently residing in the four western European countries in which the incidents we surveyed earlier took place dwarfs the number of Jews who resided in western Europe before the Second World War. Even at the height of the Dreyfus Affair, from 1896 to 1906, the number of Jews in France, a population that had lived there for centuries, was around eighty thousand, or 0.2 percent of the population. As we have seen in chapter 2, that number is exceeded by Muslims in France by a very substantial factor; approximately five to six million Muslims live in France today. Fear does not depend on numbers. In Germany in 1933, there were approximately five hundred thousand Jews, or 0.75 percent of the population. Still what the Nazis termed the "Jewish conspiracy" was in their minds a subtle form of control by a tiny minority. Those who fear the Muslim conquest of Europe see millions of Muslims among them.

The second distinction between these two forms of European religious and ethnic hatred, separated by a century, is the reality of armed attacks on civilians by Muslim extremists in Europe. However anti-Semites sought to portray the "Jewish conspiracy," that imagined threat did not include the use of bombs, guns, axes, and knives. It is true that the Nazis pointed to something they termed "Judeo-Bolshevism" to conflate Jewish bankers with Communists, but the standard anti-Semitic diatribe was over Jewish money, not bombs.

In contrast, money is not the central issue in European concerns about Islam. Instead, Muslims attached to a worldwide web of fundamentalists have called attention to themselves by engaging in bloody acts of terrorism. These acts are hardly the distorted figments of twisted

Islamophobic imaginations. They have happened in London and Madrid in spectacular and deadly fashion, and elsewhere sporadically. The terrorist attacks on New York and Washington were developed in Hamburg. When public opinion polls show Europeans linking Islam and terror, they are disclosing real reactions to real events, whereas the Nazis term *Judeo-Bolshevism* was always pure and malevolent fiction.

That said, there are some affinities between Islamophobia and anti-Semitism among some extreme groups in Europe. Each form of prejudice has been used by some Europeans to define who they are by reference to who they are not.[38] Each defines some facets of European identity as rooted in vaguely defined Christian beliefs and practices, which Muslims and Jews could never share and have been said to actively despise and reject. Both groups have remained, to anti-Semites and Islamophobes alike, in some sense as self-defined outsiders in Europe, even though their coreligionists had lived in the Balkans and elsewhere in Europe for more than a millennium. The place of Turkish Islam in Europe is ignored in such diatribes, too, as is the lingering and fertile genius of Moorish Islam in domestic and public architecture of post-1492 Christian Spain. At a time when nationalists feel besieged and worried by what they see as the incursion of the new Europe into older practices and traditions, discomfort about a changing world is almost certain to provoke instances of what Albert Hirschman termed the "rhetoric of reaction."[39] To some on the extreme right, the past was always a better place to be.

In conclusion, let us attempt a rough definition of Islamophobia. It is best understood as a pithy and memorable blanket term covering the slide from a sense of difference to distaste to prejudice among those confronting the presence of Muslims in their societies. Many of those who emphasize religious and cultural differences never take the next step toward Islamophobia. Much of what is pilloried as Islamophobia does not qualify as such. But when prominent people speak of essential differences between European Christianity and Islam, they risk encouraging others to move toward the next step in this slide.

Concern about Islam in Europe emerges from within political debate. It starts with rational analyses of Muslim immigration to Europe and Muslim practices with respect to family life, gender differences, and religious law, and it very frequently stops there. But even some responsible and thoughtful critics of Islam open the door to others who take several steps further, moving toward—and sometimes reaching—a combination of fear and hatred of Islam.

Seeing true Islamophobia—here defined more carefully than the Runnymede Trust's report as "an irrational and excessive fear of Islam and/or Muslims"—as the end of this line is useful in two ways. The first is that the process is neither inevitable nor irreversible. There is nothing that requires the move from criticism or intellectual rejection of some facets of Islam to irrational and excessive fear or even hatred of Muslims, nor that the direction be one way. Secondly, those who see that their intellectual, rational arguments about certain practices of some Muslims can be used for nefarious purposes can and do change their language or urge those misinterpreting them to think again.

A focus on process enables us to see how powerful certain catalysts are in shifting the terrain of the discussion of Islam from the reasonable to the irrational. This is hardly new in population debates, but it is a matter for concern nonetheless. The debate over immigration in Europe is one such powerful catalyst, which existed long before radical Islam came to the fore. As we have shown in earlier work, this catalyst is particularly powerful when linked to discussions of low or declining indigenous fertility.[40] But since the 1980s the arrival of Muslim immigrants in Europe on a large scale has presented what many people construe as multiple threats to European culture and security. It is not a giant step from this set of perceptions, some rational, some exaggerated, to the view that Muslims in Europe, growing strong through immigration and higher fertility, are engaged in a form of demographic takeover or conquest.

In April 2006, Muammar al-Gadhafi, the late Libyan ruler, added fuel to the fire by saying just that. Islam will take over Europe within a few decades, without any need for violent force, he told the Arabic satellite network Al Jazeera: "We have 50 million Muslims in Europe. . . . There are signs that Allah will grant Islam victory in Europe—without swords, without guns, without conquests. The 50 million Muslims of

Europe will turn it into a Muslim continent within a few decades. . . . Allah mobilizes the Muslim nation of Turkey, and adds it to the European Union. . . . Europe is in a predicament, and so is America. They should agree to become Islamic in the course of time, or else declare war on the Muslims. . . ."[41]

To be sure, it would be foolish to take the word of a demagogue as a guide to Muslim opinion, whether in Libya or elsewhere. But the fact that he made such a statement is important. Al-Gadhafi's rhetoric contributed to the slide from rational to emotive considerations of this issue. What major public figures say in public matters.

Let us also consider the case of Pope Benedict XVI to show the distinction between reasoned debate about Islam in Europe and Islamophobia. Before he became pope, Cardinal Ratzinger called negotiations with Turkey over membership in the European Union "a grave error" and "anti-historical," since Turkey's Islamic character rendered it a "permanent contrast to Europe."[42] In fact, the pope changed his mind on this point three years later and said so publicly on the eve of an official visit to Turkey.[43] The pope has many roles, and one of them is that of diplomat, and in that respect he may choose to respond to diplomatic necessities. As pope, Benedict XVI also delivered an address to the Catholic University of Regensburg,[44] in which he cited a medieval text juxtaposing the Christian belief in conversion through reason with the Muslim belief in conversion through force. On this topic he proceeded to present a learned discourse, but when cited in the popular press, the niceties tended to get lost. The scholar's rigor vanished, to be replaced by press stereotypes. The key point here is not that the pope presented Muslims as fundamentally different from Christian Europeans, but that he associated Islam with conversion through force, a position easily separated from learned discourse in the overheated atmosphere in which the presence of Muslims in Europe today is posed. It was not his intention to do so, but even the pope can lubricate the path along which many others slide into prejudice.

True Islamophobia, irrational and excessive, becomes more possible when Islam is treated as an essence, something unified, unchanging and threatening in character. One way to understand its force is to show how fear becomes encapsulated within language itself. True Islamophobes use adjectives that impute ideas or actions from the fundamental character or essence of different groups. The frequent and preferred use of adjectives rather than nouns is one stylistic form that distinguishes Islamophobes from those who object to what some Muslims do or believe.

Let us consider the following argument. Many people in Germany wrote about Jews, but anti-Semites wrote about the "Jewish threat." In turning a statement about people into a statement about a facet of the behavior of the people in question, emotive associations easily enter the discussion. In Israel, "immigration of Christians" in Hebrew carries different connotations than does "Christian immigration." It is possible that adjectives carry emotion or inflection in some languages that nouns do not convey on their own. Thus the phrase "immigration of Muslims" may describe a set of events; "Muslim immigration" may give a particular set of attributes or consequences to immigration itself. In this rhetorical grammar, immigration when it is Muslim in character is portrayed as a threat to the receiving states and communities. Islamophobes may use the adjective *Muslim* or *Islamic* to connote essential differences between subcategories of the noun in question, in this case *immigration.*

Hence immigration by Christians to Europe may be distinguished dramatically and categorically from immigration by Muslims, when the conversation starts by distinguishing Christian and Muslim immigration as two categorically different matters. The first is by definition benign; the second may be seen as less than neutral in character and, among extremists, malignant. The key point here is that the language used in much of the discussion of Muslim immigration to Europe after 9/11 has room in it for reason and for prejudice. The political context matters, here as elsewhere.

Guilt by association is always a dangerous game to play. It does matter that the 9/11 plot was hatched in Germany by radical Muslims. Yet this tells us nothing about the ideas and political tendencies of 99 percent of Muslims in Hamburg or elsewhere in Europe. Spectacular instances of terrorism create doubt about all Muslims, but rational people stop short of turning doubts into blanket prejudice. Angry and ignorant people do not.

Violence against Muslims

When we write of Islamophobia, real or imagined, we need to recognize that it describes ideas and criminal acts both. The attacks of 9/11 did not create Islamophobia but they propagated its spread in a host of ways. There were well-documented incidents of anti-Muslim violence before 9/11, reflecting long-standing patterns of hatred of Muslims of whatever race. But true Islamophobia is multifaceted. Some of its adherents may be offended by the color of Muslims' skin, though Islam is famously color-blind. Others focus on the nature of Muslim beliefs and practices and the supposed threat they pose to the broader society in which they live.

When eleven mosques in Britain were attacked in the aftermath of the terrorist bombings of London in July 2005, and when six mosques were set alight in 2006, we entered a domain beyond race. It was not black or brown men, but Muslims and Arab Muslims, more specifically, who slaughtered more than three thousand people in New York in 2001, or who killed nearly two hundred and injured eighteen hundred Madrid train commuters in March 2004. In response to these mass murders, Muslims throughout Europe became targets in a manner that both drew upon and departed from conventional xenophobia and endemic racism.[45]

Again, it is important to note that the incidence of anti-Muslim violence was already of concern in Europe before 2001. In 1997 the European Union established a European Monitoring Centre on Racism and Xenophobia, which began collecting data on discrimination and violence against Muslims throughout the EU. Three years later, the Council of Europe's European Commission against Racism and Intolerance drew attention to a rise in crimes against Muslims living in Europe. On the basis of carefully researched national reports, the commission came to the following conclusions. Note the language and recommendations, formulated well before September 2001:

> Concerned at signs that religious intolerance towards Islam and Muslim communities is increasing in countries

where this religion is not observed by the majority of the population;

Strongly regretting that Islam is sometimes portrayed inaccurately on the basis of hostile stereotyping the effect of which is to make this religion seem a threat;

Rejecting all deterministic views of Islam and recognising the great diversity intrinsic in the practice of this religion;

Firmly convinced of the need to combat the prejudice suffered by Muslim communities and stressing that this prejudice may manifest itself in different guises, in particular through negative general attitudes but also, to varying degrees, through discriminatory acts and through violence and harassment; . . .

The commission recommended that member states

- Ensure that Muslim communities are not discriminated against as to the circumstances in which they organise and practice their religion;
- Impose, in accordance with the national context, appropriate sanctions in cases of discrimination on grounds of religion;
- Take the necessary measures to ensure that the freedom of religious practice is fully guaranteed; in this context particular attention should be directed towards removing unnecessary legal or administrative obstacles to both the construction of sufficient numbers of appropriate places of worship for the practice of Islam and to its funeral rites;
- Ensure that public institutions are made aware of the need to make provision in their everyday practice for legitimate cultural and other requirements arising from the multifaith nature of society;
- Ascertain whether discrimination on religious grounds is practised in connection with access to citizenship and, if so, take the necessary measures to put an end to it;

- Take the necessary measures to eliminate any manifestation of discrimination on grounds of religious belief in access to education;
- Take measures, including legislation if necessary, to combat religious discrimination in access to employment and at the workplace;
- Encourage employers to devise and implement "codes of conduct" in order to combat religious discrimination in access to employment and at the workplace and, where appropriate, to work towards the goal of workplaces representative of the diversity of the society in question;
- Assess whether members of Muslim communities suffer from discrimination connected with social exclusion and, if so, take all necessary steps to combat these phenomena;
- Pay particular attention to the situation of Muslim women, who may suffer both from discrimination against women in general and from discrimination against Muslims;
- Ensure that curricula in schools and higher education— especially in the field of history teaching—do not present distorted interpretations of religious and cultural history and do not base their portrayal of Islam on perceptions of hostility and menace; . . .
- Encourage debate within the media and advertising professions on the image which they convey of Islam and Muslim communities and on their responsibility in this respect to avoid perpetuating prejudice and biased information;
- Provide for the monitoring and evaluation of the effectiveness of all measures taken for the purpose of combating intolerance and discrimination against Muslims.[46]

This European agenda to combat already-existing prejudices against Muslims was among the casualties of the terrorist attacks of September 2001. Thereafter, incidents of violence against Muslims rose sporadically in many different parts of Europe. In 2006, Thomas Hammarberg, the European commissioner for human rights, claimed that "persisting prejudice, negative attitudes, discrimination, and sometimes violence" were on the rise in Europe.[47] He did not specify whether the rise affected Muslims in particular, but the implication was there that this was so.

A year later, the European Monitoring Centre on Racism and Xenophobia decried a rising incidence of "attacks, abuse, harassment and violence, directed against persons perceived to be Muslim and against mosques, Muslim property and cemeteries." [48] National monitoring organizations reported the same upsurge after 2001 in Finland, the Netherlands, the United Kingdom, and Denmark. By 2006, in France, the majority of hate crimes classified as "racist" by authorities were committed against people of North African origin.[49] In French legal terms, targeting a religious group and engaging in violence against members of it constitutes "racism." Whether or not the term *racism* is accurate, the violence it describes was undoubtedly on the rise, as other reports confirmed on the basis of data for 2008 and 2009.[50]

It is possible that the proliferation of such incidents were unrelated to the controversies we described earlier, or to other public campaigns of right-wing and anti-immigrant political groups throughout Europe. But it is more likely that national political figures like the late Austrian politician Jörg Haider, well known for his anti-Semitic and anti-Muslim views, provided a vocabulary and a justification for those who went out and attacked Muslims. It was only in 2007 that the Austrian police began registering what they called "Islamophobic crimes." The likelihood is that official statistics substantially have underreported such violence for years. Here the term Islamophobia has purchase, since it deals with criminal deeds, not critical words.

The Clash of Civilizations

Concerns among Europeans about Islam have their intellectual progenitors. A number of writers have followed the late Harvard political scientist Samuel Huntington in seeing the arrival of substantial numbers of Muslims into Europe as provoking a "clash of civilizations." It is worth considering their views, since on the one hand they demonstrate an unstable mix of sober comment and criticism of Islam and concern about Islamic immigration, and on the other an emotive language producing a kind of apocalyptic gloom about the decline of Europe and its conquest by Islam.

Consider the case of Christopher Caldwell, an American journalist with a deep knowledge of and familiarity with European affairs. He writes for conservative and "neoconservative" journals, and adopts a historically minded conservative profile. Entitling his book *Reflections on the Revolution in Europe*, he intentionally conjured up the ghost of the great conservative thinker Edmund Burke, whose reflections on the French Revolution condemned it root and branch. What is the parallel upheaval Caldwell sees? It is the conquest of Europe by Islam.

Using deep research into public-opinion polls, he describes rising public alarm as to the transformation of European cities and polities as a whole as a consequence of the substantial growth of Muslim populations within them. The revolution he sees is one in which a weak culture—that of "secular Europe"—is being overwhelmed by a strong culture—militant Islam. Here are examples of the way he approaches this question:

- Immigration enhances strong countries and cultures, but it can overwhelm weak ones.
- Had Europeans realized, when immigration from Turkey, Morocco, Algeria, and elsewhere began in the 1950s and 1960s, that there would be thousands of mosques across Europe half a century later, they would never have permitted it.
- [Through open immigration policies] Europe replanted the seeds of a threat that had taken centuries of patience and violence to overcome—interreligious discord, both domestic and international.
- [Muslims are] a people patiently conquering Europe's cities, street by street.
- Europe's predicament involves population decline, aging, immigration, and the steady implantation of a foreign religion and culture in city after city.

- Clearly Europe's problem is with Islam and with immigration, and not with specific misapplications of specific
means set up to manage them.[51]

These assertions illustrate well the way in which demographic issues and
a diagnosis of cultural decline are braided together in this study.

Caldwell's voice of alarm over an Islamicized Europe is part of a
somewhat wider swath, though still a small minority of elite opinion.
Such minority views, on both sides of the Atlantic, are often held in
common with criticism of multiculturalist policies.

Some critics of Muslims in Europe leave immigrants to one side
and instead chastise European leaders for selling out their principles
in return for oil and export markets. An Egyptian-born British writer
Bat Ye'or published *Eurabia: The Euro-Arab Axis* in 2005, to decry the
pusillanimous attitude of European states to their foreign relations with
the Arab world.[52] Here what might be called "Arabophobia" elided with
"Islamophobia."

No such ambiguity existed in Oriana Fallaci's *The Rage and the
Pride*, a diatribe against Muslim immigrants, published in 2002,[53] or
in Melanie Phillip's *Londonistan*, a polemic against the British Labour
government for handing the city and the country over to the Muslim
Brotherhood.[54] To his credit, Caldwell stood aside from some of the
more-extravagant language of these authors, but the difference between
them seems more a question of nuance than of conviction. To Fallaci
and Phillip, Christian Europe was dying, in part through failure to see
what was in front of its collective face, namely a population-rich Muslim world clamoring to enter its borders. The fear expressed was simple:
Native demographic decline coupled with high levels of Muslim immigration and fertility will turn Europe into Maghreb North in a generation or two. By 2050, there will be Muslim majorities in many parts of
Europe, the distinguished Islamic historian Bernard Lewis has written.[55]
Whither Europe? Toward the dark side, is the answer of Lewis and a
host of other popular writers.

Is there any evidence that these Cassandras are expressing popular
opinion within Europe about Islam, opinion ignored by political elites?
Here Caldwell is useful, presenting abundant documentation that many

Europeans do indeed see not only Arabs but Muslim populations as dark, menacing, and alien. Polling data and elite politics tend to move in opposite directions, but what matters here is the range of comment on the dangers of a growing Muslim population in Europe.

It is hard to resist the conclusion, therefore, that concern about the impacts of expansive Islam—though perhaps not Islamophobia in its true meaning—is a palpable reality in Europe, of an undetermined magnitude. It probably represents a small part of the political spectrum but a larger part of the press and Internet opinion on these matters. Once again, we confront a multicolored collage: considered reflection by some on the compatibility of Muslim culture with European norms and practices, appearing alongside emotive and exaggerated accounts of the Islamic conquest of Europe. There are in these discordant contemporary debates striking echoes of earlier exchanges about the political and cultural consequences of "demographic decline" (however configured) at times of substantial immigration. Concerns about Islam repeat the pattern evident for more than a century in Europe—the injection of ideological venom into the public consideration of questions of immigration and fertility.

In effect, the debate about Islam and the future of Europe today has given a new twist to what we previously have termed "strategic demography."[56] It has reconfigured fears of the decline of Europe through a focus on Muslim immigration to a continent whose attachment to Christian religious beliefs has in many places by and large faded away. To pessimists like Caldwell, the enemy is already within the gates; there will be more mosques than churches in the foreseeable future. The nightmare, shared by him and his allies, is the end of cosmopolitan, tolerant Europe, and its replacement by a Europe besieged and displaced by theocratic Islam. In these broad brushstrokes the Islamophobic imagination has come into its own, as a reactionary voice, crying out to save the old world, about to be inundated by Islam.

Precisely what can be done to turn the tide is not clear in these works. Stricter immigration controls; stricter controls on marriage between European residents and non-European partners; requirements that new immigrants learn the language, history, and culture of the host countries—all these have their advocates. But the problem is in part beyond policy, since the fertility of indigenous Europeans has remained below the replacement level for a considerable period of time. Thus, these authors argue, the Muslims already in Europe will outbreed their non-Muslim neighbors and take over the continent by demographic default. This embraces an older form of demographic determinism, which has existed for more than a century and which almost always proves a mistaken guide to the future.

Conclusion: Human Rights and the Dangers of Prejudice

The one clear advantage European political culture has over its pre-1945 past, as well as over some other parts of the world, is its self-conscious acceptance of human rights norms as defining membership in the European community. There is a European Court of Human Rights, whose decisions are both superior to and written into the corpus of laws of the states subscribing to the European Convention on Human Rights. Here is a useful place to return to the question as to the utility of the term Islamophobia.

The European Convention of 1950 establishes certain rights of personal and political expression as inviolable. The dignity of the individual person is the bedrock of the European legal system. Nothing individual states do can change that. Hence those criticisms of Islam or of some Muslim customs (such as full-face veiling of women, child marriage, female genital mutilation), which claim in precise ways that such practices diminish or destroy the human rights of residents of Europe, Muslim or otherwise, cannot be defined as the kind of prejudice alleged by some who use the term Islamophobia. On the other hand, criticisms of Muslims in Europe, which seek to limit their freedom of religious expression and of communal practices attached to it, do enter the domain of prejudice, and there lies the pathway to Islamophobia.

Our conclusion is, therefore, that both the uses and abuses of the term Islamophobia are best defined by reference to the human rights regime in practice in Europe today. That regime may be tested by some of the conflicts brought to the courts for adjudication, but its strengths, accumulating over sixty years, have shown that a pattern of past prejudice need not determine the range of choices available in today's multiracial and multireligious Europe.

Beck's notion of a "risk society" was not initially framed to deal with the risks of terrorism. Some see Muslims as bringing that risk with them into Europe. Others point to a risk of a different order. The murder of ninety-two young Norwegians at a summer camp of the youth division of the ruling Norwegian Labour Party in July 2011 was carried out by Anders Breivik, a right-wing militant engaged in what he termed a Christian war against the threat of the Muslim domination of Europe. Shortly before the attack, Breivik posted a long manifesto on the Web stating the reasons for his attack. "The time for dialogue is over," he wrote. "We gave peace a chance. The time for armed resistance has come."[57] It is unclear whether Breivik acted alone or as part of a European group with similar views. We cite this case simply because it illustrates what can happen when criticism of Islam mutates into the unfounded hatred embodied in Islamophobia, and because it seems unlikely that this will be the only case of truly Islamophobic violence we all have to face.[58]

The China Trajectory

T he political dimension of the modern demographic history of China is one of its essential characteristics. Modernization theory has little purchase here, since it focused on a model derived from the western European transformation of rural, agrarian societies to urban, manufacturing ones. Chinese demographic history is not simply an echo of Western patterns. Fertility decline in China happened in both the cities and in the countryside, and with the state as its guiding force.

Here *politics* means not only national policy formulation and direction but the response of thousands of village societies and millions of individuals and couples to directives emanating from a one-party state but expressed at specific local levels. Beck's concept of "risk" must be translated differently in China, in which as we shall see the boundaries between "private" and "community" spheres differ notably from those in the West. For centuries interventions in reproductive behavior that many Westerners might have considered authoritarian and intrusive have prevailed in the family decisions of Chinese couples. The risks associated with childbearing in China have included the consequences of violating norms established by extended families, by villages, by local administrators, and since the Communist Revolution of 1949 by party apparatchiks and government officials at the district, provincial, and national levels.

The startling rapidity of China's fertility decline in the 1970s happened before the formulation and implementation of what later came to be termed the "one-child family" policy. These developments took place against the backdrop of what likely was the largest man-made famine in history and the subsequent upheavals known as the Cultural Revolution. Convulsive development is one way to describe this sequence of events, in which the state is always present. In this story, ignoring politics means ignoring reality.

Introduction

The national populations of China and India, taken together, accounted for more than 2.5 billion people, and more than 36 percent of the total world population of about 7 billion in 2012. These two nations represent a class of their own, in the weight of their recent demographic histories. However it would be misleading to conclude that China and India have similar population histories over the last two generations. To the contrary, the story of fertility decline in China is radically different from that in India. China's fertility decline has not been matched in India, with the result that some projections place India's population as likely to exceed that of China within the next two decades. In this chapter we trace the history of Chinese fertility against the turbulent backdrop of three periods: the 1970s, the 1980s, and the 1990s and after. In the next chapter we turn to India.

First, we need to observe the historical trends in China's population and fertility. As of 2005, China's estimated population of 1.3 billion alone comprised more than one-fifth of the world's total (then nearly 6.47 billion) and more than one-third of the entire population of Asia (then 3.9 billion).[1] The populations of all the countries of Europe and North America taken together summed to about 215 million less than the Chinese population; indeed, the estimated population of China in 2005 was larger than the total populations—1.216 billion—of the entire list of countries counted by the UN as "more developed."[2]

Hence, it could hardly be otherwise than that if there were any substantial changes in fertility patterns in China, there would be significant impacts upon the world's average fertility rates and even greater effects on overall fertility rates in Asia. We shall see in chapter 5 that India has joined China in the class of nations with more than 1 billion inhabitants. The gap between the two Asian giants has narrowed considerably in recent decades. What separates them still is their patterns of fertility.

Since the 1970s there indeed have been major—one might even say dramatic—changes in Chinese fertility rates. Starting from very high estimates in the 1950s and 1960s—on the order of 5.8 children per woman as late as 1970,[3] total fertility rates dropped as low as 1.46 in 1997, according to official reports.[4] In the UN Population Division database, Chinese total fertility was reported in 2002 as at 1.38—nearly as low as that of Germany. Even allowing for a substantial margin of error, these data point to a truly unprecedented fertility decline in China—a decline of 75 percent in only two decades, even more rapid than that of Japan after World War II.

But beware: These estimates may be misleading. These exceptionally low rates being reported for China are almost certainly substantially lower than reality. The most likely cause is increasing proportions of births that are not being reported in the official fertility data.[5] Yet even if appropriate adjustments are made for such substantial underreporting of Chinese births, there can be little doubt that Chinese fertility rates declined rapidly during the period from 1970 to the present. Even the adjusted fertility decline in China surely remains one of the most rapid for any country in recorded human history.

There is little consensus as to the forces driving this dramatic change in Chinese reproductive behavior. The overall argument in this book is that we are living in an unprecedented period of population dynamics, and while economic forces are important, they cannot by themselves explain the steepness of the downward curve in fertility in most parts of the developing and developed world. Other elements must be considered. One is population thought and policy. Politics matters in demographic history, and the recent history of China is an eloquent case in point.

The Multiple Faces of Chinese Fertility Policy

The Chinese revolutionary government that came to power in 1949 inherited long-standing Marxist-Leninist perspectives about population issues. It may be useful to survey this history in a few paragraphs, since it underscores just how dramatic were the recent departures in Chinese Communist thinking and policy on population questions.

In the nineteenth century, Marxists viewed population and demographic changes as epiphenomena, dependent entirely upon the nature of the economic system in power. They forcefully rejected the arguments of Malthus and the other classical economists—that populations had a tendency to grow excessively and thereby lead to poverty—as misbegotten apologies for the depredations of capitalism, an economic system that empowered the owners of capital to extract large surpluses from the value of the economic goods produced by peasants and proletariat. In response to the arguments of classical economists such as Ricardo that the marginal productivity of land implied that the larger the population, the harder it would be to produce sufficient food and hence food prices would rise in real terms, Marxian theorists argued that as the real price of food rose, the rate of exploitation of labor would rise with it, ultimately producing a collapse of the social and economic system.

In short, for most nineteenth-century Marxists, population dynamics simply reflected the way expansion of the means of production ran up against limits set by the social relations of production. These economic crises were built into the capitalist system and could not be avoided. This iron determinism is evident in early Marxist writing on this subject. But over the 150 years since Marx's death, the Marxist path on population is full of zigs and zags, evident in both energetic criticism and passionate defense of established theory and dogma.

With the triumph of the Chinese Communist Revolution in 1949, the new Government of Chairman Mao Zedong initially tended toward the long-standing views of Soviet Communists. Under the new socialist system, workers of all sorts would benefit from the full value of their labor, with no pound of flesh extracted by what they saw as the parasitic owners of capital. Hence, in this view of the new world of Communist China, a population of *any* size could be supported in economic prosperity and dignity, since all would benefit from the full value of their collective labor. Mao put it this way in 1949: " It is a great thing that China has so many people. Even if the population increases several-fold we still have a solution, and the solution is production."[6]

There was no consensus on this, however; indeed there was continuing tension between the "optimists" of socialist population theory and some of China's leading economists, who argued that socialism could not dramatically improve the lives of the Chinese people unless population growth diminished. But policy moved in another direction. Jonathan Spence has shown how in the early years of the regime, measures were passed that, if anything, increased Chinese population growth. A 1950 marriage law eased divorce and remarriage; improved public health provision led to declines in infant mortality; improving health care for the elderly and better diets led to an increase in life expectancy. For a host of reasons, more people married. Monasteries and convents were closed. Prostitution was banned. And whatever political changes occurred, traditional Chinese cultural patterns favoring large families and multiple sons endured.[7] The revolution converted the state, but village norms continued to govern family life.

The "optimistic" socialist views about there being no limits on population under Communism were further challenged by the results of the first national census of the People's Republic in 1953. Prior to this census, the government estimate of the Chinese population stood at about 425 million. In part such estimates were based upon assumptions that Chinese mortality had increased while Chinese fertility had decreased during the preceding decades of war, political instability, and natural disasters. Such assumptions came into doubt when the 1953 census instead reported a population of 583 million. With an estimated undercount of approximately 5–15 percent,[8] it became apparent that the Chinese population was probably at least 600 million—perhaps 175 million larger than expected. To put this surprise "additional" 175 million Chinese into comparative perspective, the population of the United States in 1953 was about 160 million.[9]

In addition to reporting the existence of an additional 175 million residents, the data available to the Chinese government suggested that fertility rates were on the rise, also thought to be due to the ending of decades of war and instability, along with improved health-care provision and economic modernization undertaken by the new regime.[10] One apparent result was the rapid adoption by the Chinese government of the Regulation of Contraception and Induced Abortion Act of 1953, which not only legalized induced abortion but also legalized voluntary sterilization and the importation and sale of contraceptives, as well as initiating the People's Republic's first population or family-planning program.[11]

The population program begun under this act focused on urban areas, whereas most of the Chinese population lived in rural areas. This program included large-scale propaganda efforts promoting birth control, but at this stage it was a voluntary program. It also did not make contraceptive supplies easily available to the majority of the population.[12] Imported contraceptives were available in the large cities, where most Chinese did not live, and in any case the cost of contraceptives was prohibitive for the masses.

However the passage of the 1953 legislation was but one moment in the history of Chinese population policy, contested by different factions and controversial for decades. Mao was often quoted by one faction as arguing, "The more people, the stronger we are."[13] Others took a different tack. In 1956 a group of leading Chinese economists embraced concerted efforts at fertility limitation and were supported publicly in their views by Premier Zhou Enlai. Yet within a year many of these same economists were swept up in what was termed the "anti-rightist" campaign of 1957 and purged, though Zhou himself continued in power.[14]

There were other reasons the decline in Chinese fertility was deferred. In the 1950s, the insufficiency of contraceptive supplies was one inhibitor. Perhaps in part due to such shortages, official support for traditional Chinese medical practices believed to have contraceptive effects was another. When the Chinese Academy of Sciences assessed such practices, they found them to be ineffectual but did recommend other traditional methods such as acupuncture.[15]

The Great Leap Forward, begun in 1958, was to change China profoundly. It did lead to a dramatic decline in fertility, although that was hardly its intention. Its aim was to promote expansion of both agricultural and industrial production, within the framework of the People's

Republic's Second Five-Year Plan. The objective here, as Mao insisted, was sharply to increase the productivity of the thousands of small agricultural collectives (consisting of a few hundred households) recently established. This was to be achieved by merging them into far larger "People's Communes" comprising many thousands of households.

Meanwhile, national steel production would also be sharply expanded. This was to be achieved by the output of millions of backyard steel furnaces operated by peasants, who were to be released from agricultural production as a result of the anticipated productivity increases of the new large People's Communes.

By the second half of 1958, the Central Committee of the Chinese Communist Party claimed that this "new social organization," which had "appeared, fresh as the morning sun, above the broad horizon of East Asia," was a resounding success: 740,000 cooperatives had been merged into 26,000 People's Communes, covering 99 percent of the peasant population and 120 million rural households. The official claim was that rural production had increased; in some case it had doubled; in others it had increased tenfold or even "scores of times." Indeed, so great were the communes' production increases that China no longer needed to worry about excessive population. To the contrary: In the future, China would face "not so much overpopulation as shortage of manpower."[16]

Such euphoria was based not only on ideological considerations but also on the remarkable production figures being reported by rural cadres to provincial offices and thence forwarded to Beijing. Spence notes that the local cadres did not report production below the assigned quotas for fear of being labeled "rightists" or "defeatists." The 1957 antirightist purges that had swept up the leading Chinese economists who had urged fertility limitation had also removed some of the best statisticians (and demographers as well) from the state bureaus that compiled the data reported up the line. Later reviews of the reported official totals of grain production for 1958 — 375 million tons — revised them down to 250 million tons. Some Western economists later estimated the real total to have been closer to 215 million tons. The one million local backyard steel furnaces built as central to the industrial elements of the Great Leap Forward turned out to be incapable of producing high-quality steel.[17] Both the agricultural and industrial policy initiatives were catastrophic failures.

Mao, who had earlier announced that he might step down as president, did so earlier than expected, in late 1958. Liu Shaoqi, a longtime associate of Mao and one of the original five members of the Standing Committee of the Chinese Communist Party Politburo, was named president the following spring. Mao, however, retained his chairmanship of the Communist Party and of the Military Affairs Commission.

Perhaps for this reason, few Chinese leaders expressed open criticism of Mao's role in instigating the Great Leap Forward and his responsibility for its failures. The minister of defense, Peng Dehuai, was a notable exception, not only expressing his doubts informally at a leadership meeting in Lushan in July 1959, but also in a private letter he delivered there to Mao. Mao responded with a personal denunciation of Peng as fomenting a "right opportunist clique." In a speech at Lushan, Mao acknowledged he had made mistakes in creating the Great Leap Forward. Yet he noted that he was in good company: Confucius, Lenin, and Marx also had made mistakes. If the government insisted on dwelling on the negatives, he himself would lead a peasant rising to overthrow it. Mao closed on a scatological note: "The chaos caused was on a grand scale and I take responsibility. Comrades, you must all analyze your own responsibility. If you have to shit, shit! If you have to fart, fart! You will feel much better for it."[18] Peng was removed as minister of defense,[19] and it appears that Mao's attack on Peng effectively cowed other party leaders into silence for many months and even years thereafter.

With the passing of time, most Chinese leaders and intellectuals came to describe the Great Leap Forward as a disaster, resulting in tens of millions of deaths from starvation and other causes. While credible data are understandably limited, it appears that agricultural production actually *declined* rather than increased as planned, in part due to the diversion of rural labor to industry, thereby reducing the size of the harvests. There were also a series of natural disasters, including both drought and flooding, that affected large parts of China. In a 1962 speech, after the Great Leap Forward had been discredited, President Liu Shaoqi stated that the "economic disaster was 30% fault of nature, 70% human error."[20]

Yet while this disaster was unfolding in the rural areas, data sent by provincial and local officials to the state planning organizations in Beijing reported food production to be rising sharply, apparently a result of inflated reports seeking to meet ambitious targets and quotas. These exaggerated production reports in turn led to excessive amounts of grain being commandeered by the state for transfer to urban populations and for export, leaving insufficient food supplies for the bulk of the population in rural areas. Perversely enough, Chinese government agencies *exported* large quantities of grain during the years 1958–1960, apparently unaware of famine spreading in the Chinese countryside. Estimates vary widely as to the extent of excess mortality attributable to the Great Leap Forward, but most are in the tens of millions, and many within the range of 15– 40 million.[21]

The "Three Bitter Years" beginning in 1959 ultimately led to a reversal of the Great Leap Forward in early 1961. Grain exports were ended, grain imports initiated, and a series of trials and executions of local officials were conducted for providing exaggerated data.

Mao's successor as president of the People's Republic, Liu Shaoqi, proved to be a fierce critic of the Great Leap Forward. But Mao still retained his position as chairman of the Communist Party, and beginning in 1966 he had reestablished enough political support to lead the country into the convulsive Cultural Revolution. President Liu—along with Communist Party Secretary Deng Xiaoping—were denounced as "capitalist roaders," "traitors," and "scabs."[22] Liu was removed from office and expelled from the Communist Party. He died in disgrace and in prison in 1969. Eleven year later, after Mao's death in 1976, Liu was posthumously rehabilitated after Deng Xiaoping came back to power.

This economic catastrophe had direct demographic consequences. As may be seen clearly from the estimates in fig. 4.1, Chinese fertility rates during the chaos and famine of the Great Leap Forward, which began in 1958, appear to have declined sharply—on the order of 50 percent, from over six to just over three children per woman in her childbearing years. With the reversal of the Great Leap Forward policies in 1961 and subsequent waning of the famines and other deprivations, reported Chinese fertility rates rebounded as sharply as they had declined, reaching levels in excess of seven children per woman by 1962.[23] According to

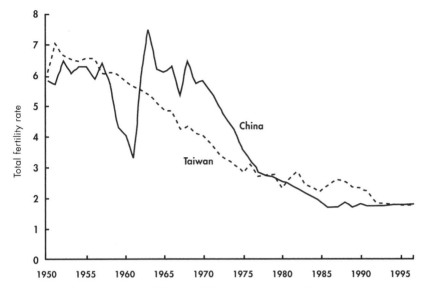

Fig. 4.1. Total Fertility Rates, China and Taiwan, 1950–1997. *Source:* From Dudley L. Poston Jr., "Social and Economic Development and the Fertility Transitions in Mainland China and Taiwan," *Population and Development Review* 26, supp.: *Population and Economic Change in East Asia* (2000), p. 41.

Peng, the conjunction of the famine of the Great Leap Forward with the subsequent baby boom alarmed the new Chinese government and led in the early 1960s to the promulgation of its second official program of birth control.[24] Like the first program of a decade earlier, this too was voluntary and focused initially on the minority of the population that was urban instead of the large majority in rural areas. Also like the first program, the second depended heavily upon campaigns of public information and propaganda.

A key goal of the program was to delay the onset of sexual activity among Chinese young adults until their mid-twenties, and it may have had some effect. For whatever reason, the limited quantitative data available do suggest that urban Chinese, especially those in the industrial metropolitan areas of the coast, did begin to reduce their fertility during the mid-1960s. According to estimates later made by Chen and Coale (table 4.1), urban fertility had declined to a level of about three children per woman in 1970–1971. Some of this decline almost certainly

Table 4.1. Total Fertility Rates, China, 1970–1990, Urban and Rural Areas

	China, All	Urban Areas	Rural Areas
1970	5.75	3.22	6.31
1971	5.40	2.83	5.96
1972	4.92	2.59	5.43
1973	4.51	2.36	4.98
1974	4.15	*1.94*	4.62
1975	3.58	*1.76*	3.97
1976	3.25	*1.60*	3.61
1977	2.87	*1.57*	3.14
1978	2.75	*1.58*	3.00
1979	2.80	*1.40*	3.10
1980	2.32	*1.20*	2.56
1981	2.71	*1.47*	2.99
1982	2.90	*1.79*	3.24
1983	2.35	*1.46*	2.61
1984	2.24	*1.31*	2.52
1985	2.12	*1.27*	2.36
1986	2.35	*1.40*	2.62
1987	2.58	*1.51*	2.87
1988	2.52	*1.47*	2.81
1989	2.35	—	—
1990	2.31	—	—

Notes: Figures in bold italics indicate below replacement level. Dashes indicate no rural/urban data for those years.

Source: From S. Chen and Ansley Coale, *Chinese Provincial Fertility Data, 1940–1990* (Beijing: Zhongguo renkou chubanshe, 1993), as cited in Isabelle Attané, "Chinese Fertility on the Eve of the 21st Century: Fact and Uncertainty," *Population: An English Selection*, vol. 13, no. 2, (2001), p. 95, table A1.

was due to factors quite remote from the birth-planning program—
especially the violence, chaos, uncertainty, and deprivations of the Cultural Revolution beginning in 1966.

Meanwhile, fertility rates in rural areas stayed high and were still
on the order of six children per woman in 1970–1971.[25] Given the pre-
dominance of the rural population, the Chinese population overall had
continued to grow during the 1960s, exceeding 800 million by 1969.

Political stability was reestablished in the early 1970s as the Cultural Revolution waned, though officially it did not end until 1976 with
the death of Mao. In 1971 the Chinese government introduced yet a third
population program. This program not only urged Chinese couples to
have fewer children overall, but also that they have them later and with
longer intervals between births. There was little or no coercion involved,
but much in the way of propaganda. One popular slogan advised, "One
is good, two is OK and three is too many." The overall program was
summarized well by its three-word slogan: "Later, longer, and fewer"
(wan, xi, shao).[26]

No study has yet been able to offer a definitive explanation for
Chinese fertility declines during the 1970s, but the declines appear to
have been real and large. Chen and Coale estimate that for the nation as
a whole, the total fertility rate declined by over 50 percent, from 5.75 in
1970 to 2.80 in 1979. The percentage decline was about the same for the
majority rural population—from 6.31 to 3.10—and a bit more, perhaps
55 percent, for the minority urban population, from 3.22 to 1.40.[27]

This 1970s decline in Chinese fertility, occurring broadly among
both urban and rural populations, was remarkable. According to one
expert, this decline constituted "the most extraordinary reduction in
fertility in a large population ever recorded in human history."[28]

While it is widely known that fertility has declined rapidly in
China, it is less well understood that this decline preceded the adoption
of the one-child-family policy in 1980. The emergence of this draconian
policy in the 1980s has tended to obscure the dramatic change that occurred in the 1970s. Almost surely the fertility declines of the 1970s resulted from some combination of socioeconomic development, changes
in cultural norms, especially at the village level, and government policies.[29] Its timing seems to have been prompted by energetic programs

to make contraception available throughout the vast expanse of China to couples wishing to control their family size, an option encouraged by intensive official propaganda promoting the virtues of "later, longer, and fewer" childbearing.

In this field, as in others, it is wise to note what people do rather than what they say. This propaganda campaign for fertility control was widely disseminated within China at the same time as the official party line, for external consumption, proclaimed an entirely different goal. The chief delegate of China to the 1974 World Population Conference in Bucharest had this to say to the delegates representing 137 participating countries: "Of all things in the world, people are the most precious. . . . Man is in the first place a producer and only in the second place a consumer. . . . The population [of Asia, Africa, and Latin America] has grown rather quickly. This is not at all a bad thing but a very good thing. . . . The large population of the Third World constitutes an important condition for strengthening the struggle against imperialism and hegemonism and accelerating social and economic development."[30]

After his return to power in 1978, Deng Xiaoping adopted a clear line favoring fertility decline. Deng saw continued population growth as a barrier that would make it impossible for China to realize its aspirations for rapid economic development. By 1980, his government had quickly adopted a new and even more energetic national birth-planning program, now generally referred to as the one-child policy, under which Chinese couples were urged forcefully to have no more than one child.

Why the urgency? The census of 1982, the most accurate in Chinese history, confirmed that the population exceeded 1 billion. According to Jonathan Spence, the leadership took the view that the "implication of this were grave, for unless population growth could be checked, even the most dramatic changes in rural and industrial production could not raise the country's standard of living."[31]

The timing here is important. Adoption of the "one-child family" policy took place *after* a decade of massive fertility decline during the 1970s. In the 1980s, under the one-child-family regime, Chinese fertility declined *less* rapidly than in the previous decade. The total fertility rates estimated by Chen and Coale show up-and-down movements during the 1980s but no obvious downward trend overall.

It also is important to note that the one-child policy, which is still in effect today (albeit with numerous modifications), has never been a truly national policy. It is more an "ideal" urged by the state, but whether this ideal is backed up by any sanctions or enforcement in different provinces and local areas appears to vary considerably across China. While it may be true that there was no national legal requirement underlying the one-child norm, it also seems to be the case that there was strong political pressure and "encouragement" in some areas. The effort was run by local government cadres; indeed, every local government had its own "Birth Planning Commission" and commissioner. Given the massive size and diversity of China, it seems certain that excessive pressure was applied by cadres in some areas. Some of these incidents have been widely reported outside China, and there have been numerous claims for political asylum by Chinese migrants on grounds of such excesses.[32] What we do not have, however, is evidence as to how widespread such excesses were and what fraction of Chinese couples they affected. (See discussion following about claims of human rights violations.)

In the thirty years that have passed, typically the one-child policy has been more energetically applied in urban than in rural areas, but even in urban areas there are notable exceptions:[33]

- Two "only-child" parents had the right to have more than one child. This was intended to address the "1–2–4 problem," that is, when one adult child must support two parents and four grandparents.
- Two parents with university master's degrees had the right to have more than one child.

Moreover, there has been considerably more flexibility in the one-child policy in rural areas, where three-quarters of the Chinese population resided. In rural areas:

- Rural couples were given official approval to have two children if the first child was female or disabled;
- Approval for second children required three-to-four-year birth spacing, and parents were penalized economically

("social maintenance fee") and by the requirement that
parents had to pay for schooling and health care;

- There were different rules for ethnic minorities (non-
Han), who were usually allowed to have two children in
urban areas, and three or four children in rural areas.

One Western expert on China's population has estimated that, under
these waivers, approximately 60 percent of Chinese women would have
been allowed to bear two children.[34] Given all of these exceptions and
variations across China, the one-child policy has likely magnified the
Chinese fertility decline, but not to a one-child average family size. Indeed, the average today seems likely to be closer to 2 than to 1.

From its inception the one-child policy of China attracted active
international criticism and intensive scrutiny as to whether it employed
coercive measures. In particular, Chinese policies in this field have been
described as in fundamental violation of basic human rights to marry
and form a family, imbedded in the Universal Declaration of Human
Rights of 1948 ("the right to marry and to found a family"[35]) and in other
UN human rights agreements. In 1968, the International Conference on
Human Rights in Teheran affirmed, "The protection of the family and
of the child remains the concern of the international community. Parents have a basic human right to determine freely and responsibly the
number and the spacing of their children. . . ."[36]

A more detailed statement of such rights was embraced six years
later in Bucharest at the 1974 World Population Conference. It was formulated as follows: "All couples and individuals have the basic right to
decide freely and responsibly the number and spacing of their children
and to have the information, education and means to do so; the responsibility of couples and individuals in the exercise of this right takes into
account the needs of their living and future children, and their responsibilities towards the community."[37] There has been repeated denun-
ciations of Chinese violations of these internationally agreed principles,
and governments such as those of the United States have required that
their contributions to international agencies such as the UN Population
Fund not be used for programs in China.[38]

There is ample evidence that China's one-child policy has embodied a stronger framework of control of marriage and reproduction than in almost any other national case and certainly more than in any major country in recent decades. There is another extreme case, in a small European country also led by a Marxist-Leninist government—that of Romania under Nicolae Ceauşescu during the 1960s and 1970s. Romania may represent an even more extreme case than China, though in the opposite direction, embodying measures designed to increase fertility rather than reduce it. Beginning in 1967, the Ceauşescu government summarily banned essentially all forms of contraception and abortion. Later, as illegal abortions increased, Romanian women were subjected to compulsory internal exams, and strong economic incentives were offered to parents of larger families. To be sure, Romania is not a country of global stature,[39] whereas what happens in China has obvious significance for international affairs and demographic trends on a global scale.

What can we conclude about the working of China's one-child policy? With wide variations across regions and over time, this policy promoted state-regulated late marriage and mandated sanction-based constraints on the numbers of children born. Most analysts have concluded that in some unknown (and likely unknowable) number of cases such policies led to excesses involving coercive abortion, sterilization, and IUD insertions. The official policy was clear that such coercive actions were unlawful. Yet as implemented at local levels, Chinese birth-planning cadres have faced fines, demotion, and dismissal if they failed to meet the numerical goals and population targets for which they were responsible. It seems clear enough that some went beyond official policy to use coercive or semicoercive methods to obtain the required results.[40]

In response, the Chinese government and those who defend its actions insisted in the 1990s—and still insist—that all governments impose coercive minima upon the age of marriage. They argue that Chinese population policies are voluntaristic and are based upon "education" and propaganda and official "encouragement." At the same time, they assert that the collective needs of the Chinese people require urgent actions to implement provisions of the previously cited UN principle that couples exercise responsibility in their reproduction "into account the needs of their living and future children, and their responsibilities towards the community."[41] They note that the Chinese government has criticized and has imposed sanctions against the excessive zeal on the part of some of its cadres, along with punishing cases of outright corruption.

In their 1999 study of Chinese demographic trends, Lee and Wang argue that these collective elements of the one-child policy since 1980 are by no means unusual in the history and culture of China. To the contrary, they argue, they represent the continuation of a very long tradition of collective demographic planning. They describe a centuries-old and unique "Chinese demographic system," quite different from that of Europe, based on four distinctive elements: infanticide; a gender-unbalanced marriage market; restraint of fertility within marriage; and widespread resort to adoption. In their view, these elements of the Chinese demographic system have never been under the control of Chinese individuals or couples. Instead, Chinese demographic patterns were regulated at the level of wider collectivities, primarily the extended family and lineage but often at village and higher levels. Hence, they contend that the policy changes that occurred since 1980 have been not changes of substance but instead a shift upward in the level of collective control over demographic behavior that has been long-standing in Chinese history—from traditional control by the extended Chinese family and village to modern control by the Chinese state. "Whereas Chinese parents in the past curtailed their fertility or killed their children in response to the dictates of household economy, today they reduce their fertility largely in response to the perceived needs and strong dictates of the national economy and increasingly to maximize their family welfare. . . . In China, demographic decisions were never individual. Decisions require careful considerations of collective needs at both ends of the social spectrum: the family and the state."[42] Hence politics in China means, among other things, the everyday negotiation of fundamental elements of family formation, a pattern of collective life that long antedated the arrival of Communism and continued through the period of fertility decline in the later twentieth century.

Post-Tiananmen Square

By the late 1980s, the "opening" and "marketization" of China forced changes in the existing birth-planning program. Chinese citizens exercised a degree of independence; they were independent at least in terms of their access to the market. The Communist Party still controlled the political system and the forces of order. While during the 1990s the Chinese government continued to seek effective state control over fertility behavior, it undertook numerous modifications designed to make the program more effective by making it more acceptable to the Chinese population. Various measures, implemented from 1993 onward, sought to improve the professional quality of program services, minimize abuses by cadres, and more effectively enforce prohibitions on the use of abortion for purposes of sex selection of offspring.

From the mid-1990s there was much greater emphasis on positive incentives more consistent with the market orientations coming to dominate economic activity. Such incentives included supplementary leave or payments in return for postponing marriage or births, for the adoption of certain contraceptive methods, and for commitments by couples to adhere to the one-child family norm.[43]

The government also forcefully proscribed the harsh measures adopted by some local governments and cadres. Indeed a list known as the "seven don'ts" was issued by the State Birth Planning Commission in 1995 and provides helpful insight into practices the government wanted to eliminate. In particular, this list prohibited those implementing birth-planning regulations from taking actions "to arrest or harm violators or their family members, to destroy property, to impound property without due process, to add fees and levy fines at will, to detain associates or retaliate against complainers, to refuse permission for a legal birth in order to meet population plans, and to organize pregnancy checks of unmarried women."[44]

The government also formally embraced the goals enunciated by the 1994 UN International Conference on Population, held in Cairo, on improving reproductive health and the status of women. The former included provision of reproductive health services via birth-planning clinics, while the latter focused on increased education and economic participation for women, especially in poor areas.[45]

The government led by Premier Zhu Rongji in 1998 continued this trend. The longtime minister of the State Birth Planning Commission, Madame Peng Peiyun, was promoted to a vice-chairmanship of the National People's Congress—nominally the highest legislative body in China, the leadership and membership of which is effectively determined by the Communist Party. In 2001, after much consultation at various levels, the Chinese government for the first time formally adopted a national law on the state planning of population and births. Prior legislative efforts had been frustrated by a lack of agreement about how uniform a set of national legal provisions on population and births could be in the large and diverse populations of China's regions and provinces. Other disagreements focused on whether such a national law should (or could) specify the number of children allowed and which contraceptive methods Chinese should use at different stages of life. The stalemate had continued for two decades, until 2001, with the result that legal provisions were limited to the provincial level and framed by regulations and the general "guidance" of the national government's policy goals.

The 2001 law therefore represented a significant departure, but agreement was possible only by keeping the new law quite general and continuing to delegate the details to the lower-level legislatures and national regulations.[46] It formalized the long-standing state institutions involved in population and birth planning, but at the same time restrained their actions by law. It emphasized that the Chinese constitution required citizens to limit their childbearing in the public interest but also that they have a right to reproduce. It encouraged, but did not require, late marriage, deferred childbearing within marriage, and the target of one child per couple. It promoted the use of contraception and voluntary sterilization rather than abortion but allowed the latter as a last resort in cases of contraceptive failure. It permitted the levy of a "social compensation fee" and the use of the Chinese practice of "criticism and education" for those who bore an unauthorized child, but it prohibited open state coercion such as criminal penalties for those who had more than one child. It required that officials "should conduct administration strictly in accordance with the law, should enforce the law in a civilized manner, and must not infringe upon citizens' legitimate rights and interests." It strictly prohibited the practice of prenatal sex selection via ultrasound and selective abortion.[47]

Enforcement of such provisions was another matter in the complexity of modern China. In particular, while the 2001 law did provide for citizen appeals and litigation against a government agency they considered to have violated their legitimate rights, it is difficult to know whether such actions have been truly available to those wronged by unlawful practices.[48]

Sex Ratio at Birth: The "Missing Girls of China"

In addition to sustained international controversy about coercive or less than wholly voluntary elements of China's population policies, many people have drawn attention to a related controversy as to whether China has promoted large-scale use of selective abortion, infanticide, or abandonment of girls. In most human populations, the ratio of male to female births ("sex ratio at birth") usually falls in a narrow range of 103 to 107 males per 100 females. In China, however, the official data on births for 2010 show a sex ratio at birth of 118.[49] These and other data have led to concerns about what some call the "missing girls of China."

It should be noted that Asian countries other than China also show sex ratios that are higher than in other world regions. In Taiwan, for example, the sex ratio is reported to be 110; in S. Korea, 108. Still, the reported sex ratio at birth of 118 in China is exceptionally high.

There is broad agreement that traditional Chinese culture embodies a strong preference for male children. The literature points to a variety of elements: Sons are better able to help their peasant parents with arduous farmwork; Chinese culture provides powerful pressures upon sons (but not daughters) to care for their dependent elderly parents in retirement; and Confucian traditions mandate that girl children upon marriage become part of the groom's family and that daughters cannot inherit, hence the absence of a male child would lead to the inheritance of the parents' landholdings by other male members of the family.

However, Zhao has convincingly argued that this does not necessarily imply that to have a large number of sons is better than having few, as often interpreted from the popular Chinese saying "More sons, more happiness and prosperity," often heard at weddings.[50] To the contrary, under traditional Chinese inheritance practices, wealthy families with many sons often divided their property equally among them, thereby reducing the individual wealth of their heirs. Even Malthus noted this point in one of the later editions of his *An Essay on the Principle of Population*—that a rich Chinese family would be likely to have more surviving children, hence more sons among whom its wealth would eventually be subdivided, and hence fewer rich heirs in later generations.[51]

A range of explanations has been put forward to account for the available Chinese data about the sex ratio at birth and in the early stages of life:

1. *Differential abortion:* The argument here is that traditional Chinese preferences for male offspring, combined with the pressures of the one-child-family policy, has led Chinese couples to selectively abort female pregnancies. Technological advances do seem to have made it easier for Chinese parents to act upon such birth preferences. There are many reports of increased access in recent years to ultrasound testing that allows determination of the sex of the fetus in early pregnancy, including itinerant services provided from mobile vans. Once sex is determined prenatally, parents may choose to abort female fetuses. The magnitude of such practices is not known. They are illegal in China but apparently available via black markets.[52]

2. *Infanticide:* A second explanation focuses on the differential practice of infanticide for female babies—the joint product of male preference, the one-child policy, and new economic incentives in rural areas.[53] It should be noted that infanticide also may have been common in eighteenth-century Europe. See, for example, the street scenes portrayed in the engravings of William Hogarth, in which the demise of multiple babies and young children is portrayed.

Das Gupta reports differential probabilities of survival for female conceptions based on the existing sex composition of the family.[54] Female fetuses conceived in families that already have a daughter have steeply higher probabilities of being aborted or of dying in early childhood than do boys in general or than do female fetuses conceived in families without older daughters. The primary effect seems to be on the second (and higher) birth orders. The sex ratio of first births is within the historical range for China, whereas if the first child is a girl, some (unknown) fraction of Chinese couples having a second child seem to take measures aimed at increasing the probability of a male birth. An alternative interpretation is the earlier suggestion of Coale that Chinese couples were likely to terminate their childbearing when they had borne their desired number of sons.[55]

3. *Abandonment and adoption:* Child abandonment, often to state-sponsored orphanages, has also become common in China. The numbers of such "orphans," mostly girls, is large and has been growing—from less than two hundred thousand in the 1970s to more than five hundred thousand in 1987, from about 1 percent of live births to about 2.5 percent. A large majority of adopted Chinese children are girls, approaching a 3:1 female-to-male ratio by 1987. By one estimate, adoptions accounted for half of the so-called "missing girls" in the 1980s.[56]

4. *Underreporting of female births:* Given the pressures of the one-child policy, some parents who desired a son but bore a daughter may have avoided or delayed reporting their girl's birth to the authorities. There are anecdotal reports of urban Chinese couples who have left female babies with relatives in rural areas so as to keep open the opportunity of bearing a boy in the city.[57]

5. *Higher mortality of females due to hepatitis B:* Recent reports provide an alternative biological/medical explanation for the high sex ratio at birth in China. Oster notes

that (a) the sex ratios of births to women who are carriers of the hepatitis B virus are as high as 155, and (b) that 10 –15 percent of the Chinese population is infected with hepatitis B. She concludes that around 75 percent of the "missing" girls in China may therefore be due to this viral infection.[58]

In a 2004 paper, Banister summarizes and assesses the existing evidence;[59] her paper predates and hence does not discuss Oster's biological/medical explanation. Banister argues that the sex-ratio phenomenon is a real one, not driven by underenumeration of girls. Indeed, she notes that a high ratio of male to female children is traditionally Chinese in a very real sense, having been a distinctive characteristic of China for centuries if not millennia. In the past the distorted ratios were due to "female infanticide immediately after birth (drowning, exposure, suffocation, abandonment) or by untimely childhood deaths through selective neglect or maltreatment of girls."[60] During the first three decades of Communist rule, this long-standing phenomenon of exceptionally high male–female sex ratios in infancy declined dramatically, presumably due to strong discouragement of such practices by government officials pursuing policies of gender equality. However, with the implementation of the one-child policy, the distorted sex ratios began to reappear. Initially there was a reappearance of female infanticide practices, but over the past two decades, sex-selective abortion came to replace sex-selective infanticide,[61] as high-quality ultrasound diagnostic technologies became available throughout China. By the mid-1980s ultrasound technology allowed fetal genitalia to be visualized at month four or five, and the ready accessibility of legal abortion allowed couples to choose to selectively abort female fetuses in the second trimester.[62] As to implications, Banister argues that while a sustained shortage of females is not a catastrophe, it is undesirable in that it represents a violation of basic human rights and may contribute to social disruption, personal unhappiness, and reports of the abduction, rape, forced marriage, and bondage of hundreds of thousands of Chinese women.[63]

The Chinese government forcefully asserts that gender-selected abortion, abandonment, and infanticide all are illegal in China. Nonetheless, there has been much criticism expressed by advocacy groups, especially Western religious groups opposing abortion and/or contraception. In addition, the US State Department and NGOs such as Amnesty International have argued that China's population policies contribute to infanticide. In 2004 hearings before the House International Relations Committee, Arthur Dewey, US assistant secretary of state for the Bureau of Population, Refugees, and Migration was quoted as stating that China's "coercive birth-planning regime [has had] extremely negative social, economic and human rights consequences . . ." including "female infanticide in rural areas where there is a strong desire for male heirs, imbalances in the sex ratio that has been estimated to be as much as 122 boys for every 100 girls, soaring rates of female suicide, and human trafficking."[64] An extended debate in the UK House of Lords focused on these issues in 1996, with several speakers also drawing upon reports emanating from Amnesty International.[65]

In their book on the history of demographic practice in China, Lee and Wang conclude that it is not surprising that as Chinese fertility rates have declined to very low levels in recent years, there appears to have been increasing use of sex-selective abortion. Such actions, they argue, represent less a dramatic change than a continuation of old cultural norms in a more humane form: in effect, continuation via prenatal technological interventions of traditional Chinese practices that previously resulted in far higher mortality rates among young female children, whether from infanticide or neglect and abandonment. In the past, they note, "In some Chinese populations, families regularly practiced infanticide to regulate the number and sex of their children, with recorded rates for some years as high as 40 percent of female births."[66]

Concerns about demographic aging and distorted sex ratios at birth have led to a flurry of discussion about whether the time was approaching for China to modify its population policies. These debates were amplified by results from the 2010 Census of China released in April 2011. In its summary of the census findings, the official *People's Daily* newspaper reported that demographic increase from 2000 to 2010 had slowed to 0.57 percent from the 1.07 percent rate of the preceding decade, and the paper quoted the director of China's National Bureau of Statistics as stating, "The rapid growth of our population has been controlled effectively thanks to the family-planning policy that started in 1980." The *People's Daily* headline, however, was that a "crisis looms as China's population growth rate slows," due to an "upward aging population trend" and "the skewed gender ratio among newborns."[67] An active debate is under way in China about whether its population policies should be gradually modified, the outcomes of which cannot be predicted.

It is evident that recent demographic history in China is a very complex amalgam of dirigiste policies and older practices. Politics happens at many levels, here as elsewhere, and an appreciation of cultural norms related to the family is essential if we are to understand population dynamics in the world's most populous country.

Fertility Decline and Social Security in China

Until very recently, most elderly Chinese received support primarily from their adult children. While there have been social insurance pension systems in place since the 1950s, these have been primarily in urban areas, where only a minority of Chinese population resided. Benefits have been available primarily for government employees and employees of state-owned enterprises with more than one hundred workers. In the rural areas, where 75 percent of the Chinese population resided, social insurance was far more limited, with almost all support for the elderly provided by adult children and "social relief" systems aimed at the destitute and truly dependent.

One nearly inevitable result of the dramatic fertility declines during the 1970s and 1980s is that the age structure of China is now in the process of a dramatic shift—toward an "older" configuration, that is, rapidly rising proportions at higher ages. The percent of the Chinese population aged sixty and over is projected by the UN to increase from about 10 percent in 2000 to 20 percent in 2025 and more than 30 percent in 2050.[68]

It is important not to overinterpret such numbers, however. The boundaries between vigorous adulthood and aged dependency are far from fixed; with the improved health and rising prosperity being experienced in China, persons aged seventy in 2050 are likely to be in far better condition than those of the same age in 2000. Nonetheless, the projected shifts in the proportion of the Chinese population of higher ages are very large and very rapid when compared with most other countries.

The rapid fertility decline also means that the increasing numbers of Chinese couples aging into their late sixties and seventies will on average have fewer adult children on whom to call for support. Hence there has been much concern (verging on a type of "moral panic," according to some scholars[69]) that the future needs of China's burgeoning elderly population will not be met.

In addition, China faces these challenges in the absence of a well-developed social insurance system. Development of such systems in the industrialized countries of Europe, North America, and Asia took many decades, after Bismarck inaugurated the first social insurance system in Germany in 1889. The US Social Security system was not established until nearly a half century later, in 1935. Given the rapidity of the other changes underway in China, it seems likely that the Chinese government will need to accelerate these developments. In 1997 the Chinese government unified the long-standing formal sector pension system that was based upon state-owned and collectively owned enterprises into a system based jointly upon a "social pool" that would provide a basic pension and a supplementary pension based upon personal accounts. The base pension was planned to provide eligible retirees with about 20 percent of the average monthly wage (varying by regions). This base pension would be adjusted in line with an urban price index and average wage increases. Personal accounts would be accumulated from a deposit by each employee of 11 percent of wages, with a monthly supplementary pension to be drawn from this personal account at the rate of 1/120 per month of the accumulated sum.[70]

In 1999 the coverage of the base pension system was expanded to include urban employees of enterprises with private and foreign investors. In 2000 the government established a "national social security fund" to provide a pool of capital invested "on market principles," to provide a financial reserve for the basic pension system. According to a Chinese government White Paper, financial capital for this fund has come from multiple sources: "reducing state shareholding, stock ownership assets, funds from the central budget, funds raised by other means approved by the State Council, and investment returns."[71] By the end of 2003 this fund had accumulated assets exceeding 130 billion yuan.

Then, in 2002, the basic pension system was again extended to include "all those who were employed in a flexible manner in urban areas." By 2003, more than 155 million Chinese were enrolled in the base pension system—a huge number to be sure, though still well under a third of the total Chinese urban population of about 515 million in that year.[72] In addition, enterprises were encouraged to set up annuities for their employees, to which both the enterprise and the employee make contributions. In 2003, some 7 million people participated in such supplementary annuity funds operated by their employers.[73] The 2001 population law authorized the incentives of preferential pension provisions for those who fully complied with the goals of the state birth-planning policies, but it left the details (and the financing) of such provisions to local governments.[74]

The Chinese government's 2004 White Paper on pension policy proposed a further phased expansion of the national pension system. The plan described by the White Paper continued to differentiate between pension provisions for the urban and rural populations. For the former, the expressed goal was to expand the current system from government employees and the formal sector to "all eligible employees" in urban areas. It also proposed that funds for the basic pension be raised through multiple channels in the future, including contributions from enterprises, from employees, and subsidies from all levels of government.

One major ambiguity surrounding urban pension provision is the large and growing "floating population" (or *liudong renkou*) of Chinese urban areas. The 2000 Census of China defines this population as those who have resided in the destination of their migration for at least six months but lack local household registration status (*hukou*) required for ready access to education, housing, health care, pensions, and formal employment.[75] Until about three decades ago, the *hukou* system effectively limited internal migration in China, especially from rural to urban areas.

Over the past two decades, these controls have been substantially weakened by the market reforms that now make it possible for unregistered migrants to obtain the necessities of life, such as food rations. The result has been very rapid growth of the "floating population," concentrated heavily in urban areas in the economically most dynamic cities and towns of the coastal regions of China. Examining only those migrating between counties, for example, this intercounty subset of the total floating population is estimated to have increased from about 7 million in 1982 to about 79 million in 2000.[76] Analysis of tabulations from the 2000 census indicates that if information about intra-country migration available in the 2000 Census is included, the total floating population was about 144 million.[77] Initial reports from the 2010 census indicate that rapid growth has continued, with a 2010 floating population of more than 261 million (19.5 percent of the total population).[78] To date, the Chinese government has not formally addressed how it plans to deal with provision of pensions for this largely urban population lacking in formal residency licenses.

As to the bulk of the Chinese population residing in rural areas, the government plan has been far more cautious. It proposed only "experimenting" with personal accounts based on the principle that "the premiums are paid mainly by individuals themselves, supplemented by collectively pooled subsidies and supported by government policies."[79] However, by 2003 only 54 million of the roughly 775 million rural population were part of this program. In 2004 the government (financed jointly by central and local governments) began to provide rural couples over age sixty who had borne only one child (or two girls) with a special pension of 50 yuan per month.[80]

The Chinese government appears to be moving toward creating the institutions and financial resources needed to provide basic pension provision for its population. It will nonetheless be a very considerable challenge to do so, given the rapidly of the shifts now under way in the Chinese age structure and the fact that the bulk of the current Chinese population in rural areas continues to be dependent upon family support in old age.

Conclusion

The pace of demographic change in recent Chinese history is staggering. This brief discussion of the more salient elements of the story can only suggest some similarities and some dissimilarities with the story presented in other parts of this book. In China, the notion of "risk" faced by couples of reproductive age has long included unusually interventionist roles played by village norms in the unfolding of various strategies of family formation. Moreover, the roles played by the central state since the Communist Revolution have framed China's recent demographic history in a host of ways that make this story a distinctive one. The Communist Party of China runs what is effectively a federation of huge regions, which if they were to spin off from Beijing's control would dwarf most of the world's independent states. The central government sets parameters, but their meaning is decided at much lower levels of aggregation. This makes China's recent history a house of many mansions. And to understand the way it works, a large dose of humility is an indispensable asset.

Population and Politics in India

Many of the classic studies of modernization and population dynamics have taken India as their field of study. Such research has enriched our understanding of many facets of demography and development, and yet there has been a consistent tendency toward overly narrow thinking in many of these works—especially the assumption that demographic change is overwhelmingly determined by economic factors. While economic factors are indeed important, we offer an alternative perspective, that greater attention should be paid to political developments to account for the way in which fertility decline has become a global phenomenon. In the important case of India, politics is part of the story of differences in pathways of fertility decline in different regions of the same country.

In this chapter, we first offer a rough sketch of post-1980 demographic developments in India and then turn to population policies and the controversies surrounding them. The Indian story is one in which the intrusion of the state and international agencies into the realm of family formation took on a striking form and force that separates it from other national stories we survey in this book. India is also a case demonstrating truly exceptional levels of diversity within the same country. The changing and variegated Indian experiences in the politics and policies of population provide abundant evidence that we need to define politics as something that happens on many levels, and that population policies almost always fail when they appear from on high.

In terms of Beck's notion of the "risk society" as it relates to reproductive decisions, India offers a case of dizzying degree of variation and complexity that cannot be easily generalized. In some regions and among some groups in India, the status of women of reproductive age is so low that their decisions about childbearing are determined essentially by their husbands and mothers-in-law. In other settings in the same country, for example in Kerala, the status of women is far higher, women are themselves more educated, and high levels of out-migration by men leads to far more independent decision making by the women themselves.

The large variations across India in the nature and methods used to implement population policies that often were described as "national" adds a further element of variation in risk. In some Indian settings the risks to women's health and family security posed by high fertility have been palpable. In other cases and time periods, especially during the "Emergency" discussed in some detail later in this chapter, the risks became quite high for couples that refused to comply with fertility *diktats* from local officialdom. Paradoxically, the unusually heavy reliance in India upon male sterilization rather than female methods of fertility regulation meant that these risks sometimes fell most directly upon men rather than women, though the effects could be felt by all members of their families.

Demographic Profile since 1980

In terms of population size, India currently is the second largest country in the world. The United Nations Population Division estimates a 2010 population for India of 1.224 billion, representing about 17.7 percent of the global estimate of 6.896 billion for that same year.[1] This compares with a comparable estimate of 1.341 billion for China.

Because India's population is growing considerably more rapidly than that of China, most projections show India to be on a demographic trajectory to exceed China's population size within a couple of decades. For example, the "medium variant" of the UN's 2010 projections suggest that India's population would reach 1.458 million by 2025, exceeding China's projected population size (1.395 billion) for the same year.[2] (However, see discussion to follow of the substantial uncertainties surrounding the future of fertility in India.)

India is by far the largest parliamentary democracy in the world. The estimated 2010 population of the second largest parliamentary democracy, the United States, at about 310 million,[3] is only about one-quarter the size of India's. The combined total of the twenty-seven parliamentary democracies that are member states of the European Union is estimated at just over 501 million at the beginning of 2010.[4]

India is comprised of twenty-eight states, some of which contain populations that are larger than those of almost all countries in the world. For example, the state of Uttar Pradesh had a 2001 population of 166 million, a population size exceeded by only 5 of the 192 countries belonging to the United Nations: China, United States, Indonesia, Brazil, and Pakistan.

In terms of land area, India is the seventh largest country, following only Russia, Canada, China, United States, Brazil, and Australia. However, India's land area accounts for only about 2.3 percent of the world's, compared with its population of more than 17 percent of the global 2010 total.

Fertility and Population Growth in India

Fertility in India was high in the period immediately following World War II; the UN total fertility rate estimate was 5.90 in 1950–1955.[5] During this period, the newly independent government of India established its first formal national family-planning program.[6]

There ensued a relatively slow fertility decline, which by 2000–2005 had reached the level of 2.96, representing a 50 percent reduction from the level fifty years earlier.[7] The Demographic and Health Survey's fertility estimate pointed to a further decline, to 2.68 for 2005–2006.[8] For this two-year period contraceptive prevalence was estimated at 48.2 percent of married women aged fifteen to forty-nine, of which most (that is, 42.8 percent of the total) were using modern methods.[9]

As to the coming decades,[10] a wide range of future fertility rates are plausible for India (see graph for India, fig. A.9, in appendix A). The median projection, based on the United Nations Population Division's new probabilistic models,[11] shows a continuing gradual fertility decline through 2050, at which time the total fertility rate would be just below 2.0. However the high and low boundaries of the 95 percent projection intervals for that same year are very different—as high as 2.5 and nearly as low as 1.0—illustrating the high levels of uncertainty surrounding the median projection for a country such as India.

Using these variants, the UN's projected population size for India in 2050 ranges from a low of 1.457 billion to a high of 1.953 billion, with the medium-variant projection indicating a population size of 1.692 billion in that year.

With respect to demographic growth rates, the medium-variant projection shows growth rates declining from 1.43 percent per year in 2005–2010 to 0.33 percent by 2045–2050. Comparable projected rates for the "low" and "high" projection variants are, of course, much lower and much higher respectively.

Diversity

The leitmotif of India is not only its gigantic population size but its extreme diversity along many dimensions—geographic, social, linguistic, cultural, economic, and certainly demographic.

The range of geographical characteristics within the borders of India is remarkable. Its northern states are dominated by the high Himalayas; indeed many of the world's highest peaks are located within the borders of India, along with similar high mountains in bordering Pakistan, Nepal, and Tibet. Yet India's southern and eastern states contain many tropical coastal plains, some of which contain large populations living on land close to sea level.

High levels of diversity of a social and cultural character also are evident both in official data and in casual observation. While India is often seen as a predominantly Hindu nation, it is best understood as a multireligious and multilingual country, with very large differences among and within its twenty-eight states along these dimensions. Over four-fifths of, or 828 million, Indian residents report themselves as Hindu, yet there are 138 million Muslims in India—the third largest Muslim population in the world, behind only Indonesia and Pakistan. In addition to its large Muslim population, the Indian census data show tens of millions of Christians, Sikhs, Buddhists, Jains, and other religious groups.

Although the absolute number of Muslims in India is large, they represent only a small minority—about 13 percent—of the population, about the same percentage as African Americans in the United States. Nonetheless there have been persistent alarums sounded by Hindu nationalists, who forecast that Muslims' higher fertility rates will lead inexorably to a Muslim majority in India. While much of this advocacy comes from Hindu fundamentalists who favor a principle of Hindutva (Hinduness), which would require all Indians to accept a Hindu ethos, related views have been espoused by the Bharatiya Janata Party (BJP) that led the governing alliance from 1998 to 2004.[12]

It is true that fertility rates among Indian Muslims tend to be higher than those of Indian Hindus, which has led some Hindu nationalists to forcefully oppose family-planning programs, which they argue are more likely to lower fertility among Hindus than among Muslims. To give a sense of the level of emotionality that can result, consider the following exhortation from a 1971 book on Hindus and family planning: "Oh Hindus realize your strength! Do not get sterilized whether you are male or female. Do not follow family planning as advocated by our stupid Government, and do not restrict your children to 2 or 3. Oh Hindus, Hinduism is your ancient homeland. If you get sterilized and do not have more than 2 or 3 children, you will lose this homeland to non-Hindus in about 80 years. Therefore have [at] minimum 5 to 6 children to perpetuate your absolute majority in Hindustan."[13]

In demographic terms, a Muslim majority in India is highly implausible. In the 1951 Indian census, the first after the 1947 partition of British India, Muslims represented about 10 percent (as compared with Hindus at 88 percent and Christians at 2 percent) of the population enumerated within the boundaries of India.[14] Over the ensuing six decades this percentage has increased, but only to about 13 percent.

Linguistic diversity is even greater. The Indian census of 1961 counted a remarkable 1,652 spoken languages, most of which were subsequently classified under 15 language groups specified in the Indian constitution, along with 91 other languages.[15]

There is also—uniquely relevant in the Indian case—the complex, centuries-old, and distinctive social stratification system based on
"caste." The subject is a controversial and volatile one in India, attended
by passionate political disputes and sometimes by violence. Even the
terminology can evoke fervent debate. The subtleties and sensitivities
involved require that all exercise great care in their interpretations of
caste in India.

Most analysts seem to agree that there are hundreds, even thousands, of categories of caste and subcaste in India. Panandiker and
Umashankar, for example, report that among Hindus alone there are
"2,378 main castes, subcastes, or jatis," and "about 3,743 backward castes
in India." They note further that the "1981 Census of India lists 1,086
scheduled castes."[16]

Generally, Indian castes are defined as in-marrying kinship groupings to which membership of individuals accrues by birth. Many castes
are associated with occupations, which therefore also tend to be passed
on from father to son. These occupations range from the high-status
priestly castes of the Brahmins, through middle-status castes associated
with farmers and artisans, to low-status castes typically associated in Indian tradition with ritually "impure" occupations, such as those dealing with dead animals, leatherwork, human excrement, cremation, and
scavenging. Various terms are used for such low-status castes, including
scheduled classes, untouchables, harijans, or *dalit.*

While there is no simple relationship between caste rank and economic status, members of higher-status castes tend to have higher levels
of income and wealth than do those of low-ranking castes. Discrimination on the basis of caste is prohibited under the Indian constitution,
and indeed there are provisions for "affirmative action" designed to up-
lift their status. The traditional caste system is more evident in rural
areas than in urban conurbations.[17]

Under such circumstances it is not surprising that fertility rates appear to be somewhat higher among the *dalit,* or low-status castes, than
among the rest of the Hindu population. Average fertility among Indian
Muslims is even higher.[18] Such comparisons are subject to all kinds of
confounding factors, such as the fact that Indian Muslims are differen-
tially located in northern states, in which fertility rates for Hindus are

higher than for Hindus in southern states, or that *dalits* may consider conversion to Islam (or Christianity or Buddhism) to escape their low status in the Hindu caste system.[19] This is a complex and contentious subject, which we can only touch upon here.

Recent Economic Growth Trends in India

Until 1990, India was a country in which a large fraction of the population lived in profound poverty. An analysis by the World Bank[20] assessed Indian poverty trends from 1981 to 2005. Using the World Bank's preferred "poverty" boundary of individuals living on less than US $1.25 per day (expressed in terms of Purchasing Power Parity, or PPP),[21] the report indicates that a 1981 population of 420 million, or about 60 percent of the Indian population, fell into this category.[22]

Beginning about a decade later, the Indian government implemented major reforms in its economic policies, and thereafter Indian economic growth accelerated. The GDP of India grew at an annual rate of 5.1 percent from 1990 to 1995, 5.8 percent from 1995 to 2000, 7.0 percent from 2000 to 2005, and 8.7 percent from 2005 to 2008.[23] Adjusting for population growth, India's GDP per capita for the same time periods also showed an accelerating growth trend: 3.1 percent; 4.0 percent; 5.4 percent; and 7.1 percent annually.[24]

In part due to demographic increase, these rising rates of Indian economic growth have not reduced the absolute numbers of Indians living in poverty, though the percentages in poverty actually have declined substantially. The World Bank's analysis shows 456 million Indians, or 42 percent, were in this category in 2005.[25] Compared with 1981 figures, the absolute number increased by about 36 million while the percentage of the total population impoverished declined from about 60 to about 42 percent.

One effect of recent economic growth has been a widening of inequality at the national level. One widely circulated report by the McKinsey Global Institute takes a sanguine view about the implications of such trends, based upon its forecast that the Indian "middle class" will grow dramatically over the next decades.[26] After noting that only about 5 percent of Indian households fell into this category in 2005, it asserts that by 2025 this number will have burgeoned to 128 million households,

accounting for 583 million persons and 41 percent of the projected population for that year.[27] However, even this optimistic report acknowledges that the gap between rich and poor in India has been widening
and will continue to do so.[28]

The evidence available also suggests large disparities in economic
growth across Indian states and regions, disparities that if anything have
been growing since the economic reforms of the early 1990s led to accel-
eration in overall economic growth in India. Analysis of annual rates of
growth of gross State Domestic Product (SDP) shows that dispersion in
economic growth rates across states increased greatly during the 1990s.[29]

During the 1980s the fastest growing state (Rajasthan) exceeded the
growth of the slowest growing state (Kerala) by a factor of less than 2.
During the 1990s the fastest growing (Gujarat) exceeded the slowest
(Bihar) by a much larger factor of 3.5. Indeed, such large disparities in
economic growth were even greater if differences among the states in
their rates of population growth were taken into account by examining
per capita data on state economic growth. Here the ratio of highest-
to-lowest growth was again about 2 in the 1980s, but as high as 7 in
the 1990s (for the pair of Gujarat and Bihar). However, high economic
growth rates in the 1990s were not concentrated in only one part of the
country, and the poor economic growth performance of Kerala in the
1980s was followed by accelerated growth in the 1990s, which brought it
up only slightly below the national average.[30]

Another study reported similar findings and suggested that state-
level investment disparities in education and agricultural productivity
widened during the 1990s.[31]

Differential Fertility in India

Significant fertility differentials persist among Indian states and more
generally among regions of the country. In particular, fertility rates
are substantially higher than the national average in many of the large
population states in the northern, central, and eastern regions of India,
while notably lower and indeed below-replacement fertility rates (usually defined as about 2.1) have appeared in large-population states in
the southern region. Table 5.1 presents the relevant data by region of

Table 5.1. Total Fertility Rates in 2005–2006 and Population in 2001 for Regions and States of India

Region and State	TFR 2005–2006	Population in 2001, Rounded (millions)
NORTH		
Rajasthan	3.21	56.5
Punjab	*1.99*	24.4
Haryana	2.69	21.1
Delhi	*2.13*	13.9
Jammu and Kashmir	2.38	10.1
Uttarakhand	2.55	8.5
Himachal Pradesh	*1.94*	6.1
CENTRAL		
Uttar Pradesh	3.82	166.2
Madhya Pradesh	3.12	60.3
Chhattisgarh	2.62	0.9
EAST		
Bihar	4.00	83.0
West Bengal	2.27	80.2
Orissa	2.37	36.8
Jharkhand	3.31	26.9
NORTHEAST		
Assam	2.42	26.7
Tripura	2.22	3.1
Meghalaya	3.80	2.3
Manipur	2.83	2.2
Nagaland	3.74	2.0
Arunachal Pradesh	3.03	1.1
Mizoram	2.86	0.9
Sikkim	*2.02*	0.5
WEST		
Maharashtra	*2.11*	96.9
Gujarat	2.42	50.7
Goa	*1.79*	1.3

(*continued*)

Table 5.1. (*Continued*)

Region and State	TFR 2005–2006	Population in 2001, Rounded
SOUTH		
Andhra Pradesh	*1.79*	76.2
Tamil Nadu	*1.80*	62.4
Karnataka	*2.07*	52.9
Kerala	*1.93*	31.8
INDIA, TOTAL		
	2.68	1028.6

Note: Total fertility rates that are highlighted are at or below replacement level for India.
Source: From International Institute for Population Sciences (IIPS) and Macro International, 2007, National Family Health Survey (NFHS-3), 2005–2006, India, vol. 1, Mumbai, IIPS; Jacques Véron, "The Demography of South Asia from the 1950s to the 2000s: A Summary of Changes and a Statistical Assessment," *Population* (English ed.) 63 (1), 2008, pp. 9–90.

the country, with states located in each region listed in order of their population size.

As may be seen, Uttar Pradesh in the central region is by far the largest Indian state, with a population of 166 million in 2001. Its reported total fertility rate was 3.82 in 2005–2006. Bihar, in the east, with 83 million in population, reported a total fertility rate of 4.00; and Rajasthan in the north, with a population of close to 57 million, had a total fertility rate of 3.21—all to be compared with the national average of 2.68 for the same year.

At the same time, all of the four Indian states in the south, most with large populations, registered much lower fertility rates; indeed all were below replacement as of 2005–2006. Kerala, the most well known of these southern states, with a population of nearly 32 million, reported a total fertility rate of 1.93. The two largest states in the south, Tamil Nadu, with 62 million inhabitants, and Andhra Pradesh, with 76 million, reported even lower total fertility rates of around 1.80.

The only states in the northern and northeastern regions of India with below-replacement fertility were Punjab, Himachal Pradesh, and

Sikkim, but of these, two have only small populations (Himachal Pradesh at 6.1 million and Sikkim with a tiny 0.5 million).

Finally, one Indian state in the west with a large population, Maharashtra, reported replacement-level fertility, and Goa reported below-replacement fertility, though it has a population of only 1.3 million.

The above suggests a caveat for any discussion of Indian fertility patterns: National averages of fertility rates for the whole of India disguise the important fact that hundreds of millions of Indians live in states, primarily in the south and to a lesser extent in the west, in which fertility rates now are at or below replacement. Meanwhile fertility rates in populous states of the northern, central, and eastern regions were much higher.

Analysis of such differences is greatly complicated by the reality that the states in the southern region of India also differ markedly in many other respects. Disentangling these social, economic, cultural, political, and historical threads is a daunting, perhaps impossible, task in the present study.

A 1992 field study of a large multicultural resettlement colony (described by the author as "a slightly glorified slum") compares recent migrants to Delhi from the northern state of Uttar Pradesh and the southern state of Tamil Nadu. The results were derived from interviews with both the heads of household and married or previously married women in these households. [32] These interviews were modeled broadly after the World Fertility Survey Core Questionnaire,[33] with added sections focused on women's status and autonomy, and on women's knowledge, attitudes, and behaviors related to health and family planning. There was also a subsequent six-month longitudinal follow-up in which households with at least two living children below the age of twelve were visited every two weeks to collect information on children's activities, consumption, illnesses, and treatment.

The women in the study who had migrated to Delhi from Tamil Nadu reported distinctly lower levels of fertility and child mortality than did the comparable sample of migrant women from Uttar Pradesh. Moreover, while child mortality among girls was substantially higher than that of boys in the Uttar Pradesh sample, this was not the case for the Tamil sample. The lower fertility rates among migrants from

Tamil Nadu appeared to result from an earlier halt to childbearing, both through voluntary sterilization and contraception. These differentials in turn were explained by greater exposure and interaction of Tamil women with people outside the household as well as greater female autonomy in domestic decision making compared with the more-restricted and less-autonomous horizons for women from Uttar Pradesh. While such field studies do not pretend to "explain" macro-level differences in fertility rates among Indian regions and states, they do offer useful insights and controls for what otherwise are outcomes of multiple possible forces.

Caldwell and his colleagues provide an account of a countervailing force tending toward higher fertility in the South Indian state of Karnataka. There, the weakening of traditional means of fertility control—in particular postnatal sexual abstinence of two years—to roughly six months tended toward higher fertility. Here is another instance of the complexity of pathways and causes of population growth in India.[34]

A Brief History of Indian Population Policy

India achieved independence in 1947. Until 1950 it retained the British monarch as nominal head of state ("Dominion" status); since then India has been a republic, though still part of the British Commonwealth. In late 1951 the new republic adopted its first Five Year Plan, which included a formal policy aimed at reducing the country's rapid population growth rate (about 2.0 percent per year at that point) as an essential step toward development. The Indian Family Planning Programme, initiated the following year, was one of the first such government-sponsored programs in the world, and by the 1960s it had become the largest.[35]

Implementation of the family-planning provisions of the first Five Year Plan, however, was very uneven, since under the federal political structure of the Indian republic the central government in New Delhi had little power to enforce its declared population policy. This was broadly true of all policies promulgated by the central government and increasingly so during the 1960s, when the trend was one of decentralization of political power to the states. In his classic book *Asian Drama*, Gunnar Myrdal described India as a "soft state" in which "policies decided upon are often not enforced, if they are enacted at all, and . . . the

authorities, even when framing policies, are reluctant to place obligations on people."[36] Implementation of family-planning programs happened almost entirely at the state level, while the central government
provided financial support and encouragement. In many Indian states,
including some of those with the largest populations, political support
for the government's population policy during the 1950s and especially
the 1960s was limited, and implementation was weak.

Indira Gandhi was the daughter of Jawaharlal Nehru, the first and
longest-serving prime minister of independent India, who died in office in 1964. She unexpectedly became prime minister in 1966 following the sudden death of then Prime Minister Lal Bahadur Shastri, who
succeeded her father and in whose cabinet she had served as minister of
information and broadcasting. At that point the ruling Indian Congress
Party included both a socialist faction led by Mrs. Gandhi and a conservative faction led by Morarji Desai, whom she defeated in the 1966 party
leadership election with the support from the president of the Indian
National Congress.

During the first few years of her prime ministership, Mrs. Gandhi
did little to reverse the trend toward the decentralization of political
power in general, nor did she seek to implement more energetic family-
planning programs than those of her predecessors. Her conservative opponent Desai had joined her government in 1967 and later had become
deputy prime minister, but relations between the left and right factions
of the Indian Congress Party continued to deteriorate. In 1969 there was
a formal split, with the faction controlled by Indira Gandhi becoming
the Congress (R) Party (later renamed Congress (I) Party, with the *I* for
"Indira"). Desai's faction renamed itself the Congress (O) Party, with
the "O" standing for "Organisation".[37]

In the parliamentary elections of 1971, Gandhi's Congress (I) Party
established control over the national Parliament. In the following year
it also gained political control over many states in state elections. During much of this year Indira Gandhi expressed strong support for those
fighting a war in East Pakistan seeking separation from West Pakistan.
This war erupted after more than a year of internal political conflict in
Pakistan following the election of 1970. Ultimately the conflict led to
a military intervention by India, which, after a short (two-week) war

between India and Pakistan, culminated in surrender by Pakistan and the reconstitution of East Pakistan as an independent state, Bangladesh.

Following Mrs. Gandhi's success in the brief 1971 war with Pakistan and in the 1971 and 1972 elections, she began to reassert the authority of the central government of India. The 1972 state elections represented not only successes for her party but set the stage for the establishment of unusual personal control over state government leaders. Myron Weiner, an authority on Indian politics, noted: "Most of the chief ministers who assumed power in the states after the Congress victories of 1972 were the personal choices of the prime minister . . . The new chief ministers were completely dependent upon the prime minister for their positions. Several chief ministers who had dominated the state party machinery for decades were removed, replaced by young leaders more personally loyal to the prime minister."[38]

During the years following the state elections in 1972, data emerging from the 1971 Census of India made clear that instead of India's population growth rate declining as had been forecast, it had increased to about 2.3 percent per year.[39] These results were alarming to the nation's elite, almost all of whom shared the view that India's population growth was too high to allow for successful economic development.

The year 1975 was one of domestic political turmoil in India. In Bihar, J. P. Narayan, who had been a close associate of Mahatma Gandhi, led a campaign of nonviolent resistance to the central government of Indira Gandhi. In Gujarat, a loose coalition of parties that was later to coalesce into the ruling Janata Party succeeded in defeating the Congress Party. The growing unrest was fueled by declines in food production, rising food prices, and the negative economic effects of the dramatic increases in world oil prices during 1973–1974.

On 12 June 1975, political turmoil was transformed into political crisis when a judge in the Allahabad High Court nullified Prime Minister Indira Gandhi's reelection to the lower house of the Indian Parliament. This controversial decision was in response to repeated claims by political opponents that her Congress (I) Party had engaged in electoral fraud during the 1971 election. The court determined that Mrs. Gandhi's campaign had used illegally certain elements of government machinery in support of her election.[40] The judge's ruling that nullified her election would have had the effect of removing her from the position of prime minister, since no longer would she have been a member of Parliament. The decision also excluded her from political office for a six-year period.

The Gandhi government responded quickly by advising the Indian president to proclaim an "Emergency" under Article 352 of the Indian constitution, a provision that had been invoked only twice before, in both cases during wartime—during the India-China War in the 1960s and during the India-Pakistan War in 1971. Then President Fakhruddin Ali Ahmed followed the government's advice and formally declared a "State of Emergency" on 26 June 1975, two weeks after the Allahabad court ruling. The president's proclamation of the Emergency had to be approved by parliament within six months, and could be renewed for successive six-month periods by parliamentary action. Both were reasonably assured given the large parliamentary majority held by the Congress (I) Party.

The Indian constitution provides that during a State of Emergency, both the fundamental rights of individuals guaranteed by the constitution and the federal system of government may be suspended. The Gandhi government used these emergency powers to ban opposition parties and to arrest thousands of protesters and protest leaders such as J. P. Narayan and his associates. It invoked direct control by the central government over states such as Tamil Nadu and Gujarat, then ruled by opposition parties. It imposed censorship upon the Indian press.[41] Later it amended the constitution to insulate Gandhi from any legal liability from the electoral fraud case that had led to the judicial nullification of her 1971 election to Parliament. The State of Emergency lasted for twenty-one months, after which the government called a national election. To the surprise of many, this election led to the defeat of Indira Gandhi's party by the Janata Party, the previously loose coalition of parties that had emerged stronger from its opposition to the Emergency.

Shortly after the formal declaration of an Emergency in 1975, the government promulgated a Twenty Point Programme designed to increase economic growth, improve public services, and reduce poverty and illiteracy. This program contained little or no attention to Indian population and family-planning issues. Policies on these topics appeared only months later, with the completion of a parallel Five Point Programme developed by the prime minister's younger son, Sanjay Gandhi.

During this period the prime minister assigned leadership of what had become a Twenty-five-Point Programme to Sanjay Gandhi. He proved to be a committed proponent of energetic family-planning programs, which he made a centerpiece of his many speeches and reportedly promoted even more forcefully in numerous private discussions with Indian leaders at both national and state levels.[42] Sanjay and his mother, the prime minister, were well aware of the reluctance of many state governments to adopt measures to help reduce high rates of population growth. In October 1975 the health minister wrote to Indira Gandhi, "The problem [of rapid population growth] is now so serious that there seems to be no alternative to thinking in terms of introduction of some elements of compulsion in the larger national interest."[43]

With support from key members of the ruling party, from his mother down, Sanjay Gandhi led the successful effort to amend the Indian constitution in 1976 to provide the central government with enhanced powers for implementation of population policies. The health minister's 1975 call for "elements of compulsion in the larger national interest" was echoed by the prime minister in January 1976: "We must now act decisively, and bring down the birth rate speedily too. We should not hesitate to take steps which might be described as drastic."[44]

A new National Population Policy was adopted by the Indian cabinet in April 1976. It contained numerous detailed goals on family planning and population policy, including:

- Increased central government funds to state governments and nonprofit agencies that were providing family planning services;
- Tying federal-to-state funding to the effectiveness of family-planning program performance;
- Raising the legal age at marriage;
- Increasing female literacy rates;
- Increasing payments to "acceptors" of sterilization;

- Adoption of regulations to encourage small family norms within the civil service;
- And—last but not least—authorizing state governments to pursue compulsory sterilization policies.[45]

In his angry five-hundred-plus-page historical treatment of international efforts to reduce the high demographic growth rates that became prominent after World War II, Connelly argues that this newly aggressive Indian population program of 1976 was aided and abetted by bilateral and multilateral aid donors. First, he suggests that the seeds of the Indian program were planted in a 1972 meeting of senior officials of the leading aid agencies, during which he states that "together they would lay out a new strategy to control the population of the world."[46] (Participating agencies included the Swedish International Development Agency (SIDA), the Population Council, the Ford Foundation, the World Bank, the International Planned Parenthood Federation (IPPF), the United Nations Fund for Population Activities (UNFPA), and the US Agency for International Development (USAID).)

According to Connelly, the new strategy developed at this high-level 1972 meeting included a decision to reduce international population assistance to ministries of health, which generally had low status in developing countries and had proved to be relatively ineffectual with family-planning programs. Instead, those laying out a new strategy to "control the population of the world" decided to deploy the World Bank's considerable leverage with the high-politics ministries of finance and planning in such a way as to "make governments work with UNFPA."[47]

Second, Connolly asserts that although the Gandhi government had decided in 1974 (that is, before the Emergency) to suspend both its sterilization camps and extra incentive payments for "acceptors," it reversed this decision in response to the UNFPA's offer of its largest grant ever to India—$40 million. It was, in Connelly's words, "the usual dog's breakfast, only bigger, with vehicles from UNDP, a training program from UNICEF, and so on. But the single largest part, $14 million, was for 'expansion of sterilization program.'"[48]

Third, with respect specifically to the Indian government's new population policy announced in 1976, Connelly points an accusatory finger at two international aid agencies in particular: the World Bank and the Swedish International Development Agency (SIDA). He acknowledges that these donors did not initiate the coercive policies embraced by the Indian government, but he asserts that they responded to these policies by increasing their support to the Indian program.[49] He reports, for example, that in December 1976 SIDA decided to provide an additional $17 million to a population project in India that it operated jointly with the World Bank, and he quotes the Bank's advisor as stating that while it would not support compulsion, "civilized and gentle pressure should be used."[50] Connelly also claims that although the US aid agency USAID had closed its office in India and as a matter of policy did not support incentive programs, the head of its population program "met with WHO officials and signaled that USAID wanted to support the Indian program"[51] and that USAID rapidly expanded its support for voluntary sterilization programs during the same year the new Indian program was promulgated. Connelly's interpretation of the roles played by international aid agencies represents one extreme of a wide range of views as to the provenance of the Indian program, but they do warrant at least a mention here.

Under the rubric of this new national policy, and with strong urgings from Sanjay Gandhi and his associates, many Indian states chose to adopt numerous new measures, though the governments of some states demurred. In many ways these efforts were based upon the experiences and infrastructure of the existing national family-planning program, though Sanjay made it clear that all government agencies, not only the Ministry of Health and Family Planning, had to be involved and also that all would be assessed on the basis of the program's success. For the first time, the policy was being implemented with the application of political will and abundant pressure on the part of top government leaders.

A dizzying variety of state government approaches resulted. Many were directed specifically at state government employees, thereby signaling the commitment of the state leadership to the program. Examples included:

- The establishment of numerical state targets for sterilization procedures, with subtargets allocated to different state agencies;
- Support for mobile sterilization camps to make sterilization on a large scale easily accessible to rural populations.[52]

Different states developed positive incentives to encourage smaller families, directed at either individuals or communities, for example:

- Increasing levels of money payments for acceptors of sterilization in many states;
- Offering salary increases for state government employees undergoing sterilization (Andhra Pradesh);
- Providing loans to sterilized people or those with small families (Orissa);
- Irrigation water at subsidized prices to villages meeting sterilization targets (Madhya Pradesh).[53]

There were negative incentives too, applied either to the individual or the community:

- Limiting maternity leave for female state employees to the first two births (Himachal Pradesh);
- Travel support for no more than two children of state employees (West Bengal);
- Excluding those with more than three children from state government jobs, with the exception of those who were sterilized (Rajasthan);
- Denial of public food rations to families with three or more children (Bihar);
- Loss of a month's salary by teachers who were not sterilized (Uttar Pradesh);
- Reduced pay for family-planning/health workers not achieving acceptor targets (Uttar Pradesh);
- State legislation enabling compulsory sterilization of couples with three or more children (Maharashtra),[54]

though this legislation was never ratified by the central government.[55]

As in the past, many policies were announced but never put into practice. In some cases these were Potemkin programs intended to show responsiveness to central government wishes. In other cases the policy intent was real, but the bureaucracy proved impenetrable or found creative ways to frustrate the relevant programs.

The Gandhi government's strong focus upon sterilization was hardly without precedent. In some parts of India family planning advocates had long promoted sterilization as an efficient mechanism of fertility regulation, in view of the acknowledged weakness of health services in parts of rural India. Nor was there anything new in the central government providing state governments with numerical targets for such sterilizations, although under the previous "soft state" setting these had rarely been reached and there was little or no effort to enforce them. Suddenly, under the Emergency, the desultory became the overzealous, albeit with enormous variation among the states and local areas of India.

The most committed, and sometimes overcommitted, states were in the "Hindi heartland," Hindi-speaking states of northern and central India with close ties to the Nehru/Gandhi dynasty: the Union Territory of Delhi; Haryana; Himachal Pradesh; Madhya Pradesh; and Uttar Pradesh (the Gandhi's longstanding political base). Meanwhile states in which other parties held control and the Gandhis had little influence declined to respond to the central government's new policies. In particular, the Communist government of the southern state of Kerala, which had broken with Mrs. Gandhi over the roles being played by her son Sanjay, openly and publicly opposed the policy. Tamil Nadu, the South Indian state to the east of Kerala that had long been controlled by a regional party opposed to domination by the north, did little in response to the new policy. The troubled far-north state of Jammu and Kashmir, with its two-thirds majority of Muslim citizens and its government dominated by a Kashmir nationalist party, not only ignored the new policies but also rejected the central government's offer of cash incentives for sterilization adopters. G. M. Shah, a leading Muslim politician in Jammu and Kashmir who had served as its chief minister from 1984 to 1986, put it in these evocative words: "The government has hatched a conspiracy to reduce the Kashmiri Muslim population. . . . Our State had an 82 percent Muslim population in 1947; it is now [1989] a mere 54 percent as the 1981 census figures reveal. We should reject the government's family planning program. This is aimed at further reducing the Muslim population in Kashmir. Every Kashmiri Muslim should have four wives to produce at least one dozen children."[56] The percentages claimed by Shah were in error: Only 57 percent of the state's population was Muslim in 1947, and that had risen to 64 percent in the 1981 population.[57] But what matters here is not the accuracy of the claimed "evidence," but the nature of the claim about the Indian Family Planning Programme.

While there is some uncertainty about the reliability of the data produced regarding this program, there is little doubt that sterilizations rose sharply: The numbers reported rose from 1.3 million (1974–1975) to 2.6 million (1975–1976) to 8.1–8.25 million (1976–1977). Of this last figure some 75–80 percent (6.5 million) took place during the six-month period from July to December 1976. Given that the "stock" of Indians who had been sterilized in the prior twenty-five years was estimated to be about 14 million, the increase of 8.1–8.25 million during 1976–1977 represented a more than 50 percent expansion. In the state of Uttar Pradesh, closely tied to the Gandhi government, sterilization numbers rose from less than 175,000 in 1975–1976 to 837,000 a year later.[58]

There were numerous reports, many of which were later confirmed after the Emergency, of pressure, threats, and outright physical coercion in support of achieving numerical sterilization targets, especially in the more-aggressive areas of central Indian states such as Uttar Pradesh with close ties to the Gandhi government.[59] Depending on the time and place, villagers in such regions were subjected to pressures ranging from hassles to compulsion, supported by incentives and disincentives that were both authorized and unauthorized by central or state government policies. One summary offers the following examples, ranging from more-effective enforcement of existing laws to draconian coercive measures:

- Heightened enforcement against the "time-honored village tradition of ticketless travel" on Indian railways: Railroad ticket inspectors, seeking to meet their supervisors' sterilization quotas, began to assess large fines against those without tickets unless they agreed to be sterilized.[60]
- Families with children received visits from local schoolteachers pointing to the contribution of smaller families to the mother's health and the children's well-being. Teachers who made such visits were more certain to receive their salaries.
- Labor contractors told would-be employees that they required a sterilization certificate. Such contractors would thereby meet the sterilization quota imposed on them by the state public works department.
- The availability of heavily subsidized food at government "fair price" shops depended on those with large families agreeing to sterilization.
- Local police would no longer overlook the activities of petty criminals unless they agreed to undergo vasectomy.[61]

In one extreme and infamous case, in the Muslim village of Uttawar in Haryana, a state near Delhi, there was a police roundup of about four hundred men arrested on suspicion of possession of illegal arms or threats of violence. Most were freed after they agreed to be sterilized.[62]

It is true that cases such as these likely affected relatively small numbers. However, far larger numbers appear to have responded with avoidance strategies to the episodic appearance of forceful and politically directed sterilization "drives" in their local areas. Many slept in their fields for a few nights or weeks and avoided local travel on buses and trains. In a particularly balanced and judicious summary of an understandably emotional and volatile issue, Gwatkin wrote as follows in 1979:

In sum, the Indian family planning program clearly involved coercion. The duration of such activities was relatively brief, probably lasting no more than a few weeks in any one location; they were concentrated primarily in a few parts of the country relatively close to New Delhi; they doubtless affected no more than a very small portion of India's total population. But at the same time, the available evidence suggests strongly that the frequency of indisputably coercive practices significantly exceeded the "isolated incident"; that many thousands of people at the very least experienced extremely unpleasant treatment at the hands of police and other government authorities; that millions more were subjected to strong indirect pressures, feared they might experience direct coercion, and altered their normal activities in order to avoid it."[63]

Those who acted coercively did not do so on the basis of explicit instructions from the highest authorities, which rarely existed, but rather in response to the intense political pressure exercised by the party in power and its agents. Mrs. Gandhi's followers put into practice what they saw as her will and that of her son Sanjay, and did so forcefully. Their aim was to obtain extraordinarily large numbers of sterilization acceptors immediately, with no excuses tolerated for failure to comply and with few questions asked about how compliance was achieved. As Gwatkin notes, "The program's excesses resulted less from consciously coercive intent than from the metabolism of the Indian political system driven by a mindless top-level enthusiasm for family planning, unconstrained by a concern for the other values that might be violated. . . ."[64]

In a lengthy two-part set of articles published in the Canadian journal *Pacific Affairs* in 1982–1983,[65] Vicziany argues that most studies draw too sharp a contrast between Indian family-planning practices before and during the Emergency, and that the excesses of the sterilization programs during the Emergency are criticized as "coercive" only because commentators had misinterpreted the earlier Indian programs as "voluntary."[66] To the contrary, she argues, Indian family-planning programs since the 1960s had been "deeply coercive, even without resort to physical force,"[67] "that the Indian birth-control program was never genuinely voluntary in character and that a great many of those who submitted to vasectomy do so under coercion of one kind or another,"[68] and that "the poorer, the weaker, and the laboring strata of society were affected disproportionately."[69] It is only fair to note that this criticism is in part definitional. Vicziany's preferred definition of *coercive* is far broader than actions involving "compulsion" specified in Gunnar Myrdal's classic 1968 work *Asian Drama*, holding instead that the financial incentives and other long-standing components of the pre-Emergency Indian Family Planning Programme were intrinsically "coercive."[70] The most excessive elements of pre-Emergency family planning reached their maxima in local districts in which the district collector—the most powerful government official at local levels, with supervisory authority over all local civil servants—led the effort.[71] Hence the mobilization of all levels of government during the twenty-one months of the Emergency produced similar excesses.

It is hardly surprising that by early 1977, opposition to the many excesses of the Emergency, and especially to those of its population program, had become very widespread. In January 1977 Indira Gandhi relaxed the Emergency, released her political opponents from jail, and called a general election for March of that year. Gandhi may have believed that her government would be returned to power in view of the obstacles faced by a fractured and suppressed political opposition, but the loose coalition of parties that had formed as the Janata Movement coalesced into a formidable opponent under the leadership (again) of J. P. Narayan. Janata won a majority of seats in the March 1977 election. Indira Gandhi herself was defeated in her own constituency election.

The new Janata government moved quickly to distance itself from the population programs led by Sanjay Gandhi. The Indian Family Planning Programme was renamed the Family Welfare Programme, and the pressures and incentives that had led to coerced sterilization were denounced and eliminated. The number of officially reported sterilizations declined precipitously from the 8.1–8.25 million in 1976–1977 to just over 1 million in 1977–1978.

In the years that followed family-planning and population policy became anathema to political parties and leaders alike, even including Indira Gandhi. She returned to power in the elections of January 1980, but in June of that same year her son Sanjay was killed in a flying accident. Indira Gandhi served as prime minister until she was assassinated by her own bodyguards in 1984.

Despite the searing experience of the Gandhis' population program during the twenty-one-month Emergency in 1975–1977, voluntary family-planning programs have continued. They have never again, however, been pursued as a high priority; indeed, successive governments have exercised great caution in their implementation.[72] The programs are the prerogative of the central government, but it still lacks the capacity at local levels to implement them directly. The central government's role is generally limited to including population policy as part its Five Year Plans for national development and to providing financial support to state governments; these policies depend upon the states for implementation. Given that the states of India vary greatly in their politics, their level of economic development, and their demography, this is a recipe for highly variable policy implementation.[73]

In the period since Mrs. Gandhi's assassination, single-party rule from the center is less evident, and there is more coalition politics involving multiple parties representing regional elites and populations. Representatives of the lower castes have emerged, especially in the economically lagging but demographically large states of the north. In some cases these diverse leaderships are hostile to the central government's urgings about population policy.

Meanwhile, quite different regional elites that are in power in South Indian states, such as Tamil Nadu, have expressed fear about the numerical preponderance of the regions of the Indian north. Southern politicians have denounced what they saw as a northern strategy to use demographic growth to gain political domination over the more-developed regions of the south.[74] In these southern states there was, as we have seen, much lower fertility than in the north. Here is a domestic example of the kind of reasoning from "strategic demography" that has been prominent in national debates about the implications of low fertility in many Western countries.[75] The suspicion of some is that those—be they countries in Europe or the Middle East, or subnational states in India—with larger populations and higher fertility rates use their demographic advantage to maximize their political position vis-à-vis less-fertile and less-populous neighbors.

Moreover, there is continuing opposition from leaders of India's large Muslim minority to central government programs to reduce fertility. Some see this as a reflection of Muslim theological ambivalence about voluntary male sterilization (vasectomy), in widespread use since the 1960s in predominantly Hindu India.[76] Others emphasize Muslim-Hindu differences in women's autonomy and socioeconomic status. Yet a careful analysis finds that "pervasive Muslim-Hindu differences in fertility intentions and in the risk of an unwanted child" cannot be adequately explained by differences in socioeconomic status and women's autonomy, and concludes that the most likely explanations lie in a minority group response among Indian Muslims and their leaders, in which fertility becomes a marker of group identity.[77]

One possible conclusion is that the remarkable diversity of India, combined with the federal and democratic nature of the Indian political system, has tended to increase the role of identity politics. This, combined with the memory of the excesses of the Emergency, has notably weakened the earlier national consensus about the importance of population policies for the nation's future well-being.

A new National Population Policy was announced in February 2000. It emphasized that there would be no coercion, and that implementation would be decentralized—a "bottoms-up approach" according to the Department of Family Welfare's secretary. The new policy included a series of incentives including US$11 for the birth of a girl. Its medium-term demographic goal was a total fertility rate at replacement level by 2010. By 2010 it was evident that this goal was not going to be reached. The long-term goal of the policy, a nongrowing Indian population by 2045, therefore came into question, though it was far too soon to conclude that it could not be reached.[78]

The Special Case of Kerala

No discussion of population policy in India would be complete without at least some special mention of Kerala. Although demographic increase in Kerala was one of the highest in India during the 1950s, during the 1970s it began to decline, reached replacement level in the late 1980s, and since then has been among the lowest reported by Indian states. The early and rapid fertility declines in Kerala were not consistent with the expectations of demographic transition theory. During the period of fertility decline, Kerala was a state characterized by low per capita income, weak economic activity in both agricultural and industrial sectors, and high rates of unemployment.[79]

In most discussions of this phenomenon, Kerala's early fertility decline is attributed to its long-standing emphasis on primary education and literacy (especially for women), public health, and social equity. Kerala's literacy rate—91 percent—is the highest of any state in India, where the average is about 65 percent. The same is true for the high literacy rate of females in Kerala: 88 percent, versus 54 percent for all of India.[80] In part this is due to Kerala's distinctive history and culture, in part due to its politics.

As to history and culture, the literature on Kerala points to adoption of a matrilineal system followed by Kerala's upper-caste Hindus and ruling class that provided unusually high status to women and girls; to the unusually progressive policies pursued by the Maharajas of Kerala from the eighteenth to the twentieth centuries; and to the strong commitment to education instilled in Kerala by its Christian missionaries (indeed Saint Thomas the Apostle is said to have arrived and preached near Cochin, on the coast of what is now Kerala, in A.D. 52.)[81]

As to matters political, Kerala, along with two other Indian states, was long led politically by the Communist Party of India (Marxist), currently the lead party of one of the two major political alliances, the Left Democratic Front (LDF). The state government of Kerala has invested heavily in continuing traditional Keralan support for literacy and universal education, while also instituting policies supporting land reform, public health, and minimum wages for agricultural workers.[82]

What is often not mentioned in discussions of Kerala's early and rapid fertility decline is that the state was also a leader of intensive family-planning programs beginning in the 1970s. Indeed, Kerala was the originator of the Indian "vasectomy camp." Beginning in 1971, Kerala organized mobile field hospitals to provide vasectomy services to men, accompanied by energetic publicity campaigns and large monetary incentive payments in both cash and goods equivalent to more than a month's salary for an unskilled worker.[83] These vasectomy camps were later to serve as models for similar efforts promoted by the Gandhi government, notwithstanding the fact that the Communist Party of India was a strong opponent of this Congress (I) Party government.[84]

Finally, there is another unusual demographic element in Kerala that also has received less attention than have education, literacy, and social equity: Kerala is the source of very large-scale out-migration to other countries, and especially to the oil-rich Gulf States. As of 2008 there were an estimated 2.5 million Keralans working in the Gulf States, primarily in Saudi Arabia and United Arab Emirates,[85] compared with about 31.8 million persons resident in Kerala. Some 44 percent of the 2.5 million Keralans resident outside India are Muslim, disproportionately high given that Muslims represent less than one-quarter of the Keralan population.[86] Lengthy marital separations surely reduce fertility rates directly, and large volumes of remittances being sent to Kerala by Keralans abroad—on the order of US$4 billion in 2003, representing some 22 percent of Kerala's net domestic product—alleviate poverty among migrants' family members remaining in the state.[87] According to one study, "Migration has provided the single most dynamic factor in the otherwise dismal scenario of Kerala in the last quarter of the twentieth century. It is one of the positive outcomes of the Kerala Model of Development. Kerala is approaching the end of the millennium with a little cheer in many of its homes, thanks to migration and the economic returns that it brings. In Kerala, migration must have contributed more to poverty alleviation than any other factor including agrarian reforms, trade union activities and social welfare legislation."[88]

Conclusion

This brief survey of Indian demographic history highlights, in one dramatic and controversial case, how much politics can matter in this field. Here, politics means national authority, but it also means the way in which other, nonelected "experts" working for foreign aid agencies and other NGOs operate within developing countries. In the Indian case, there is considerable evidence that at certain times elected Indian officials, with encouragement from the World Bank, SIDA, USAID, and other international agencies, exerted pressure on Indian families to restrict their fertility. In both cases, that of Mrs. Gandhi's government and that of various international assistance programs, those with power and resources sought to persuade poor people that it was in their interest to restrict their fertility, by sterilization if possible, and by other means if necessary. This is politics as paternalism, backed up by law and cash.

In the long term, this kind of top-down politics failed in India. The reason for its failure relates not only to the cruelty or heavy-handedness of its implementation, but also to the multidimensional nature of political power. Top-down efforts have almost always failed to raise fertility levels in the short term; efforts from the top to lower fertility almost always fail, too, although the case of China may represent a partial exception (see chapter 4).

Such efforts from the center are more productive when they act symbiotically with politics at the local level, as was the case in China. Demographic inequalities almost always intersect with political contestation. Local elites may have their own demographic agendas that run counter to those of other regions or of the central government. Some groups may see large and rapidly growing populations as sustaining or increasing their political power. Here there is little to separate Indian politics from the politics of Europe before the Second World War or the Middle East over the past decades. In the Indian case, what we term "strategic demography" takes place within a single country; in other global regions, the balance of numbers is usually measured between countries.

In a nation with the astonishing variety that characterizes India, few generalizations make sense. But one that may survive scrutiny is that, as in most other parts of the world, politics starts within the household and has immediate relevance at the level of the neighborhood and the village. At times, regional politics can enter everyday life and make a difference, but it is only very rarely that national programs or efforts can bear fruit. They do so only when they coincide with what is already going on at the "ground level" where most of us live our lives.

The failure of the Gandhis' program of top-down enforcement of family-planning initiatives does not prove that politics is irrelevant to demographic developments. On the contrary, it shows that politics at the national or international level is but one way in which societies organize themselves and construct frameworks in which to promote the well-being of their citizens. In this field, of greater importance than governments are households and the networks they construct in order to survive and, when possible, to prosper.

In between the household and the nation are states and regions, and their particularities—histories, cultures, political institutions— may have more to tell us about the different fertility patterns in India than does any analysis of the national state as a whole. The case of Kerala provides an example within India of early and rapid decline to fertility levels below replacement, notwithstanding Kerala's concurrent low income and high unemployment. Kerala is also an Indian state with long-standing government by a Communist Party and with a pattern of large-scale out-migration to the oil-rich states of the Persian Gulf. It is of course well-nigh impossible to disentangle the effects of history, culture, politics, literacy, social equity, and out-migration as they may have affected fertility rates in Kerala. Indeed, even the politics of Keralan Communism may reflect how people, at the local level at certain times and places, expressed their desires for a better future for their children.

All we wish to derive from this example is to say that politics is more than the national contest for power over the central state. It happens at multiple levels at once, and the closer to the household and village it gets, the more likely it will be that policies that may have been formulated at any level of authority will be converted into the material conditions of fertility decline. Symbiotic politics means just that: the braiding together of programs with patterns of everyday life, negotiated in families, villages, towns, and cities in a myriad of ways. The example of India shows how this is so, and how in some cases, when governments try to enforce changes in fertility behavior, they not only fail but pay the price of political defeat for doing so.

In the People's Republic of China, politics operates differently. There, central government policies are linked to local life in a host of ways unknown in India. The Indian and Chinese cases show, in opposing ways, that in any effort to understand the globalization of fertility decline, we ignore politics at our peril.

Japan

Family Structure, Abortion,
and Fertility since 1945

Although fertility rates in Japan in recent years have been relatively close to those of its much larger East Asian neighbor China, the postwar history of fertility decline in these two countries was remarkably different. Japan industrialized much earlier and experienced low fertility rates during the 1930s, but, in addition, the immediate postwar history of Japan reflected three political, demographic, and economic vectors: direct occupation by foreign powers, in this case controlled by the Supreme Command Allied Powers (SCAP), led by the US military; dramatic fertility declines based on widespread abortion rather than contraception or sterilization; and what eventually came to be called the Japanese postwar "economic miracle"—sustained and rapid export-led economic growth that established Japan as the second largest national economy in the world by the late 1960s.

These unique and dynamic postwar experiences gave a distinctive Japanese inflection to Beck's concept of a "risk society." In the immediate postwar years, as we shall see, the risks attached to childbearing in Japan were defined by the deep postwar economic crisis and desperate poverty that have often been forgotten. Later, the risks associated with marriage and childbearing appeared to have more to do with conflicts between rising aspirations among young women and continuing cultural norms regarding family obligations in Japan.

Japanese fertility declines in the immediate postwar period were notably rapid. Indeed, until the dramatic fertility declines in China during the 1970s and 1980s (see chapter 4), postwar Japan was the most remarkable case on record of fertility decline in a country of substantial size. The history of six decades of Japanese fertility patterns since World War II may be seen in fig. 6.1.

In only eight years, from 1949 to 1957, the total fertility rate of Japan fell by fully 50 percent—from 4.3 to 2.1; that is, from moderately high fertility to "replacement level" fertility in less than one decade. In the early 1970s, this dramatic decline was followed by an increase in the number of births, which some in Japan call the "Second Baby Boom"; there was also a small increase in the total fertility rate, to slightly above 2.1.

Subsequently there was a second-stage decline in Japanese fertility, at a slower pace to be sure, but to very low levels indeed. By 1995 Japanese fertility had declined below 1.5, and by 2005 below 1.3, placing Japan among the small group of countries with the lowest fertility rates in the world. The lowest recorded total fertility rate for Japan was 1.28 in 2005, after which it has been increasing. The most recent official estimates, for 2010 and 2011, show a total fertility rate of 1.39.[1]

Japanese media and political discussions now resonate with animated debate about low fertility rates, their implications, and whether any governmental actions should or could be undertaken to affect them. Some alarmist predictions see "the last Japanese switching off the lights sometime in the next century."[2] There have been calls for increases in childbearing by Japanese couples and for increased immigration to Japan. In early 2007, the Japanese minister of health, Hakuo Yanagisawa, provoked a national political firestorm by speaking of Japanese women as "birth-giving machines and devices." Something may have been lost in translation, but the English-speaking press quoted Minister Yanagisawa as stating, "Because the number of birth-giving machines and devices is fixed, all we can ask for is for them to do their best per head."[3]

Our discussion of Japanese fertility trends rests on the English-language material on the subject. This is a drawback in all comparative

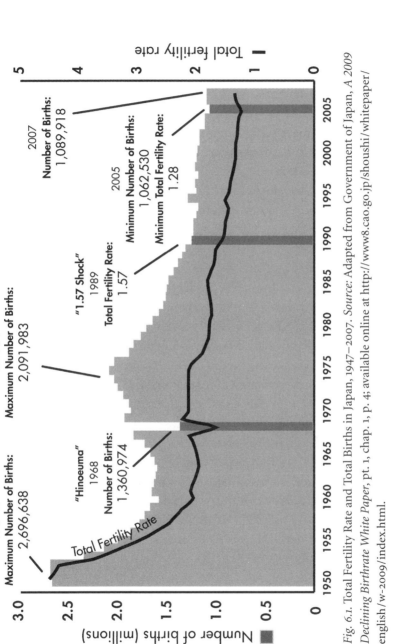

Fig. 6.1. Total Fertility Rate and Total Births in Japan, 1947–2007. *Source:* Adapted from Government of Japan, *A 2009 Declining Birthrate White Paper,* pt. 1, chap. 1, p. 4; available online at http://www8.cao.go.jp/shoushi/whitepaper/english/w-2009/index.html.

work covering a broad range of countries, cultures, and language groups. But with the advice of Japan specialists, we have presented the best available data and interpretation of an important and distinctive case of global fertility decline.[4]

Before discussing the postwar fertility decline in Japan, however, it should be emphasized that Japanese fertility rates had been on a declining trajectory for at least two decades before World War II. Writing from the perspective of 1947 and with the benefit of ready access to Japanese census and birth registration data from 1920 to the end of World War II, two prominent American demographers, Irene B. Taeuber and Frank W. Notestein, estimated that the gross reproduction rate for Japan had declined by about 17 percent from 1920 to 1937, a slower decline than that in Europe, but still nontrivial.[5]

The history of the Japanese fertility decline is similar to that in other countries, in that it is exceptionally difficult to disentangle the forces that affect human reproduction in general and fertility rates in particular. All agree that we need to pay particular attention to what are termed "proximate determinants of fertility."[6] Specifically, these include age of entry into sexual life and frequency of sexual activity, whether marital or nonmarital; contraception; induced abortion; and infertility (what English-speaking demographers call "infecundability") related, for example, to breastfeeding practices or the incidence of some venereal diseases.

Noriko Tsuya has provided a very useful analysis of Japanese fertility behavior within this framework. Her analyses of Japanese data on proportion married, contraceptive practice, induced abortion, and breastfeeding show that over the two decades following World War II, the proportion married was always the most important element in limiting overall fertility rates in Japan. In addition, during the period of most rapid fertility decline, from 1950 to 1960, the significance of both induced abortion and contraception rose substantially. Subsequent to 1960, the proportion married continued to be important, while the relative impact of contraception rose and that of abortion declined.[7]

The postwar history of Japanese policy toward abortion and contraception is a convoluted one, but it is here that we find one central feature of the particular character of Japanese fertility decline. Subsequent to the fertility declines of the 1920s, the increasingly militarist Japanese governments of the 1930s embraced pronatalist positions motivated by imperial aspirations, although Drixler notes that these were not very energetically pursued.[8] Moreover, the Japanese invasion of Manchuria in 1931, followed by its reconfiguration as the new Japan-dominated (though nominally independent) state of Manchukuo in 1932, was motivated in substantial part by the search for access to additional land for Japanese emigration and raw materials for the burgeoning Japanese economy. The same could be said for the later Japanese invasions of British colonies in Asia (Malaya, Singapore, Burma) and of the US-controlled Philippines.

By the end of World War II, much of the Japanese economy lay in ruins. About 25 percent of Japan's national wealth had been expended on the war, and inflation rates were high. Estimates of war-related deaths vary, but most agree that approximately two million Japanese military and up to one million civilians died as a result of the war.[9] After 1945, nearly six million Japanese soldiers and settlers were repatriated to Japan from China and other Asian countries by the victorious Allied Powers. Meanwhile, some 20 percent of the national housing stock had been destroyed, and closer to 60 percent in Tokyo and Osaka. In 1946 the minister of finance warned that ten million Japanese were in danger of starvation.[10] According to one academic analysis undertaken at the International Christian University in Tokyo,

> Extensive areas of the large cities were in ruins, many people still lived in air raid shelters, railway stations, and makeshift houses lacking even the elementary facilities for family life. Humiliated by their defeat and discouraged by the scarcity of food and the widespread lack of employment, the municipal authorities were inclined to adopt a fatalistic attitude that prevented normal efforts to improve living conditions. . . . Before the war Japan and its colonial possessions were self-sufficient in food production. Now 20 percent of the food supply of the nation must be imported from abroad. . . .

Students of Japan's industrial problems generally agree that there will be great difficulty in increasing industrial production sufficiently to maintain even the present standard of living for an expanding population.[11]

Such concerns about a looming demographic catastrophe facing Japan were shared by postwar Japanese political elites, many of whom "feared that the population growth, seemingly out of control, would render Japan incapable of economic recovery. . . ."[12]

Warren S. Thompson, a prominent American demographer and longtime researcher on East Asia, voiced deeply pessimistic views at that time. In what must surely represent one of the clearest examples of the inability of even distinguished social scientists to forecast the future, Thompson wrote in 1949 that it was

> . . . extremely questionable whether the increase in productivity to be expected in Japan during the next decade and the expansion of foreign trade which should accompany it will be large enough to provide any substantial improvement in the level of living once the subsidy furnished by the United States is withdrawn.[13]
>
> . . . Hence I find myself highly skeptical regarding the outlook for the future of Japan. As a man of humane sentiments, I hope that the conclusions expressed above are wrong in two respects: (1) that I have magnified the difficulties Japan will encounter in increasing production and foreign trade and emigration, and (2) that I have underestimated the speed with which the Japanese will reduce their birth rate. However when I try to weigh objectively the probabilities I do not believe I have made these errors. Hence I find myself very apprehensive regarding Japan's future. A real catastrophe involving millions of persons may be in the making and it may very well be precipitated by the rather sudden withdrawal of American support from the economy of Japan before the Japanese have been able to make any workable adjustment of population to resources.[14]

Luckily for Japan, developments subsequently proved Thompson's gloomy prognosis wrong. As in Europe, domestic human capital and capital investment, both Japanese and international, created one of the most robust moments of growth in the history of capitalism in Japan as well as in postwar Europe.

Whatever the successes of the 1950s and 1960s, Japan in the late 1940s did face very real economic crises, and there were credible concerns that major epidemics would devastate the dense and undernourished Japanese population. This possibility led the Supreme Command Allied Powers (SCAP) led by General Douglas MacArthur to undertake large-scale preventive actions. Of the population of about 72 million at the end of the war, all were vaccinated against smallpox, most against cholera and typhoid, and a third against tuberculosis.[15] In anticipation of serious food shortages, SCAP arranged for large quantities of grains and other foodstuffs to be imported from the United States.

The occupation authorities energetically expanded the collection of demographic data to inform planning, programming, and rationing for the occupation. SCAP undertook a remarkable series of no fewer than six censuses within the five-year period 1945–1950—almost immediately after the September 1945 surrender, followed in short order by repeated censuses in November 1945, April 1946, October 1947, August 1948, and October 1950. It also began to use the existing Japanese vital registration system for monthly monitoring of demographic events, especially trends in mortality and morbidity but also fertility.[16] In the end, there were none of the epidemics that had been feared, and indeed mortality rates declined rapidly. The crude death rate declined from 17.6 per thousand in 1946 to 12.0 in 1948; the latter rate was well below those that preceded the war.

Meanwhile, the return of large numbers of Japanese soldiers led to a sharp increase in fertility rates by the late 1940s, which, combined with the rapid mortality declines, led to accelerating population growth. Together the combination of large repatriations, declining mortality, and rising fertility produced an increase of almost eight million in the population of Japan between 1945 and 1948.[17]

By 1947, three members of the postwar National Diet of Japan— still operating under the control of the Allied Powers—introduced legislation to amend the 1940 Eugenics Protection Law, in which the previous militarist government had legalized abortion for eugenic purposes. This initiative was primarily Japanese in character. It was introduced jointly by three members of the Socialist Party, Dr. Tenrei Ōta, Shidzue Katō (who also was married to a minister in the Socialist Party cabinet of 1947), and Dr. Masako Fukuda. Ōta and Fukuda both were obstetrician-gynecologists who supported access to contraception and abortion. Indeed, in 1934 Ōta had developed an intrauterine contraceptive device (IUD) still known as the Ōta Ring, an improvement on an earlier German IUD known as the Gräfenberg Ring. Use of the Ōta Ring, along with most other contraceptive devices, had been banned by the prewar Japanese government (similar bans on contraception were imposed by its Axis ally Germany). Ōta himself had been jailed for promoting family planning,[18] and later changed his name and went into hiding.[19]

The proposed 1947 bill continued many of the eugenic provisions of the 1940 law and strengthened provisions for eugenic sterilization,[20] but it also authorized government support for a network of clinics offering to Japanese citizens an array of modern means of voluntary birth control. The bill did not pass the Diet in 1947, due in part to delayed agreement by SCAP for its introduction.[21] After the Socialist Party government lost power to a more conservative government in 1947, the bill's three Socialist cosponsors agreed to have it introduced into the upper house of the Diet in 1948 by another obstetrician-gynecologist, a conservative named Yasaburō Taniguchi.[22] By the time Taniguchi's amended version of the Eugenic Protection Law was passed in 1948, the clause authorizing birth control clinics had disappeared. Connelly suggests that this omission "bore the fingerprints of bureaucrats in the Health and Welfare Ministry."[23] The bill as amended did continue legal access to voluntary abortion in Japan, but only on grounds of rape, hereditary defects, or to protect the health of the mother.

The role played by SCAP authorities in the evolution and ultimate passage of Japanese law in this domain has been differently interpreted. One American expert argued that SCAP had strongly stimulated the birth control movement. Ōta stated, "But for their [SCAP's] support, no such law would have been enacted," although other Japanese birth control proponents believed that the occupation had suppressed the birth control movement. Irene B. Taeuber, an American expert on Japanese demography, described the SCAP posture as active avoidance of any involvement in population policies, which she described as "militant neutralism."[24]

The most authoritative treatment of this debate in the English-language literature, by Deborah Oakley, concludes that the movement leading to adoption and later amendment of the 1948 law was led by Japanese activists and interest groups, was opposed by conservative Japanese religious groups, and was allowed to proceed by a SCAP posture that she describes as "protective neutralism." By this she meant that "Instead of actively *avoiding* action, as alleged by the term militant neutralism, the Americans were actively interested, facilitative, and sometimes openly directive, using a strategy that protected Japanese population policy from interest group pressures outside the Japanese political system."[25] These pressures from outside included political groups in the United States, the hierarchy of the Catholic Church, and the Soviet Union. MacArthur himself may have wanted to avoid involvement in the issue as a threat to his plans to run for the Republican presidential nomination in alliance with Catholic conservative politicians. The pope had admonished a meeting of Allied Forces doctors to "never countenance the deliberate frustration of nature's priceless power to generate life."[26] Moreover SCAP was formally responsible to a Far Eastern Commission in which the Union of Soviet Socialist Republics (USSR) had veto power (as did the United States, United Kingdom, and China). Oakley and others suggest that SCAP's refusal to become involved in the Japanese political debate about a new Eugenics Protection Law limited the ability of the USSR to claim that the American-dominated occupation was violating international legal principles established by the Nuremburg Trials.[27]

According to Connelly, however, General Crawford F. Sams, the US general directing the Allied Powers' Public Health and Welfare Section, took the lead on issues related to fertility and mortality. He ensured that the amended bill was not vetoed by the occupation. Sams had his own reservations about its provisions but believed that any legislation on this topic "had to be seen as a purely Japanese initiative."[28]

In a later interview, Sams noted that the neutral position was entirely intentional: Any "attempt to force limitation of families [on the

Japanese] . . . would place the U.S. and other occupying powers in the position of justifiably being charged with genocide."[29] In another interview, Sams noted that introduction of the 1948 Eugenics Protection Law by private members of the Diet rather than by the normal process of submission by the Welfare Ministry ensured that it would not be seen as coming from the occupation, which controlled the ministry. "This was to avoid what would have been a worldwide furor, because the Catholics would have been in on it for sure, and so would the Communists, in charging genocide."[30]

However, cosponsor Shidzue Katō was greatly embarrassed by the modifications made to the original draft bill she had cosponsored, especially the elimination of the birth control clinics that had been part of her original bill. Her embarrassment did not render her silent; to the contrary, according to the account by Hopper, Katō vented her frustration at a 1948 meeting with a Rockefeller Foundation mission to the region: "'We have to face this problem, but unfortunately most people from the Prime Minister to the masses of people do not think seriously about this matter; they do not think about it at all.' She [Katō] had warned the last two prime ministers, but they had no plans and no ideas, apparently waiting in vain for U.S. guidance. How could occupation officials pretend to be neutral about birth control, she asked, when they pushed public health campaigns and thus population growth disproportionate to Japan's natural resources? 'How,' she asked, 'can you be thinking of human welfare?'"[31] In early 1949, at the invitation of occupation officials, the American demographer Warren Thompson traveled to Japan as an advisor to SCAP on demographic questions and charged as well with drawing attention to population issues among both Japanese elites and the public.[32] Thompson, one of the originators of demographic transition theory, had earlier written specifically about the demographic challenges facing the Pacific region.[33]

Thompson's efforts may have had some effects in focusing attention on the subject among Japanese leaders, especially with respect to contraception. At the time of his arrival, the Health and Welfare Ministry still had not approved any contraceptives under the 1947 law.[34] Thompson's consultations were followed shortly by an announcement by Prime Minister Shigeru Yoshida in April 1949 that birth control was "a fundamental solution to Japan's population problem."[35] Within a few months the Yoshida cabinet had created a new Council on Population Problems, which in November 1949 recommended continued attention to moderating the birthrate but also that contraception should be emphasized over abortion.[36] In that same year the Health and Welfare Ministry modified its limitations on contraception and approved twenty-seven different contraceptives, and the Japanese parliament began to revise the 1947 law to include contraceptive provision at government clinics.

However, the 1949 actions with the most demographic significance were Japanese in origin, embodied within the Japanese Diet's decision to broaden the grounds for legal voluntary abortion to include economic hardship.[37] This legislative amendment had little to do with the occupation, having been led instead by a group of Japanese obstetrician-gynecologists known as Nichibo (formally, the Japan Association for Maternal Welfare). Nichibo was organized in 1949 by the same Diet member, Yasaburō Taniguchi, who had succeeded in having the 1948 Eugenic Protection Law passed. In 1949 he succeeded in obtaining Diet passage of an additional clause to Article 14 of the 1948 law that allowed abortions "if the continuation of pregnancy or childbirth is likely to seriously harm the mother's health for physical or economic reasons."[38] At the time Taniguchi stated that the "economic reasons" criterion applied only to women who would qualify for public assistance, a position later incorporated in the Ministry of Health and Welfare's regulations. But in practice these limitations were not enforced either by doctors or by the ministry, and nearly all abortions in Japan since 1949 have cited this economic criterion.[39]

In 1952 Taniguchi and Nichibo sponsored another amendment. This further expanded access to abortion by transferring the right to approve a woman's request for an abortion from a "Eugenic Protection Committee" to independent medical specialists approved for this purpose.[40]

In the years immediately following the 1949 amendment, there was a dramatic surge in the official number of abortion procedures. The published data, generally seen as an underestimate, show the numbers increasing from about three hundred thousand in 1949 to more than one million in 1955. Independent researchers' estimates range from two to four times higher than these official numbers.[41] In the medium term the 1949 amendment had a far greater effect on birthrates than any modifications of policies relating to contraception.

Supreme Commander MacArthur did not embrace the new measures announced by the Japanese government in 1949, even though Thompson reported that MacArthur had agreed with his view that "the home islands could not support even their present population, emigration was no solution, and . . . powerful incentives for smaller families would make it impossible to stop the nascent birth control movement. But he was skeptical that it could be accelerated, and therefore concluded that there was 'no need to take active measures.'"[42] Connelly's interpretation is that MacArthur's skepticism was motivated by his presidential ambitions, evident after the Allied Catholic Women's Club of Tokyo (whose members were mostly wives of US personnel) protested public statements by Thompson. Some action was taken in response to such protests. The occupation officials who had engaged Thompson as an advisor were reprimanded and ordered to sign a reassuring letter to the Allied Catholic Women's Club of Tokyo.[43]

However, in 1949 MacArthur could have exercised his right as supreme commander to veto the extension of access to abortion for "economic reasons." He did not do so, and this inaction may have been the key role played by SCAP in this policy domain. This may have reflected continued commitment by MacArthur and his staff to ensure that policy making in this area was genuinely Japanese. Another possible explanation is the American authorities did not anticipate the ensuing surge of abortion procedures in Japan. Finally, by 1949 the general known as the "Emperor's Emperor" and the "American Shogun" already had relinquished some of his previously unilateral control over Japan to the Department of State and then to Japanese political leaders, as his attention shifted to the threatening developments in Korea. The formal cession of occupation control of Japan occurred in 1952.

This brief survey of post-1945 Japanese population history is derived solely from English-language sources. A fuller account using Japanese materials would be necessary before reaching any authoritative conclusions. And yet it seems clear that while the American presence and some facets of Americanization had a bearing on Japanese marriage patterns, the initiative for the relevant changes, especially with respect to the legalization of abortion for economic reasons, were Japanese in origin. [44]

From 1949 onward, as noted earlier, there was a dramatic decline in Japanese fertility rates. By 1957 the total fertility rate of Japan had declined to slightly below 2.1, a reduction of more than 50 percent from the level of 4.3 in 1949. Japanese fertility then stabilized at around the 2.1 level for more than a decade before declining further in the 1970s.

There was one notable and interesting exception to the relative stability of Japanese fertility rates during the 1960s, a kind of "natural experiment" that demonstrated the strong ability of Japanese couples to control their fertility. Japanese fertility experienced a sharp downward spike to 1.58 for the single year of 1966, an episode driven by the Japanese zodiac calendar. Each year in this calendar is symbolized by one of twelve animals and one of five elements. The year 1966 was the Year of the Fire Horse (Hinoeuma), an astrological event that occurs once every sixty years, that is, in 1846, 1906, and 1966. It had been widely believed in Japan since the eighteenth century that Hinoeuma was a most inauspicious year for a child to be born, and especially so for a girl child. Rohlfs, Reed, and Yamada report a 22 percent decline in the size of the birth cohort for that single year, 1966, effected primarily via contraception and abortion. They noted that the birth registration data are clouded to an unknown extent by likely but hard-to-measure misrepresentation of birth year, especially for births occurring toward the end of 1966. The decline of female births in 1846 was greater than the decline of male births in that year; such differences were reduced in 1906 and essentially vanished in 1966.[45] This experience subsequently became more significant, with the so-called "1.57 Shock," discussed later.

The years 1973–1974 were those of the first oil crisis, which had particularly threatening implications for Japan, given its nearly complete dependence upon imported oil. In these years, Japanese fertility rates again turned sharply downward, declining to about 1.7–1.8, a level that was sustained for most of the period 1976–1988. A further decline then ensued, with fertility rates reaching 1.4–1.5 by the mid-1990s. Since the mid-1990s, a decade of unusual economic stagnation in Japan, there has been a further small decline, to a stable level of about 1.3–1.4 over the decade to the present.[46]

The graphic for Japan (A.10) in appendix A summarizes reported Japanese total fertility rates from 1950 to 2010, followed by the array of the UN Population Divisions probabilistic projections of plausible future fertility rates to 2100. This figure highlights the initial stage of fertility decline in the 1950s, the later fertility declines in the 1970s, 1980s, and 1990s, and the relatively stable but very low fertility rates from 2000 to 2010.

The graphic also shows alternative projection scenarios going forward from 2010, serving as illustrations of the range of plausible pathways for future Japanese fertility. (As noted earlier, we believe it wise to focus on these forward projections up to 2050 rather than 2100, given the large uncertainties involved especially in the later decades.) As may be seen, the median fertility projection (the heavy line) suggests a gradual increase in the currently very low total fertility rate in Japan, rising from about 1.3 to about 1.8 by 2050. The range of uncertainty is indicated by the 95 percent projection intervals (the dotted lines above and below the median projection line), which show an upper bound as high as 2.5 and a lower bound as low as 1.3 in 2050.

Some Demographic Particularities of Japan

It is important to understand that the period total fertility rates calculated for all Japanese women followed a markedly different pattern from the actual number of children born to Japanese married women. Between 1975 and 2005, the total fertility rate for all women (TFR) declined by more than one-third, from 1.91 to 1.28, followed by a small increase.[47] Meanwhile, the actual number of *children ever born to married women aged forty-five to forty-nine* (that is, the completed family size of this cohort of women at the end of their childbearing years) was nearly constant over this same rough period; it was 2.2 in 1982, 2.1 in 1997, and 2.2 again in 2005.[48] Moreover, repeated surveys of first-married Japanese women undertaken over two decades, between 1977 and 2005, showed little sign of declines in the number of children they intended or expected to bear. In 1977 that number was 2.17, rising to 2.23 in 1992, and declining to 2.11 in the most recent survey in 2002—certainly consistent with the view that the expected family size of married Japanese women had not changed very much.[49]

Hence, both the expected and actual completed family size of married women were stable over the same period in which substantial declines in total fertility rates took place. The declines occurred primarily because the age at marriage and proportions never married among Japanese women of prime reproductive age changed substantially over this period, in some ways dramatically so. As may be seen in table 6.1, the mean age of brides at first marriage increased from 25.0 years in 1977 to 28.2 years in 2006—a very substantial increase given that the mid-20s are usually the peak years of childbearing.[50] The age at first marriage for Japanese men also increased, but to a lesser extent, so the average difference in age at marriage for men and women declined.

Evidently marriage has been increasingly deferred, to a substantial degree, by young Japanese women over the past quarter century. Yet this measure of the average age at marriage is but one crude indicator of a dramatic sea change under way in Japanese marital behavior. Even more striking, perhaps, are data on the trends in the proportion of Japanese women of reproductive age who have never been married (see fig. 6.2).

Table 6.1. Age at First Marriage, Japan

	Male	Female
2006	30.0	28.2
2001	29.0	27.2
1997	28.5	26.6
1987	28.4	25.7
1977	27.4	25.0

Source: From National Institute of Population and Social Security Research, *Population Statistics of Japan 2008*, Tokyo, 2008, table 6-12.

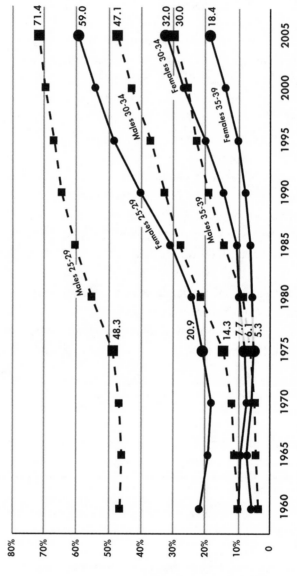

Fig. 6.2. Percentage Never Married, by Sex and Age Group, Japan, 1960–2005. *Source:* From Government of Japan, *A 2009 Declining Birthrate White Paper (Summary),* p. 5.

Consider the following remarkable numbers: Among Japanese women aged 30–34 in 2005, nearly one-third (32.0 percent) had never been married. For those aged 25–29, nearly three in five (59.0 percent) had never been married.[51] As may be seen in fig. 6.2, the percentage of never-married females in both of these prime ages of childbearing have shown distinctly rising trajectories over the past three to four decades.

These very high percentages of never-married Japanese women in the prime years of reproduction may be usefully compared to data from other industrialized, urbanized, and prosperous countries. In some, for example Canada, the Netherlands, the United Kingdom, France, and the United States, such percentages are typically much lower—roughly in the range of 30–40 percent never married among women aged 25–29, and 60–70 percent for ages 20–24.

In a few industrialized countries, and especially Nordic countries such as Iceland, Norway, and Sweden, the high percentages of women never married are similar to those in Japan. There are, however, important differences in the fertility outcomes in the two cases, since in those Nordic countries with high percentages of women never married, on the order of one-half or more of births reported occur outside of marriage.[52]

In Japan, in stark contrast, the percentage of births reported outside of marriage in 2006 was only about 2 percent.[53] It seems apparent that in the Nordic countries, nonmarriage is not a strong impediment to childbearing. Meanwhile, in Japanese society marriage is a virtual sine qua non for reproduction.[54]

Japanese demographers concur that fertility declines during the immediate postwar period were related most prominently to abortion and contraception, but that subsequent fertility declines over the past two decades are due mainly to recent declines in the percentage who are married among women in the key reproductive years of 20–29. According to a 2008 summary by Shigemi Kono, former director of Japan's National Institute for Population and Social Security Research, "Almost all of the decline in Japan's fertility rate between the mid-1970s and the early 1990s is explained by decline in the proportion of reproductive-age women who are married. Evidence of declining marital fertility has emerged only very recently."[55] MacKeller and Horlacher, citing previous research by Ogawa, Retherford, and Yashiro, conclude, "It is not declining marital fertility, but rather the growing tendency to delay or forgo marriage that has been the main source of the post-1973 fertility decline in Japan."[56]

Jones provides a valuable analysis of these marriage patterns for Pacific Asia, including Japan.[57] He points to a "striking trend toward delayed marriage and in many cases a failure to marry at all" that is common across this region, with the notable exception of China, a trend he terms "flight from marriage."[58] He notes that while this trend is also evident in much of Europe, a simple comparison of the percentage of reproductive-age women who are single in these regions would be "highly misleading" because of the high percentages of cohabiting couples in Europe versus the apparently low levels in this category in much of Pacific Asia. In order to make more credible comparisons of Pacific Asian marriage patterns with those of Europe, he develops a measure of "effective singlehood," in which the "never-married" or "single" category is adjusted to exclude nonmarried women who are currently cohabiting or have ever cohabited. In effect, he suggests that cohabitation in Europe has replaced a substantial fraction of living arrangements that would previously have been marriages, but that the same is not true for most of Pacific Asia.[59]

A comparison of Japan and Sweden illustrates the importance of these adjustments. As may be seen in table 6.2, for men and women combined aged 25–34 in 2000, the percent "single" in Japan was 49 percent, versus 72 percent in Sweden. However, taking account of high cohabitation rates in Sweden, the "effectively-single" percentage (those who are single and who have never cohabitated) is calculated at only 13 percent. Data on cohabitation in Japan are weaker, but Jones notes that the previously rare phenomenon has been becoming more common and that the proportion ever-cohabiting among Japanese women born in the 1970s appears to be on the order of 20 percent. Though this estimate is not strictly comparable to the numbers for Sweden given earlier, it does suggest that the population "effectively single" in Japan is likely lower than the 49 percent reported as single, though still far higher than Sweden's estimated 13 percent.[60]

Table 6.2. Comparison of the Percentage of Single, Never-Cohabited (Europe), and the Percentage of Single, Never-Married (Pacific Asia) Men and Women Combined, Ages 25–34, 2000

Country	% Single	% Single, Not Currently Cohabiting	% Single, Never Cohabited
Europe			
Sweden	72	33	13
Denmark	63	31	14
Finland	57	28	17
Great Britain	43	32	16
Ireland	55	39	32
France	61	30	15
Belgium	41	26	20
Luxembourg	35	20	11
Netherlands	53	31	23
East Germany	54	32	17
West Germany	50	25	19
Austria	48	26	13
Spain	56	45	41
Portugal	39	34	32
Italy	66	59	55
Greece	44	34	29
Pacific Asia			
Japan	49		
South Korea	38		
Hong Kong	52		
Taiwan	42		
Singapore	38		
Singapore Chinese	41		
Singapore Malays	28		
Singapore Indians	27		

(continued)

Table 6.2. (*Continued*)

Country	% Single	% Single, Not Currently Cohabiting	% Single, Never Cohabited
Malaysia	31		
Malaysian Chinese	42		
Malaysian Malays	25		
Malaysian Indians	32		
Thailand	28		
China	11		
Philippines	34		
Indonesia	18		
Myanmar	33		

Source: Adapted from Gavin W. Jones, "Delayed Marriage and Very Low Fertility in Pacific Asia," *Population and Development Review* 33, no. 3 (September 2007), table 3; available online at http://www.jstor.org/stable/25434630.

This "flight from marriage" in Japan is likely a major factor underlying the declines in Japanese fertility during the 1980s and 1990s. There is no definitive explanation available for these recent remarkable trends in marriage patterns among Japanese women of reproductive age. To be sure, they have occurred over the same period that has seen rising education and labor-force participation of women, but which is cause and which is effect is unclear. Other changes beyond rising education and workforce participation are evidently also underway.

One is the apparent weakening of the traditional arranged marriages and family value system. Another is the rising proportions of (unmarried) young adults residing with their parents (a pattern also visible in Italy), which may be related in part to the combined effects of the high cost of housing, the scarcity of mortgage credit, and the low wages of younger Japanese generations compared with older generations.

Many Japanese researchers point to a tightening "marriage squeeze" for younger Japanese women. By this they mean that young

Japanese women, whose education levels have risen more rapidly than those of males, have experienced increasing difficulty in finding marriageable males with culturally suitable levels of education or occupational status. Marriage norms in Japan are such that men tend to marry women who are younger and less educated than they are, whereas women tend to marry older, more educated men with better economic prospects. In addition, there may also be a "values gap," in which educated Japanese men of marriageable age have been slower than educated young Japanese women to embrace gender equality related to careers, housework, and childrearing.[61] This gap naturally raises questions about the compatibility of careers, marriage, and motherhood for educated young Japanese women. In particular, those who wish to pursue careers may believe that marriage must be deferred until they have established themselves in careers, and that if they do marry they may wish to remain childless.[62]

Jones has usefully summarized underlying factors that have been affecting marriage patterns in Pacific Asian countries. Of those he discusses, the following seem likely to apply to the case of Japan:

- Women's reluctance to marry men whose economic prospects are uncertain. Young Japanese males in particular have experienced deterioration in their prospects of finding regular full-time employment during the extended period of economic stagnation in Japan since the collapse of Japan's "bubble economy" in the 1990s. Those young males in the so-called NEET category (Not in Education, Employment or Training) are particularly disadvantaged with respect to marriage and fatherhood in a society such as Japan with its relatively rigid gender roles.[63]
- Rising education levels among women, with more highly educated women deferring marriage in order to establish themselves in careers, and these careers raising the economic opportunity costs of marriage and childbearing.
- A "marriage squeeze" for more educated urban women, due to more rapid education gains among women coupled with social norms favoring "hypergamy," i.e., women

expected to marry up whereas men often prefer younger and less well educated wives.

- Women's concerns that if they marry they will be responsible for elder care of two sets of parents in view of Japan's small family average family size.
- A "values gap," in which more educated Japanese women have adopted feminist values that are not as commonly held by Japanese men of marriageable age.[64]

Finally, with respect to childbearing within marriage, it seems plausible that the massive urbanization of Japan has had the indirect effect of weakening support from multigenerational stem families, while alternative sources such as publicly provided day care have not yet become common.

As we have seen in chapter 2, on European fertility decline, one possible framework within which to place Japanese experience is that of the "risk society." It may be that young professional women see childbearing as a risk, endangering their prospective careers and financial security. Given that a period of rising real incomes has been followed by a period of greater economic uncertainty, recent cohorts of Japanese women may stay out of marriage, and thereby of childbearing, as a form of risk control. This is simply a conjecture consistent with Beck's theory of risk aversion, but one that is well established in popular discourse in Japan. If this is so, it is one more indication that there is room for greater attention to the examination of policy changes in the overall story of fertility decline.

Implications of Japanese Fertility Trends

As a result of the fertility trends and levels described earlier, the age structure of Japan currently is undergoing a shift toward the older ages, the process often called "demographic aging." Due to the rapid decline of fertility after the war combined with very long life expectancy, this trend is more pronounced than that of any other country—indeed perhaps more rapid than that of any large population in human history, although projected aging patterns for China suggest that Japan may be eclipsed in this regard during the current century. As recently as 1990, Japan was the member country of the Organisation for Economic Co-operation and Development (OECD) with the lowest percentage of its population aged sixty-five years and over, at about 12 percent.[65] By 2009 this had increased to nearly 23 percent, and if key assumptions underlying official government demographic projections for 2050 were to be realized, it would rise to nearly 40 percent by 2050.[66]

The underlying demographic forces in Japan are different from those of the United States and some other industrialized countries, such as Australia and Canada. Unlike these, Japan did not experience a sustained postwar baby boom that produced a large generation that is now "aging." Put another way, Japan's present age composition does not contain exceptionally large baby-boom cohorts that are now approaching their mid-sixties. Instead, it is the remarkably steep fertility decline experienced since around 1950 that is by far the most important cause of demographic aging in Japan. To this must be added the exceptional increases in elderly life expectancy. Remaining life expectancy at age sixty-five is nearly twenty-four years for Japanese women and nineteen years for Japanese men.[67]

There is much concern in Japanese policy circles about the economic implications of further demographic aging. The concerns generally fall within the following five categories of impacts:

1. Declines in the (very high) Japanese savings rate;
2. Slowing of labor-force growth;
3. Possible impacts upon productivity;
4. Fiscal stresses on Japan's pension systems; and,
5. Rising health-care expenditures.

With respect to *declines in Japanese saving rates*, Japan has for decades been notable for its exceptionally high rates of national savings, at least until the latter part of the 1990s. Fig. 6.3 shows the national savings rate for Japan compared with that of the United States from 1956 to 2000. Japanese national savings peaked at about 25 percent of Net National Product around 1970, well over twice that of the United States in the same period. During the late 1980s and early 1990s, the rate in Japan

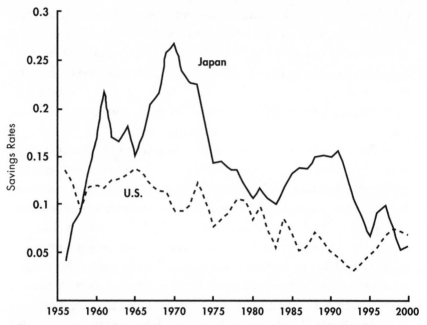

Fig. 6.3. Net National Savings Rates as a Percentage of Net National Product, Japan, 1956–2000. *Source:* From Kaiji Chen, Ayşe İmrohoroğlu and Selahattin İmrohoroğlu, "The Japanese Saving Rate," *American Economic Review* 96, no. 5 (2006), p. 1851; available online at http://pubs.aeaweb.org/doi/pdfplus/10.1257/ aer.96.5.1850.

exceeded 10 percent (again twice that of the United States for the same period), before declining to about 5 percent in the late 1990s.[68]

What is called "national savings" may be divided into public and private savings. *Public* savings consists essentially of savings and investment by governments. The obverse would be "dis-savings" and "disinvestment," that is, when governments run operating deficits and/or privatize government-owned capital assets. During the periods of very high national savings in Japan, public savings were strongly positive. These rates of public savings have been declining in recent years, and there is general agreement that the trend is toward deficit as demands grow upon the large public pension and health systems, even if there are substantial reforms in the public pension system.[69]

Meanwhile gross *private* savings rates in Japan were high during the 1970s, 1980s, and 1990s, generally in the range of 25–30 percent of

GDP, before turning downward in the first decade of the twenty-first century. In contrast, comparable rates for the United States rarely exceeded 20 percent over the same period, and were declining sharply toward the end of the 1990s.[70]

Private savings incorporate those by households and those in the business sector. Both have been high in Japan, but with different trend lines. Household savings rose sharply in the early 1970s and then began a steady decline for the ensuing twenty-five years, while business-sector savings in Japan showed almost exactly the opposite trend.[71]

As may be seen in table 6.3, notwithstanding the long decline in the household savings rate in Japan, it remained among the highest of those in industrialized countries until 2000, although by 2003 it had declined well below the rates for France, Germany, and Italy.

Many economists believe that Japan's rapid postwar fertility declines produced a decades-long "demographic dividend" that was an important factor in Japan's "economic miracle" of rapid economic growth, enabling it to become what was at the time the world's second largest economy. Specifically, during the Japanese economic boom of the 1970s and 1980s, the population age structure included large cohorts

Table 6.3. Net Household Savings Rate in Percentages, 1985 – 2003, for Selected Industrialized Countries

	Japan	USA	UK	France	Germany	Italy
1985	16.5	9.2	6.9	8.9	12.5	21.5
1990	13.9	7.0	5.6	7.8	13.9	24.0
1995	11.9	4.6	7.0	11.2	11.2	17.9
2000	9.5	2.3	3.5	10.9	9.7	9.2
2003	6.3	1.4	3.9	11.1	10.7	10.5

Source: From Charles Yuji Horioka, "Are the Japanese Unique? An Analysis of Consumption and Saving Behavior in Japan," in Sheldon Garon and Patricia L. Maclachlan, *The Ambivalent Consumer: Questioning Consumption in East Asia and the West* (Ithaca, NY: Cornell University Press, 2006), p. 117. Reproduced in Sheldon Garon, *Beyond Our Means: Why America Spends while the World Saves* (Princeton, NJ: Princeton University Press, 2012), chap. 9, ms. p. 19.

of young adults born before the fertility decline, who, because their own fertility rates were declining so rapidly, had relatively small numbers of dependent children requiring financial support. Hence they were able to save substantial fractions of their incomes in bank accounts (even though interest rates were low), funds that then became available also at low interest rates for investment in the Japanese economy and for investment overseas.[72]

While this may be true, factors other than demography likely accounted for much of the high household savings rate in postwar Japan. In particular, Garon describes a striking array of explicit government policies designed to encourage budgetary caution and savings among Japanese households. The postwar Japanese government transformed wartime savings campaigns, described as "virtually compulsory" by the occupation leadership, into voluntary but forceful campaigns to promote household savings, which the government described as essential to the very survival of Japan as an independent nation.

Accompanied by "strident appeals to economic nationalism," successive postwar Japanese governments promoted no fewer than nine official "National Salvation Savings Campaigns" as key elements of "a do-or-die struggle to finance export industries and restrain consumption of imports."[73] Japanese government officials carefully studied the savings promotion policies of postwar European governments and adapted many of these approaches to the circumstances in Japan. These included a vast array of policies, institutions, and associations designed to promote and incentivize household savings, including: "model savings districts," "national savings associations," "Children's Banks," and a "Central Council for Savings Promotion."

The most prominent official promotion of household savings was led by the Japanese post office. It provided easy access to household savings accounts at its more than fifteen thousand branches (later expanded to some twenty-four thousand). It also developed a system in which its mail deliverers collected small amounts of savings for deposit in post office accounts. Unlike most savings programs operated by Japanese commercial banks, these post office savings accounts were guaranteed by the Japanese government, and often paid higher-than-market interest rates. Moreover, postal savings accounts that were below specified sizes were exempted from taxes, and post office employees actively assisted depositors in establishing multiple savings accounts below these limits to avoid triggering taxation on the earnings of their savings. The Japanese post office became, and remains today, one of the largest financial institutions in the world.[74]

Meanwhile, government agencies, women's associations, and magazines and other media encouraged and assisted Japanese housewives to maintain household account books. Garon describes what was involved as follows:

> The methodical housewife-saver became a cultural icon in postwar Japan as perhaps nowhere in the West. . . . During the 1950s more and more wives recorded the details of family finances in standardized account books issued by housewives' magazines and government agencies. By 1965 half of all surveyed households reported they kept account books (41 percent of them regularly). They would continue to do so at those levels for the next twenty-five years. Keeping a typical Japanese account book was not for the languid. Each day, one recorded income and then itemized expenditures into ten or more categories including taxes, food, housing, utilities, clothing, health, education, self-cultivation and entertainment, transportation and telephone, socially obligatory expenses, and one-time special costs. Food expenditures were further divided into the subcategories of rice, side dishes, eating out, and "treats." At the end of the day, literally, the diligent housewife calculated the cash balance as well as outstanding debts and amounts deposited in savings. Account books from the 1990s further instructed users to record all credit card purchases.
>
> The excruciating demands of the account books prompted some women to refuse to keep them. Yet the bigger surprise is how many Japanese women utilized the ledgers more or less as designed. According to official surveys from 1973 to 1984, roughly half of those surveyed who kept accounts replied that they recorded income and expenditures

every day. Another one-fifth claimed they itemized expenses daily but calculated balances monthly. The remaining one-quarter budgeted on a monthly basis."[75]

Hence while the rapid postwar declines in Japanese family size likely did produce a "demographic dividend" that contributed to high household saving rates in Japan, it is apparent that there were many other powerful forces underlying this savings phenomenon.

In recent years, concerns have been expressed that over the near-to-medium-term future, the low fertility rates of the past decades will lead to far smaller rates of household savings, as the size of the working-age population grows very slowly or declines, and the numbers of dependent elderly increase as the large young-adult cohorts of the economic boom period age into retirement. The general theoretical perspective underlying such an expectation is the "life cycle model of consumption," in which households acquire savings and other assets during their working years and then "dis-save" during their retirement years.

The evidence in support of such forecasts is quite mixed, however. The OECD's *Economic Outlook* reports, "there is an absence of convincing evidence, particularly in Japan, that savings rates of older people are substantially lower than those observed for the working-age population."[76] There has been little evidence of declining household savings rates in similarly aging populations in Germany and other European countries. Household savings rates in Japan have indeed declined since the late 1990s, but Garon concludes that the main reason for this has been declining household incomes. In addition, campaigns by the Japanese government to promote savings have waned since 2000, with the government urging Japanese households to invest rather than save, while continuing to minimize the accretion of household debt.[77]

Slowing of Japanese Labor-Force Growth

The low fertility rates of the past decades also have led to concerns about possible declines in the size of the Japanese labor force over the next few decades. In response, Japanese government policy has encouraged the export of low-productivity employment to lower-wage Pacific Rim countries such as China and Korea. Yet at the same time, other policies have tended to support sectors of the Japanese economy, such as the wholesale and retail trades, which are relatively inefficient, while at the same time creating disincentives in the tax and social insurance systems that work against labor-force participation by married women with children. Moreover, labor-market discrimination against women tends to concentrate those who do work in relatively low-productivity employment.[78]

There are, of course, ample pools of ready workers in low-wage countries of Asia that could be imported easily to work in high-wage Japan, should that be desired by the Japanese electorate and government. Indeed, as Japanese fertility has continued at very low levels, some—especially business leaders—have begun to call for such measures.[79] This has been a subject of active, sometimes passionate, debate in Japan, a debate that we will address later.

Finding Appropriate Responses to Low Fertility

Public opinion polls undertaken by the Japanese government in 2004 and 2009 (see fig. 6.4) suggest that a substantial majority of Japanese believe that recent very low fertility rates and resulting trends toward demographic aging are highly undesirable.[80] Official concern appears to have been raised dramatically by what is widely known in Japan as the "1.57 Shock." This refers to the total fertility rate of 1.57 that was recorded in 1989. This produced a "shock," or what Shirahase refers to as "a wave of panic," because it breached the previous low in the total fertility rate that had been registered in 1966, which had generally been understood to be an aberrational and hence temporary one-year downward spike due to the zodiac Year of the Fire Horse.

In response, the Japanese government in the 1990s began to adopt what has become an impressively ambitious range of policy "countermeasures against declining birthrate," to be discussed in the following section.[81] As may be seen in fig. 6.1, since then the total fertility rate continued to decline slowly, reaching levels comparable to those seen in Germany and Italy.

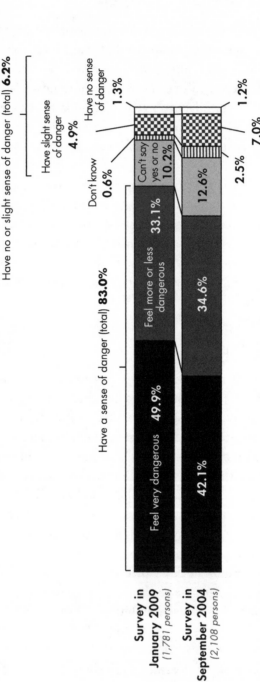

Have no or slight sense of danger (total) **6.2%**

Have slight sense of danger **4.9%**

Have no sense of danger **1.3%**

1.2%

Have a sense of danger (total) **83.0%**

Don't know **0.6%**

Can't say yes or no **10.2%**

Feel more or less dangerous **33.1%**

12.6%

Feel very dangerous **49.9%**

2.5%

7.0%

34.6%

42.1%

Survey in January 2009 *(1,781 persons)*

Survey in September 2004 *(2,108 persons)*

Fig. 6.4. Public Opinion in Japan as to whether Respondents Feel a Sense of Danger about Low Fertility, 2004 and 2009.
Source: From Government of Japan, *A 2009 Declining Birthrate White Paper,* p. 19.

MEASURES INTENDED TO INCREASE MARITAL FERTILITY

Legislation known as the Declining Birthrate Society Countermeasures Basic Act was adopted in 2003. This act was implemented via an ambitious number of specific measures intended to gradually increase Japanese fertility rates. The primary thrust of these measures, and the bulk of the governmental budgets allocated to them, has been to rebalance work and family life in Japan and to subsidize child care and other services for families with young children.

They include the following:

1. "To Raise Self-independent and Strong Children" (including enhancing education and skills and dealing with youth unemployment);
2. "Reviewing Working Styles to Support Balance between Work and Family" (including child-care leave, reemployment for women after childrearing, and balancing working hours to achieve work-life balance);
3. "Understanding the Importance of Life and Family" (including deepening understanding of societal structures that support worry-free childbirth and childrearing);
4. "New Support and Unity for Raising Children" (including provisions for child care, preschool, and after-school education; children's health; support system for pregnancy, maternity, and perinatal health; enhanced child allowances; changes in tax system to support families with children).[82]

The Japanese government's 2009 White Paper emphasizes that an important goal of these measures is to eliminate the gaps between the hopes expressed by young Japanese adults regarding marriage and childbearing as compared to their actual marital and fertility behavior given the material conditions they face. It notes that recent national fertility surveys show that about 90 percent of unmarried Japanese express "a wish to be married in due course," and that both male and female persons who are already married or hope to become married consider a family of two children to be desirable. The government estimates that if these hopes were to be fulfilled, the Japanese total fertility rate would increase to 1.75 by 2040.[83]

The effectiveness of these measures remains to be seen. Their emphasis upon modifying work-life imbalances and child-care limitations in the lives of married Japanese couples of reproductive age is both understandable and ambitious.

As described, the government's measures so far have apparently paid much less attention to some of the key factors that may explain the unusually low rates of marriage of Japanese women in their peak child-bearing years of twenty to twenty-nine. There are indications that these marriage patterns are related in part to the irregular employment opportunities that have been available to young adult males,[84] an issue that bedevils not only Japan but also a number of European countries with very low fertility rates. A related issue that also has differential negative impacts is the high cost of housing suitable for young families with children; several measures to address this are mentioned in the White Paper, but their effectiveness is unclear.

IMMIGRATION

An alternative to raising fertility rates in Japan would be to increase international migration. It would be very easy for the Japanese government to attract large numbers of additional immigrants, in view of the large economic differentials among Asian countries. However, the mixed history of Japanese society with foreign migrants, coupled with the compositional effects of large-scale immigration in a society with very low fertility rates, means that this approach is problematic in terms of how it would be received by the Japanese public.

In fact, the number of "foreigners" residing in Japan has been growing at about 4 percent per year for the past two decades, though this growth rate relates to a very small base. As of 2006 the total "stock" of the registered foreign-born in Japan was just over 2 million. While this corresponds to an increase of about 50 percent over the preceding decade, it still represents less than 2 percent of Japan's estimated population of about 128 million. About 80 percent of these 2 million were from only four countries: Korea, China, Brazil, and the Philippines.[85] In addition, there are on the order of 250,000 illegal or unauthorized foreign residents. Chinese nationals, a group that is increasing especially rapidly, are thought to constitute nearly one-third of all foreigners in Japan.[86]

Proponents of increased immigration to Japan point to its sustained low fertility rates, which have led (albeit only very recently) to a small decline in Japan's population; by one estimate, the Japanese population declined by some 183,000 between 2008 and 2009—a significant number of individuals to be sure, though also a truly tiny percentage (about one-tenth of 1 percent) of a mid-2008 Japanese population of more than 127 million.[87]

More importantly, Japanese fertility rates have been so low for so many years that essentially all demographic projections posit a decline in the size of the Japanese population. If, for example, fertility and immigration rates were to remain low for the next four decades, the population size would drop to about 100 million by 2050. Moreover the age structure of the resulting smaller population would shift toward an older median age and a higher percentage of the population over age sixty-five. Finally, according to one projection by the Health, Labor and Welfare Ministry, the Japanese labor force of 2030 will likely be about 10 million smaller than the 66 million of today.[88]

Some in Japan argue that for such reasons the admission of substantial numbers of international migrants should be embraced, as a way to moderate the projected population decline and shift toward an older population. As in many other countries, among the leaders of such advocacy for expanded international migration are Japanese corporate leaders, including the leading Japanese business federation, the Nippon Keidanren.[89] Meanwhile, there is no consensus about increasing immigration among Japanese politicians, senior civil servants, and media editors; collectively these elites remain cautious and ambivalent. Some urge increased admissions of foreigners, but only for high-skilled workers and preferably those with Japanese language skills. Others point with alarm to the problems (high unemployment in Europe, especially for youth; riots in France; radical Muslim communities) they see in European countries with large populations of foreigners, and argue that the large and sustained immigration practices allowed by countries such as the United States, Canada, and Australia are inappropriate for Japan. Still others blame foreigners in Japan for a rising wave of crime.[90]

It is only fair to note that Japan's historical experience with immigration has not been a particularly positive one, though also not terribly negative. Japanese colonial conquests of a century ago led to the importation—sometimes through force—of migrants from China and Korea. Their Japan-born descendants, known as Zainichi, now number about 465,000, are still designated as Special Permanent Residents, and often do not have Japanese citizenship.[91] Many are reasonably well integrated into Japanese society, and some have become economically successful, especially in real estate and gambling establishments. Yet there continue to be currents of hostility and discrimination against immigrants in Japan as elsewhere.

As noted earlier, the number of foreigners resident in Japan exceeds two million persons. In response to the 1980s economic boom, the then government of Japan did modify its visa laws to facilitate the temporary migration of *nisei*, that is, the sons or daughters born abroad to first-generation Japanese emigrants (*issei*) before World War II, mostly in South American countries such as Brazil.[92] As a result, there are about three hundred thousand *nisei* resident in Japan. Despite their Japanese ethnic origins, they face complaints about their inability to speak Japanese and about their distinctly non-Japanese behavior patterns such as alleged "noisiness," "laziness," "untidiness," and so on.[93] In recent years the Japanese government sharply restricted the availability of visas for "entertainers." It did so in response to international criticism that Japanese organized crime was using these visas for human trafficking for its sex trade.[94]

While there is much controversy surrounding past, current, and possible future international migration to Japan, there is general agreement that plausible levels of future migration cannot be a credible response to concerns about very low fertility rates. A much-discussed 2000 report by the United Nations Demographic Division, entitled *Replacement Migration: Is It a Solution to Declining and Ageing Populations?*[95] used a varying set of fifty-year demographic projections[96] to estimate the number of immigrants that would be required to:

1. Prevent a decline in the total population size;
2. Hold constant the size of the population between ages fifteen and sixty-five;
3. Hold constant the "old age dependency ratio" (defined as persons over sixty-five to those fifteen to sixty-four).

In the report's case study on Japan, the calculations showed that to hold constant the "old age dependency ratio" would require the admission of 553 million immigrants by 2050; this number might be compared to the 2006 population of Japan of 127 million. Under this projection, immigrants and their offspring in 2050 would account for 87 percent of the population in Japan.[97]

This UN report led to widespread confusion and misreporting among the world's press and to equally confused criticism from many politicians. Numerous articles reported that the UN had recommended that governments in low-fertility countries shift policy toward large-scale immigration.[98] To the contrary, the UN report emphasized that its projections "are not meant to be recommendations in any way, but illustrations of hypothetical scenarios."[99] Moreover, it concluded that depending upon expanded immigration to maintain the "old age dependency ratio" in countries with very low fertility rates "seems out of reach because of the extraordinarily large numbers of migrants that would be required."[100]

ADAPTATION OF JAPANESE PENSION SYSTEM

There has been substantial discussion in Japan as to how best to moderate the fiscal stresses upon Japan's public pension system resulting from (inevitable) demographic aging. In theory, the taxes that support the public pension system could be increased, the eligibility age for public pension eligibility could be raised, and future increases in pension payouts could be constrained.

Such measures are being considered by the governments of nearly all advanced countries as they address the near-certainty of shifts in their population age structures toward higher percentages over their current official retirement ages. There are, of course, real political risks involved in such measures.

The rapid aging of the Japanese population led successive governments to implement gradual reforms in the Japanese pension system beginning in the 1980s. Like most pension policies, the Japanese system is complex and cannot be fully described here; a useful and up-to-date summary is provided by the OECD.[101] In recent years the official age for the "basic" tier of public pension has been gradually increased from sixty to sixty-five. However, until the pension reforms adopted in 2000, the larger tier of income-related pensions, called "Employees' Pension," could be claimed at age sixty under a "specially provided" option, and more than 50 percent of Japanese men and 35 percent of Japanese women aged sixty to sixty-four took advantage of this provision.[102] Pension reforms adopted in 2001 will gradually increase the eligibility age of this portion of pensions to sixty-five, but not with full effect until 2025 for men and 2030 for women.[103] Japanese political leaders have called for additional reforms that would gradually increase pensionable age to seventy, but the issues involved are politically controversial and the outcome is necessarily uncertain.[104] Policy changes adopted in 2005 and 2006 reduced or eliminated some pension provisions that previously had discouraged those sixty to sixty-four from continuing to work.[105]

Despite continuing early access to pensions, it is common for Japanese to continue to work after the official retirement age, often part-time. As a result, the "effective retirement age," that is, the average age of departure from the labor force, actually is close to seventy for Japanese men, as may be seen in fig. 6.5.[106] This of course may limit the potential effect of increasing retirement age in Japan when compared to the situation in countries with lower elderly labor-force participation rates, such as Italy. On the other hand, many of these not yet "effectively retired" are nonetheless receiving pensions, which the OECD notes may serve as an implicit wage subsidy to their employers,[107] and if so, the drain on public pension funds could be reduced if the official pension age were gradually raised toward this same age.

Reaching a national consensus on such questions will be difficult and will pose challenges to Japan's perceptions of itself and of its future. What is certain is that these debates and the choices politicians make do

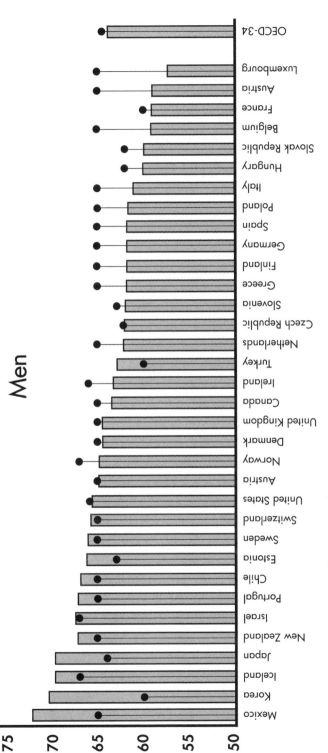

Men

Fig. 6.5. Effective and Official Ages of Retirement for Men, 2010.

Notes: The average effective age of retirement is defined as the average age of exit from the labor force during a five-year period. Labor-force (net) exits are estimated by taking the difference in the participation rate for each five-year age group (50 and over) at the beginning of the period and the rate for the corresponding age group aged five-years older at the end of the period. The official age corresponds to the age at which a pension can be received irrespective of whether a worker has a long insurance record of years of contributions. Belgium and France have different official retirement ages, but in both countries workers can retire at age 60 with forty years of contributions. In Greece, workers with thirty-five years of contributions can retire at age 58, and in Italy, at 57 (56 for manual workers). *Source:* From "Ageing and Employment Policies—Statistics on Average Effective Age of Retirement, OECD," in Directorate for Employment, Labour, and Social Affairs, *Live Longer, Work Longer: A Synthesis Report* (Paris: OECD Publishing, 23 February 2006); available online at http://www.oecd.org/document/47/0,3746,en_2649_34747_39371887_1_1_1,00.html.

matter. Population history is not simply a question of economic stimulus and demographic response. The combined political and social origins of Japan's rapid fertility declines after the Second World War must be borne in mind when projections of possible futures are discussed. Politics created the catastrophic war Japan lost; it created the new order that Japan fashioned (with American oversight) after defeat; and it will shape the future of the Japanese population, which is now, like that of many other industrialized nations, at historically unprecedented levels of low fertility.

A key argument of this book is that political change is complex and its demographic consequences frequently unpredictable. Nonetheless, the political dynamics of countries undergoing sustained low fertility are essential parts of the overall story. The demographic and political histories of post-1945 Japan are very different from those of India and China. But all three share one thing in common: Demography is shaped by politics, and not only by economic forces. Opening access to abortion on economic grounds was a Japanese political decision as well as a response to social and economic pressures. The more we keep that in mind, the better will be our understanding of today's choices bearing on Japan's futures.

North America and NAFTA

The North American Free Trade Agreement (NAFTA), which went into effect in 1994, defined "North America" as consisting of the United States, Mexico, and Canada. This is an arbitrary definition and one not followed by others, such as the United Nations,[1] but it is one with some utility in this book, which focuses on the political history of population developments in the last two decades. We do present some data on Canada, but a full discussion of the Canadian case is beyond the scope of this study.[2]

Fertility Trends

Within this NAFTA region, there have long been substantial differentials in fertility. In particular, Mexican fertility rates have been far higher than those in the United States and Canada. At the beginning of the 1950s, total fertility rates were reported in the United States at about 3.2 and in Canada at about 3.5, in both cases substantially higher than those during the 1930s. Meanwhile, in Mexico the total fertility rate was well over 6.6 children per woman—roughly double those of the United States and Canada.[3]

From these postwar rates, the three countries' fertility rates have followed notably different trajectories. Both the United States and

Canada were among the few industrialized countries that registered large and sustained baby booms, conventionally defined as beginning around 1947 and ending around 1964.[4] The peak fertility rates in both were reported in the late 1950s, at 3.72 for the United States in 1957 and at 3.92 for Canada in 1958.

Meanwhile, in Mexico fertility rates followed a very different path. Even at the peak of the postwar baby boom in the United States and Canada in the late 1950s, Mexican rates were far higher still at around 6.8. Then, as US and Canadian rates began to decline rapidly from their late-1950s baby boom peaks, Mexican fertility rates remained at these high levels for a further decade. By 1972 fertility in both the United States and Canada had declined to below-replacement levels: 2.05 in the United States and 2.01 in Canada. But Mexican fertility rates in 1972 were still in excess of 6.52.

Coincidentally, in that same year, the Mexican government reversed long-standing policy by establishing a new national family-planning program designed explicitly to lower Mexico's fertility rates. We will discuss this development below. Without implying any causal relationship, there can be no doubt from the data that a sustained and substantial fertility decline ensued. By the end of the 1980s Mexican fertility rates were generally below 3.5, and by the turn of the twenty-first century, at the 2.5 level.

The rapid pace of fertility decline in Mexico was hardly surprising. Mexico is an urbanized, industrialized, and middle-income country, for which moderate rather than high levels of fertility would have been expected. Indeed, perhaps the most surprising aspect of Mexican fertility patterns during the second half of the twentieth century was not the fertility decline that began in the early 1970s but, instead, the substantial delay in fertility declines that would have been expected to occur earlier on the basis of demographic transition theory. During the postwar period, the Mexican economy was one of the most rapidly growing, yet after fully two decades of substantial economic advances, the Mexican total fertility rate had not declined at all from the more than 6.6 level at the beginning of the 1950s. As a result of this sustained high fertility and declining mortality, by 1972 the Mexican population had grown to about 54 million, up more than one-third from its 1940 population of 40 million.

The puzzle of Mexico's lagging fertility decline was explored in 1977 by the eminent American demographer Ansley Coale.[5] He addressed "the paradox implied by the continuation of high fertility" in Mexico by first noting a variety of robust indicators of rapid Mexican development in the two decades between the 1950s and 1970s: "impressive progress: a 72 percent increase in the proportion of the population of primary school age attending school, a 26 percent increase in literacy, an 89 percent increase in per capita income at constant prices, a 38 percent increase in the urban proportion, and a 27 percent rise in the average duration of life."[6] Coale concluded that this experience of very impressive measures of social and economic development in Mexico accompanied by no sign of fertility decline must raise real doubts about the confident arguments drawn from demographic transition theory that modernization, understood as economic development, in and of itself predictably leads to declines in fertility. The latter arguments were asserted forcefully by many governments at the 1974 World Population Conference in Bucharest.[7]

The delayed onset of Mexican fertility decline appears in part to have been related to particular facets of Mexican economic development and in part to pronatalist goals that had been part of Mexican national policy for a century and half.[8] From the achievement of independence from Spain in 1821, Mexico had faced serious challenges in establishing its sovereignty and national security over the large but very sparsely populated territory it claimed as inherited from Spain. Indeed, one of the long-standing slogans of Mexican political discourse was "To govern is to populate."[9]

It is not practical here to provide a detailed discussion of the complex political history of Mexico in the decades following the 1821 Mexican revolution as it contributed to this pronatalist view. What is relevant for our purposes is that the territory of the former Spanish colonies in America that were claimed by what briefly became the first Mexican Empire and then the United Mexican States covered an enormous area of some four million square kilometers (about twice the size of modern

Mexico), but one that was populated by only six million people. Only the tiniest of Mexican populations resided in the expansive areas of the northern territories, and their exceedingly sparse settlement and long distances from the seat of government in Mexico City made the establishment of effective Mexican sovereignty nearly impossible.

In order to assert its sovereignty and effective control, the Mexican government encouraged high fertility—hence the slogan "To govern is to populate," cited above. It also sought to populate its territories by actively encouraging immigration. However, this strategy backfired in the sparsely populated northern territory then known as Tejas, since most of the immigrants encouraged to settle there came from the United States to its north and east. Cabrera reports that as of 1835, this remote northern territory of Tejas had about "35,000 free inhabitants of Anglo-Saxon extraction and 5,000 slaves, while the Mexican population in the state numbered fewer than 5,000."[10] The new United Mexican States were plagued by a long period of internal political instability and even by an 1829 invasion by Spain seeking a reconquest of its former colonies. Moreover, the capital of Mexico City was far to the south and transportation infrastructure was poor. The combination of these demographic, political, and geographical realities contributed to separatist tendencies and eventually to the declarations of independence in several Mexican regions, including Tejas as the "Republic of Texas" in 1836.[11] The consequences for the Mexican state were disastrous, ultimately compelling it to cede half of the territory it claimed to the United States.[12]

The impetus toward populating its remaining territories by encouraging both fertility and immigration continued in Mexico even after the destructive Mexican civil war of 1910–1921. By the 1930s, however, a new kind of Mexican nationalism under President Lázaro Cárdenas (president from 1934 to 1940) was codified in the General Population Law of 1936. Under this law, Mexican population growth was still promoted but primarily by raising natural increase among Mexicans: promoting marriage and fertility and reducing high levels of infant and child mortality. The General Population Law also included provisions on migration, measures to encourage Mexican nationals to repatriate from abroad, to limit further emigration of Mexicans, and to allow continued inflow of non-Mexican immigrants but in reduced numbers.[13]

These policies continued through the 1940s and 1950s, and indeed could be judged a success in that the population of Mexico grew very rapidly. In 1936, when the General Population Law was promulgated, the Mexican population was an estimated 18.4 million. By 1950 its population had increased to 26.3 million, by 1960 to 35.0 million, and by 1970 to more than 50 million.[14] Indeed, in the 1960s the population of Mexico was increasing by about 3.5 percent per year,[15] a figure approaching the maximum rate ever seen in a large human population.

During the 1960s a number of leading development economists and others in Mexico had begun to consider such rapid demographic increase to present a serious impediment to economic development, and urged adoption of a new population policy that included voluntary family-planning programs as important components.[16] Among the most prominent of these was Dr. Victor Urquidi, a leading Mexican economist and president of the elite research institution El Colegio de Mexico. Urquidi was a close advisor to Luis Echeverría—the leader of the left-of-center elements of the long-ruling PRI Party[17]—who in 1969 became the party's candidate for the Mexican presidency.

In his successful presidential campaign in 1969, Echeverría embraced again the long-standing nationalist mantra of "To govern is to populate."[18] But in 1972, two years after his inauguration as president of Mexico, Echeverría announced an energetic and official national family-planning program, intended to support voluntary means of fertility regulation that would substantially lower fertility rates in Mexico. Although there had long been concern that such a policy would be forcefully opposed by the Mexican Catholic Church, in fact the church did not express opposition, at least not in public. Some attribute this silence to the Mexican church's "great tolerance regarding the contraceptive practices of its congregation."[19] Others reported that before announcing his new population policy in 1972, President Echeverría summoned church leaders, informed them of his decision, and made it clear to them that he expected to hear of no opposition to the policy from the church.[20] In 1974, the government created a National Population Council to coordinate the family-planning activities of multiple government agencies, and the Mexican constitution was amended to guarantee the right of Mexican men and women to control their family size voluntarily.[21]

The Mexican government's family-planning program established during the Echeverría presidency continued under his successors. It not only provided Mexican couples with ready and low-cost access to modern contraception but also sought to encourage demand for such methods via ambitious programs of mass communication and sex education. These efforts included support for now-famous Mexican *telenovelas* or "soap operas" intended to effect social change, pioneered by the Mexican TV producer Miguel Sabido. Sabido's popular production *Acompáñame* focused on family planning and was a popular phenomenon in Mexico for a full decade, from 1977 to 1986; many believe it succeeded in legitimizing family planning to millions of Mexican viewers.[22] While no causal effects can be demonstrated, over this period Mexican fertility rates did decline substantially.

The total fertility rate in Mexico had declined to 2.7 by the year 2000 and to below 2.3 in 2012.[23] Apart from this dramatic decline in national fertility rates, during the second half of the twentieth century, Mexico was characterized by dynamic changes in many other aspects of its demography that are beyond our scope here. There was massive rural-to-urban migration, with the metropolitan area of Mexico City becoming one of the largest in the world. Related to this internal migration were large regional differences in economic development and prosperity. Rural farmers generally registered low productivity increases, while industrialization expanded rapidly in urban area; at the same time the Mexican oil industry grew rapidly.

Mexican Migration to the United States

During the twentieth century, and especially during its last quarter, Mexico became one of the most significant countries of out-migration in the world. As we have seen, until the mid-1970s Mexican fertility rates remained high, notwithstanding steep declines in mortality and rapid social and economic development. The predictable demographic result was very substantial population growth: The population enumerated in Mexico grew from about 28 million in 1950, to 52 million in 1970, to 100 million in 2000, and 113 million in 2010.[24]

Moreover, the Mexican-*born* population actually was considerably larger than the population enumerated within Mexico. According to relatively reliable US Census Bureau estimates, some 11,478,000 persons born in Mexico were residing in the United States in 2009, representing nearly 30 percent of all immigrants in the United States.[25] If we accept the above estimates as credible, they mean that as of 2010 the Mexican-born population resident in Mexico *and* in the United States totaled on the order of 124.5 million, of which about 113 million lived in Mexico. In addition, there are smaller but still-significant numbers of Mexican emigrants in countries other than the United States. The World Bank reports that Mexico is in absolute terms the largest country of emigration in the world, exceeding even countries with far larger populations, such as India and China—both well over ten times larger than Mexico. Moreover, the World Bank rates the "Mexico-US Corridor" as by far the largest migration corridor in the world.[26]

Mexico also ranks among the largest source countries of emigrants in proportionate terms: The above estimates indicate that nearly 10 percent of Mexican-born persons currently live outside of Mexico. This places Mexico in a relatively small set of countries (other than very small island states) from which a tenth or more of the native-born population has emigrated. While available data on emigration are weak, this set of countries would almost surely include Cuba, Haiti, Afghanistan, El Salvador, and (in the past) Rwanda and Bosnia and Herzegovina. As may be seen from this list of unfortunate states, the emigration of such a large percentage of a country's population usually has been a consequence of war (civil or international), political repression, genocide, or economic failure—none of which is the case for Mexico. Moreover, all of the countries on this list have far smaller populations than Mexico does: The largest is strife-torn Afghanistan, at about 33 million, while Cuba, Haiti, and Rwanda are in the 9–12 million range, and the others even smaller. (For completeness, it is worth noting that there are other countries with far larger percentages of their populations that have emigrated, but with a few notable exceptions, these outflows while large in percentage terms are small in absolute size, given the very small populations of the countries of origin, for example, small island states in the Caribbean and Pacific.)[27]

The above estimates of Mexican-born persons living in the United States also indicate very large increases over the last quarter of the twentieth century. An earlier US Census Bureau estimate of the Mexican-born population resident in the United States was only 760,000 in 1970.[28] This would imply growth of some 10.7 million over the period from 1970 to 2006, representing a fifteen-fold increase from the level of 1970.

In addition to the unusually high magnitudes of Mexican emigration, both in absolute and proportionate terms, the other unique feature of Mexican migration is the large fraction that has migrated outside of legal channels.[29] Of the 11.5 million Mexicans living in the United States, approximately 6.5 million, or some 60 percent, are estimated to be unauthorized—according to the most recent estimates based on the "residual method" pioneered during the 1980s by technical staff of the Immigration and Naturalization Service and the Census Bureau, and later at the Pew Hispanic Center.[30] Estimated trends in the overall numbers of unauthorized migrants in the United States (of which Mexicans constitute the majority) are shown in table 7.1.

Not surprisingly, the phenomenon of such large-scale and irregular migration has produced a complex patchwork of political controversies on the US federal, state, and local levels, as well as continuing disagreements and tensions between the Mexican and US governments. This is a very long and convoluted story, to which an entire book could be devoted to tell it properly. We address it in more-limited form in the following section.

US Immigration Politics and US-Mexican Relations

Political conflict surrounding the aforementioned patterns of Mexican migration has been visible and highly charged in the United States for at least the last three decades. US policies on immigration to date have been under the effective control of regional, economic, and ethnic interest-group politics, and in the fierce debate over Mexican immigration to the United States we find many ideological viewpoints that range from the center to the extremes of the peripheries.

In addition to domestic US political developments, there have been numerous bilateral discussions between the two governments. Notwith-

Table 7.1. Estimates, in Millions, of Unauthorized Immigrant Population Resident in United States, 2000–2010

Year	Estimate	Range
2010	11.2	(10.7–11.7)
2009	11.1	(10.6–11.6)
2008	11.6	(11.1–12.1)
2007	**12.0***	(11.5–12.5)
2006	11.3	(10.8–11.8)
2005	**11.1***	(10.6–11.6)
2004	**10.4***	(9.9–10.8)
2003	9.7	(9.2–10.2)
2002	9.4	(9.0–9.9)
2001	**9.3***	(8.8–9.7)
2000	8.4	(7.9–8.8)

Notes: Numbers in boldface with asterisk indicate change from previous year is statistically significant. Range represents bounds of the estimated 90 percent confidence interval. *Source:* Adapted from Jeffrey S. Passel and D'Vera Cohn, *Unauthorized Immigrant Population: National and State Trends, 2010,* (Washington, DC: Pew Hispanic Center, 1 February 2011).

standing the complex but close political and economic ties between the two countries,[31] it would be fair to say that the two governments have never been able to reach agreement as to the primary causes or the empirical impacts of such migratory movements. Given this, they also have been unable to find common ground regarding collaborative policies on the phenomenon of Mexico–United States migration.

The official US government position has been that it welcomes lawful immigration, and indeed that Mexico is by far the largest source country of legal immigrants to the United States. However, it objects to the continuing flow of unauthorized/irregular/illegal/undocumented migrants from Mexico, a flow that is even larger than the large legal migrations from the same country. The US government asserts its sovereign right to control entry of non-nationals, though it is apparent that for a variety of political reasons it does not enforce that right effectively. American diplomats have routinely argued that the US government would welcome bilateral cooperation from the Mexican government to regularize migration across the two countries' lengthy common border. They claim that cooperation about migration between two of the three members of the North American Free Trade area should be similar to cooperation in other spheres, such as security, the facilitation of trade and commerce, and the control of crime and drug trafficking.

Yet the actions of American politicians in the legislative and the executive branches have long conveyed mixed and often confusing messages about unauthorized migration from Mexico. Mexican officials understand that the Immigration Reform and Control Act of 1986 (IRCA) was passed by the US Congress only after the inclusion of amendments that rendered enforcement of its employment provisions very difficult indeed.[32] Mexican leaders know too that the US executive branch waxes hot and cold about visible enforcement, and that US judges at different levels have repeatedly intervened to reverse executive-branch enforcement actions and judicial decisions by other judges. Under these circumstances it is difficult for sophisticated observers of US politics to discern the "real" policy stance. Many Mexicans see such actions as evidence of a lack of unified commitment to enforcement of US immigration policies. From the Mexican standpoint, the US position formally is one of sovereign enforcement, but the informal reality is marked by lax and ineffective enforcement measures.

The perspectives of Mexican government officials regarding unauthorized Mexican migration to the United States are very different indeed from those expressed by US government officials. Mexican leaders emphasize arguments about basic human rights, stating that Mexican nationals are entitled to migrate internationally in search of employment, irrespective of US border controls and legal provisions enforcing them. This argument was stated most succinctly by Ernesto López Portillo, president of Mexico from 1976 to 1982: "It is not a crime to look for work, and I refuse to consider it as such."[33] A second basic human right often invoked by Mexican officials is that of family unification, which they argue should be available in the countries to which Mexican citizens have migrated whether or not such migration is consistent with those countries' laws.[34]

With regard to US requests for binational collaboration to regulate migration across the Mexico-US border, Mexican officials argue further that the Mexican constitution prohibits the government from impeding the departure of Mexicans from Mexico. Some critics see the Mexican government as actively colluding in the transfer of surplus population across the US border.[35]

Mexican representatives also state that it was the US government that initiated Mexican migration with its Bracero Programs, and point to demand for Mexican labor by US employers and the ineffectiveness of US immigration enforcement as the key drivers of unauthorized Mexican migration.[36] In economic and political terms, they argue, hard-working Mexican migrants help the United States to build economic prosperity, while their out-migration provides a valuable "safety valve" for underemployed Mexicans.

Finally, Mexican officials note that earnings or remittances sent back to Mexico by its workers in the United States represent a large and critical source of external capital flows to the Mexican economy. In the words of former Mexican President Vicente Fox, Mexican migrants sending back remittances are "heroes," indispensable to the creation of a modern and prosperous Mexico.[37]

This is a minimalist summary of a much more complex and sometimes emotional debate. Within this sea of controversy, what can be said objectively about the forces underlying the large and sustained unauthorized migration of Mexican citizens to the United States?

There can be little doubt about the validity of the Mexican claim that it was the US government that in the past encouraged Mexican migration. This was clearly evident during both World War I and World War II, when it approved the recruitment by US employers of Mexican agricultural and railroad workers as *braceros*.

It is also more than obvious that some US employers in some regions and some minority of industries actively seek to employ undocumented workers, the majority of whom are Mexican. This is most common in the US Southwest and in industries such as labor-intensive fruit and vegetable agriculture; nursery and landscaping; construction; and hospitality (that is, hotels and restaurants).

Finally, it is fair to say that the US political system has proved unable so far to agree upon policies that would allow effective enforcement of its official provisions regarding immigration. This applies generally to unauthorized migration from anywhere, but especially so for that from Mexico, given that it accounts for nearly 60 percent of the totals.[38]

On the other hand, there is also little doubt that the large influx of low-skill and low-wage Mexican workers has tended to restrain the pace of improvement in wages and benefits—below what they might otherwise have been—of US workers with similar skill levels in the same occupations and regions, including many Mexican Americans.

The Mexican government's assertion that one country's nationals have a "right" to enter another country unlawfully in search of employment is not accepted by other countries. Nor, in practice, is this same assertion accepted by the Mexican government itself with respect to nationals from other countries seeking to enter Mexico to work.

What about the argument that all migrants, authorized or unauthorized, have the right to "reunite" with their families in their country of destination? This claim is based upon a general sentence about protection of the family, in Article 16 of the Universal Declaration of Human Rights: "The family is the natural and fundamental group unit of society and is entitled to protection by society and the State."[39] In order to solidify its claim of an internationally agreed right of family unification for all migrants, lawful or unlawful, the Mexican government has for more than two decades expended considerable diplomatic effort in authoring, sponsoring, and promoting an International Convention on the Protection of the Rights of All Migrant Workers and Members of Their Families.[40] This draft UN convention was adopted in 1990 by a majority vote of the UN General Assembly. As indicated in its title, it declares a substantial number of human rights accruing to "all migrant workers and members of their families"—with no distinction between migrant workers whose presence in a country is authorized or unauthorized, legal or illegal.

The convention passed by the General Assembly contained a "self-activating" article. Its Article 87 states that the convention "shall enter into force on the first day of the month following a period of three months after the date of the deposit of the twentieth instrument of ratification or accession."[41] The twentieth ratification took place in 2003, and hence, according to the UN this convention, has now entered "into force." To date it has been ratified by more than 30 of the 193 member states of the United Nations. All of the ratifying countries are primarily countries of origin for migrants, though some of these countries also are destinations for migrants from other countries.

However, the convention has "entered into force" only within the territory of the signatory states, and not one of the primary countries to which most such migrants seek to move (mostly Western or high-income countries) is among those that have ratified it. The conclusion must be that the convention has only what some human rights activists term "normative" force, meaning that it sets a standard against which to measure the policies of individual states, though it lacks the judicial force enabling any individual to go to court to enforce it. This term of art from international legal parlance, *normative*, is a controversial one, since the terminology seems to claim that the action advocated by the measure conforms with the "norms" of a society or societies. Instead, "normative" measures are aspirational in character, and indeed they are rarely followed in practice. They are signposts toward a possible future that is desired by supporters but are not legally enforceable instruments of international law today. Their writ does not extend beyond the boundaries of those countries that accept them.[42]

As to the constitutional issues raised, the Mexican government correctly states that constitutionally it cannot prevent its citizens from leaving Mexico; indeed, this right of departure is explicitly protected by the 1948 Universal Declaration of Human Rights.[43] However, there is no limitation on a state's right to regulate such departures by requiring that they be made via officially defined ports of entry/departure: Nothing in the Universal Declaration of Human Rights mandates that a government must allow its citizens to leave a country at any location along its borders.

Finally, the large remittances sent home by Mexican workers abroad do indeed add substantially to Mexico's source of external capital, though Mexican economists debate whether these also make the

Mexican rural economy more inegalitarian or even more vulnerable than it already is to the ups and downs in the US economy.[44]

Some commentators note that if the United States actually wanted to regulate unauthorized migration from Mexico, it would adopt legislation and practices that would make it possible to do so. To those with this perspective, the demonstrable ineffectiveness of US law and practice reveals that the "true" preferences of the US political leadership is for continued unauthorized migration, even if they are unwilling to state this explicitly. This is a point worthy of discussion. But first we turn to the North American Free Trade Agreement (NAFTA) as it does, or does not, relate to demographic issues in the North American region.

Mistaken Assumptions: NAFTA and Mexico– United States Migration

Among the many and decades-old debates about Mexico–United States migration trends, perhaps the most contentious is that which surrounds US legislation to enter into the North American Free Trade Agreement (NAFTA). NAFTA is a trilateral agreement (not a "treaty")[45] among Canada, Mexico, and the United States that went into effect at the beginning of 1994. It succeeded the 1988 bilateral agreement between Canada and the United States known as the Canada-United States Free Trade Agreement.

The original proposal for what came to be NAFTA was put forward by Mexican President Carlos Salinas de Gortari and negotiated with the administrations led by George H. W. Bush in the United States and Brian Mulroney in Canada.[46] The agreement was initially agreed to by these three leaders in 1993. In the US case, such an agreement required support from Congress before it could go into effect, and NAFTA proved to be highly controversial. Bush, a Republican, was unable to gain sufficient congressional support, and hence the pending agreement was passed on to his successor, President Clinton, a Democrat.[47] Clinton embraced NAFTA and lobbied strongly for its passage. In the end his efforts led to legislative passage, but only with a majority provided by congressional Republicans after his own Democratic Party proved to be deeply split.[48]

Congressional passage of NAFTA was in doubt until the very end. As the final legislative and public debates came to a head during the few months prior to the congressional votes in November 1993, US proponents of the agreement suddenly began to argue that it would reduce the flow of unauthorized migration from Mexico. In a front-page story on 26 September 1993, *The Washington Times* reported:

> Almost overnight, the volatile topic of illegal immigration has become part of the fractious debate over the North American Free Trade Agreement.
>
> During four years of analysis on the merits or pitfalls of freer trade between the U.S. and Mexico, the matter of illegal immigration almost never came up. . . .
>
> Then quite suddenly, proponents set about wooing skeptical voters with this seductive message about NAFTA and illegal immigration:
>
> Approve NAFTA and rid the nation's borders of uncontrollable waves of immigrants seeking work in America.
>
> They painted an equally alarming alternative:
>
> Defeat NAFTA and risk even greater hordes of alien crossings as punishment for turning our back on Mexico and crippling its strides toward a free-market economy.
>
> Other pro-NAFTA heavyweights have picked up on the immigration theme.[49]

The article cites statements along these lines by former President Ford, Secretary of State Warren Christopher, and former Chrysler CEO Lee Iacocca, and then resumes its story:

> Rep. Robert T. Matsui, California Democrat, is afraid of overselling the pact's ability to stem immigration. In the short term, there could be additional illegal immigration into the U.S., said Mr. Matsui, one of the leading supporters of NAFTA. "I think the impact will be minimal, but I think there could be additional immigration in the first two or three years. . . . If NAFTA goes down, I mean the surge [of

Mexican migrants] over the next decade will be overwhelming," Mr. Matsui said.[50]

The claim that the adoption of NAFTA would reduce unlawful migration to the United States was made on both sides of the US-Mexican border. President Salinas argued that NAFTA "would enable Mexico to export tomatoes rather than tomato pickers."[51] Others in Mexico acknowledged that the forecasted moderating effects on unauthorized Mexican migration would not occur rapidly. In invited testimony before a 1993 hearing of the Subcommittee on International Law, Immigration, and Refugees of the US House of Representatives, Jorge Bustamante, president of the El Colegio de la Frontera Norte and a longtime advisor to the Mexican government on immigration matters, cited his own research on the Mexican border as indicating that "no significant impact will be felt in the phenomenon of undocumented immigration in the first five years after the signing of the NAFTA." However Bustamante went on to suggest, though in hedged language, that there would be quite large restraining effects on unauthorized migration after the first five years: "In six of ten years, the impact will be no more than a 25 percent reduction in the volume observable today. In 11–15 years, the study predicts a maximum reduction of 50 percent. This figure will increase exponentially as time goes on."[52]

US government witnesses made similar statements. Doris Meissner, the commissioner of the Immigration and Naturalization Service,[53] told the subcommittee, "Quite simply, I believe NAFTA is the United States' best opportunity to reduce illegal immigration across our southern border in the long term. Its promise of a greatly strengthened Mexican economy, with its corollary of a higher standard of living for Mexicans, presents us with the single best systemic solution to the flow of undocumented workers into the United States. By passing NAFTA, the Congress will start us on the road toward gaining control of what has seemed uncontrollable and unending. . . ."[54] Deputy United States Trade Representative Rufus Yerxa told the subcommittee:

The question we should ask ourselves is this: are we better off with NAFTA when it comes to the immigration problem, or without? The answer, clearly, is we are better off with NAFTA. Ultimately, the answer to the problem of illegal immigration from Mexico is sustained robust economic growth in Mexico. NAFTA will promote rapid economic growth. According to a review of studies by the International Trade Commission, NAFTA will increase economic activity by up to 11 percent by the end of the transition period, 2008, resulting in gains to Mexican employment and average real wages.

Well before the NAFTA, the Commission for the Study of International Migration and Cooperative Economic Development, created by the Congress in 1986 and chaired, I should note, by Ambassador Diego Asencio, who is here today, concluded that the development and availability of new and better jobs in Mexico, through measures including a free trade pact, was the only way to diminish migratory pressures over time.

Ambassador Yerxa also quoted President Clinton in the same vein:

> President Clinton said it best when he asked on October 20, "If you beat (NAFTA) will it reduce the pressure for people looking for illegal immigration? No. It will increase the pressure on people coming here."[55]

Independent analysts—most of whom were supporters of NAFTA on other grounds—were more cautious than those NAFTA advocates who were claiming impacts within five to ten years, emphasizing instead that the claimed curbing effects could not be expected until the very long term. In 1990 the US government commission cited by Ambassador Asencio—the Commission for the Study of International Migration and Cooperative Economic Development—recommended trade liberalization to accelerate economic development in Mexico as one important approach that might moderate emigration pressures over several generations, but noted that such an effect would not be likely in the short-to-medium term: "Development, if sustained, can eventually reduce emigration pressures, but it may take several generations for this process to run its course."[56]

A 1993 paper by two respected researchers on Mexican migration concluded that the likely short-term impacts of NAFTA would be *increased* out-migration by dislocated low-productivity Mexican farmers, but added, "Even with the anticipated dislocations in small-scale agriculture, future levels of total Mexican migration to the United States (both legal and illegal) almost certainly would be higher in the absence of trade liberalization."[57] Press reports at the time of the US debate on NAFTA shows that similar doubts were expressed publicly by leading experts on Mexican trade and migration, such as Sidney Weintraub, Manuel Garcia y Griego, and Jeffrey Schott.[58]

NAFTA has been in force now for nearly two decades, allowing us to make a provisional but informed assessment of these arguments. What, if anything, can now be said about its effects on unauthorized Mexico–United States migration?

The first conclusion is that implementation of NAFTA has not—at least not yet—seemed to contribute in any way to a decline in unauthorized migration from Mexico. To the contrary, the estimated "stock" of unauthorized Mexican migrants in the United States has risen sharply since NAFTA came into effect in January 1994. It is now possible to assemble a useful time series from 1986 to 2010 of the most credible estimates of the *total* unauthorized population resident in the United States, based on similar estimating techniques. As may be seen in fig. 7.1, the total estimated for 1992 is 3.4 million and 5.8 million for 1996, representing an increase of some 70 percent over the period. Yet these annual estimates for 1992 and 1996 both include unauthorized migrants from all countries, and so must be reduced appropriately to exclude those coming from countries other than Mexico. This percentage is estimated to have increased from about 31 percent to about 43 percent between 1986 and 2004, as the volumes of unauthorized migrants from other countries increased more rapidly than did those from Mexico.[59] If we estimate on this basis that about 36–37 percent of the gross estimated unauthorized "stock" in 1992 and 1996 were other than Mexican (a crude estimate, to be sure), this would imply rough totals of Mexican unauthorized migrants of about 2.35 million in 1992 and 4.5 million in 1996— an increase of about 90 percent rather than a decline.

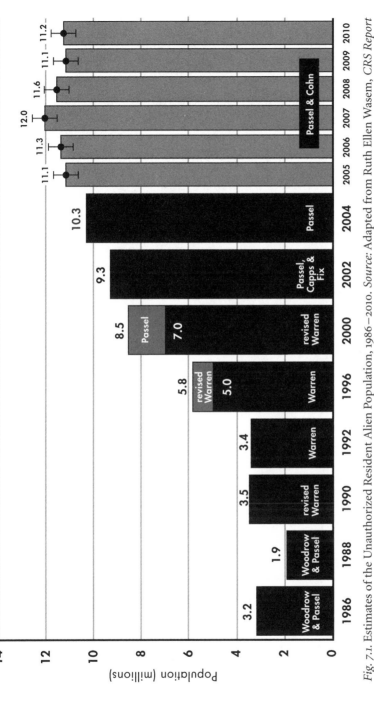

Fig. 7.1. Estimates of the Unauthorized Resident Alien Population, 1986–2010. *Source:* Adapted from Ruth Ellen Wasem, *CRS Report to Congress: Unauthorized Aliens in the United States: Estimates since 1986,* Congressional Research Service, updated 24 January 2007, order code RS21938, p. 3; available online at http://www.ilw.com/immigdaily/news/2007,0315-crs.pdf; and Jeffrey Passel and D'Vera Cohn, *Unauthorized Immigrant Population: National and State Trends, 2010* (Washington, DC: Pew Hispanic Center, 1 February 2011), fig. 1; available online at http://www.pewhispanic.org/2011/02/01/unauthorized-immigrant-population-brnational-and-state-trends-2010. See these sources for identification of the different estimates.

As to later years, Passel and Cohn have helpfully provided a time series of estimates for Mexican unauthorized migrants only for the subsequent years 2000–2010, to which the adjusted estimates for 1992 and 1996 may usefully be compared (see fig. 7.2). As may be seen, their estimates show substantial continuing increases during much of the first decade of the twenty-first century, from 4.6 million in 2000 to 6.0 million in 2004 and peaking at 7.0 million in 2007 before declining to 6.5 million in 2010. The latter decline is generally agreed to be a consequence of the deep recession in the United States that began in late 2007.

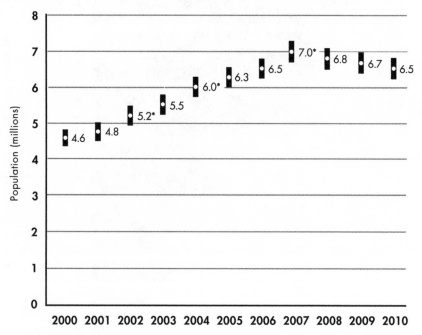

Fig. 7.2. Estimates of the US Unauthorized Immigrant Population from Mexico, 2000–2010.

Notes: Bars indicate low and high points of the approximate 90 percent confidence interval. The symbol * indicates that the change from the previous year is statistically significant. *Source:* From Jeffrey Passel and D'Vera Cohn, *Unauthorized Immigrant Population: National and State Trends, 2010* (Washington, DC: Pew Hispanic Center, 1 February 2011), p. 2, fig. 2 ; available online at http://www.pewhispanic.org/2011/02/01/ii-current-estimates-and-trends/.

Taking all of these estimates together, then, the estimated stock of Mexican unauthorized migrants resident in the United States rose from 2.35 million during the year in which NAFTA came into force to 6.5 million in 2010. Suffice it to say that the trends do not suggest that implementation of NAFTA has led over a period of a decade and half to a reduction in the number of unauthorized Mexican migrants resident in the United States. Given the confident assurances from NAFTA supporters in both Mexico and the United States that support for NAFTA was the best way to ensure a decline in unauthorized migration from Mexico, why has this not occurred since 1994? There are many possible explanations.

First, the promised reductions in unauthorized migration may simply have been based on ignorance among some NAFTA proponents of the repeated finding among immigration researchers that accelerating economic development in low-income countries tends to stimulate rather than restrain out-migration, and over a period of many decades rather than a few years.[60] To be fair it should be noted that many of the declines promised by more careful proponents were carefully hedged: "Over the long term" was a common qualifier. Even Jorge Bustamante, who, in the congressional testimony quoted above rather clearly forecast declines in such Mexican migration only five years after implementation of NAFTA, hedged his forecast by saying such declines would be "no more than a 25 percent reduction in the volume observable today . . . [and in] 11 to 15 years . . . a maximum reduction of 50 percent."[61] Framed in this way, a zero reduction or even increases in unauthorized Mexican migration would be technically consistent with such forecasts. The niceties of such hedged forecasts seem to have been lost on many proponents who cited them as expert evidence for prompt migration-restraining effects of the proposed NAFTA.

A second, more cynical, explanation is that the claims represented an effective if mendacious political marketing strategy by NAFTA proponents seeking to attract political support. The targets of such a strategy would have been those in the United States who were skeptical about NAFTA but strongly supportive of restraints on such unauthorized migration.

Third, it is possible that the Mexican peso crisis of December 1994, generally seen as unrelated to NAFTA (even though the latter came into force in January of the same year), stimulated a surge of out-migration that might otherwise not have occurred.

Fourth, as argued by many Mexicans, the rapid growth in unauthorized migration from Mexico was driven by rising demand for Mexican labor in the United States rather than by events in Mexico.

Fifth, some (mostly on the left) believe that an important goal of NAFTA was to disrupt and reduce low-productivity Mexican grain agriculture by exposing it to direct competition from highly productive and heavily subsidized US grain production, while at the same time expanding the profits of large firms engaged in grain importing.[62]

Sixth, and finally, some experts on NAFTA believe the Mexican government erred by rapidly ending tariffs on imported grain rather than phasing out these tariffs over many years as allowed by NAFTA. In this view such a gradual phaseout would have facilitated a gradual transition of Mexican farmers away from grain and toward labor-intensive fruits and vegetables.[63]

Two Yawning Gaps: US Immigration Policy and Opinion

Immigration policy in the United States is one of the most fractious and controversial issues on the national agenda. While the subject is intrinsically highly political, it has not until very recently been primarily a partisan issue, one on which disagreement is between the Republicans and the Democrats. To the contrary, the fissures have been more along the lines of region, industry, ethnicity/religion, and ideology, and the debate has been driven by active interest groups on all sides. On the key issues surrounding immigration policy, both the Democratic and Republican Parties remain divided among themselves.

Consequently, there has been political stalemate for many years, despite the fact that the ongoing system of immigration law is generally agreed to be dysfunctional. Indeed, a succession of US presidents, including both Barack Obama and George W. Bush, repeatedly has described the US immigration system as "broken."

The core sources of this legislative and political failure can been found in two yawning gaps: the gap between immigration law and practice, and the gap between elite and public opinion. Let us consider these seriatim.

THE GAP BETWEEN IMMIGRATION LAW AND PRACTICE IN THE UNITED STATES

As may be seen from the most credible estimates of the large and growing number of migrants—Mexican and non-Mexican—resident in the United States with no legal authorization, there is a wide gap between official US law and policy on immigration and the actual situation. Moreover, the large increases in the numbers of such unauthorized migrants since 1990 suggest that this gap may, if anything, have been widening over the past decades.

As might be expected, there are as many explanations for this gap between law and practice as there are points of view on the causes and consequences of international migration. We cannot address all the multiple hues of opinion on this matter, but a few are worthy of our attention.

For some, the complex rights, preferences, and procedures embodied in official US immigration law are simply incompatible with current conditions of an increasingly global economy. From this perspective, international flows of people across national borders essentially are unstoppable. Instead, these global flows of human beings are products of a particular economic moment: that of multinational corporations operating in the global economy, that of pronounced economic and demographic inequalities, that of US employers' demand for a low-wage labor force. All of these are overwhelming macroeconomic forces that are impossible to control. In such cases the best thing for a government to do is to get out of the way. It is important to note that such views can be found on both the left and the right, among "progressives" and "libertarians," and among Democrats and Republicans both. Their overall perspectives may be worlds apart, but on these issues they can often be found working in unison as truly strange bedfellows.

For others, unauthorized immigration is akin to the trafficking and use of illegal drugs. They see unauthorized migrants as knowing lawbreakers who seek to take advantage of the availability of higher-paying employment, publicly financed health and education benefits, and poorly regulated underground economies in the United States. They note that many such migrants use the services of smuggler networks to gain unauthorized entry, and that many of these smuggler networks also traffic in illegal drugs and the sex trade. The failure of US immigration policy, from this perspective, is similar to that of the failure of US drug policy: Attractive economic returns reward abuse of weak laws, and knowing law-abusers face only a corrupted US and Mexican officialdom and an apathetic and feckless US system of enforcement. Proponents of this view argue that effective control is entirely feasible, but those in charge are unwilling even to try.

For still others, all human beings are entitled to a basic human right to migrate to locations in which they can better their lot and that of their families. In this view, national boundaries are morally and ethically suspect to the extent they stand in the way of this fundamental human right. Such perspectives can be found in the teachings of some organized religions, most forcefully expressed by the Roman Catholic Church. More limited versions of this perspective attach such rights not to all human beings, but instead focus on the moral and material entitlements of those who by virtue of their place of birth are living in desperate poverty or experiencing violence and/or persecution. These people must be helped by opening the doors to a safer life in the United States.

THE GAP BETWEEN ELITE AND PUBLIC OPINION

There is a second yawning gap in this discussion, too. This one is located between the views about immigration (both lawful and unlawful) held by US economic and political elites as compared with those of the bulk of the population. All surveys of US public opinion (other than those commissioned and/or framed by interest groups) show only small minorities—commonly about 10–20 percent—favoring increased legal immigration. The March 2006 survey by the Pew Research Center for the People and the Press is typical. In response to its survey question number 36 ("Should LEGAL immigration into the United States be kept at its present level, increased or decreased?"), only 17 percent favored increasing legal immigration, versus 40 percent favoring a decrease and 37 percent favoring keeping legal immigration the same.[64] Yet a variety of organizations and members of Congress have been energetically seeking legislation to both increase legal immigration numbers and to legalize large numbers of unauthorized migrants. Such efforts continued even after the onset of the major recession that began in late 2007 and led to US unemployment rates that rose as high as 10 percent before declining to a still-painful 8 percent.

This gap between US elite and public opinion on immigration matters appears to be similarly found in other countries. Generally speaking, economic and political elites tend to be far more open to expanded legal immigration and to lax enforcement of immigration laws than are the broader publics. Anecdotal indications of this gap abound in many countries, but in the US case there are credible quantitative data as well.

In particular, in 2002 and again in 2004 the Chicago Council on Foreign Relations (now renamed the Chicago Council on Global Affairs) added a valuable feature to its regular national public-opinion surveys of American opinion on major national and international issues. These two survey studies creatively administered the same questionnaire to two distinct samples: first, to a representative sample of the entire US population, that is, "public opinion" as conventionally defined; and second, to a sample of four hundred and fifty opinion "leaders" on foreign policy issues, including one hundred congressional members and senior staff, numerous executive-branch officials, university administrators and professors, senior journalists, and leaders of corporations, unions, religious organizations, and interest groups. This methodology enabled quantitative assessment of the extent of gaps between public and elite opinion on a variety of foreign relations topics.

The Chicago Council summarizes the comparison of views on immigration in a single clear sentence: "Immigration—widely seen as a threat to low-wage American workers and as a possible source of terrorism—draws remarkably stronger reactions from the public than from leaders."[65] The most recent such comparison, from 2004, shows that among the "leaders" group some 33 percent wanted to increase legal immigration, versus only 11 percent of the public opinion sample. In the same poll, only 10 percent of the "leaders" group wished to decrease the level of legal immigration, while fully 54 percent of the public opinion sample supported such decreases (see fig. 7.3).

With respect to unauthorized/illegal migration, the 2002 report concluded: "The foreign policy goal of reducing illegal immigration is a far higher public priority [than a priority of leaders] by a 48 point margin. The public is substantially more alarmed by immigrants and refugees coming into the United States as a critical threat to U.S. interests by a 46 point margin (60% of the public versus only 14% of leaders). By large, 39 point gaps, the public is more favorable to decreasing legal immigration (57% vs. 18%) and to combating international terrorism by restricting immigration from Arab and Muslim countries (79% vs. 40%)."[66]

The 2004 report by the Chicago Council shows that negative perceptions of immigration among the US public declined somewhat from those of 2002, in part due to lessened concern about terrorism. Nonetheless, a large gap remained between the opinions held by the public and leaders, as illustrated by fig. 7.3, published in 2004.

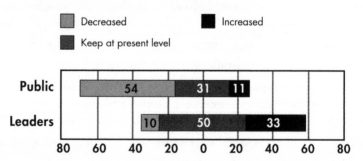

Fig. 7.3. Opinions on Legal Immigration Levels among US Public and Leaders. *Source:* From Chicago Council on Foreign Relations, *Global Views 2004: Comparing Mexican and American Public Opinion and Foreign Policy* (Chicago: Chicago Council on Foreign Relations, 2004), p. 47; available online at http://www.ccfr.org/globalviews2004/sub/pdf/Global_Views_2004_US.pdf.

COMPARISONS OF PUBLIC OPINION IN THE
UNITED STATES AND MEXICO

Also in 2004, the Chicago Council on Foreign Relations undertook an interesting comparative survey of US and Mexican public opinion on such foreign policy issues, implemented in cooperation with two Mexican organizations, the Centro de Investigación y Docencia Económicas and the Consejo Mexicano de Asuntos Internacionales.[67] The sample size in the United States was 1,195 adults; that in Mexico was 1,500 persons aged eighteen and over.[68]

Overall, the joint study described the issue of migration as "the most explosive problem between the United States and Mexico, especially the large numbers of undocumented Mexicans migrating to the United States."[69] The US and Mexican respondents expressed similar opinions about Mexican migrants, with large majorities in both countries believing they work hard, and (small) majorities believing they "respect the law"—notwithstanding the unauthorized status of a majority (see fig. 7.4). However the US and Mexican samples expressed differing opinions about whether Mexican migrants learn English (42 percent of US respondents thought they do, versus 63 percent of Mexican respondents). Similar differences of perspective appeared as to whether Mexican migrants "integrate in American life." Of US respondents, 52 percent said they do; whereas only 39 percent of Mexican respondents agreed.[70]

Comparisons of US and Mexican public opinion about primary responsibility for dealing with unauthorized Mexican migration are clouded by an unfortunate methodological disparity in the two survey questionnaires. For reasons not made clear in the Chicago Council report, US respondents were asked to choose between only two options: Should the United States or Mexico be considered more responsible? Mexican respondents however were given three options: Should the United States, Mexico, or "both" be held more responsible? Small majorities of both US and Mexican survey populations (50 percent in the United States; 54 percent in Mexico) indicated that Mexico should be seen as more responsible. Among US respondents, 45 percent said the United States should be considered more responsible. In the Mexico

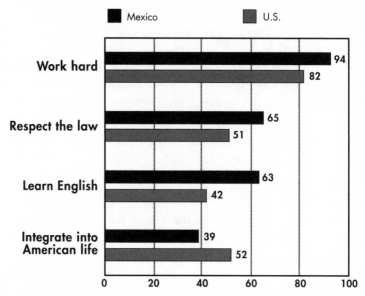

Fig. 7.4. Mexican and US Views on Mexican Immigrants Living in the United States. *Source:* From Chicago Council on Foreign Relations, *Global Views 2004,* fig. 3–5, p. 30.

sample only 21 percent of respondents said that the United States should be more responsible, while 54 percent said it should be Mexico. These comparisons are summarized graphically in fig. 7.5. But given the option of "both," some 23 percent of the Mexican sample chose this response, slightly higher than the 21 percent that said Mexico only.

The Politics of US Immigration Policy

The yawning gap between official US law and policy on immigration and actual practice is no accident. On the contrary, it is the predictable outcome of the political forces and structures that affect US immigration law, policy, and practice. Under US constitutional law and practice, it is almost universally accepted that regulation of immigration falls under the jurisdiction of the US government at the federal level and, more precisely, of the US Congress. Under this "plenary power" doctrine, it is argued that since the US Constitution grants only to Congress the

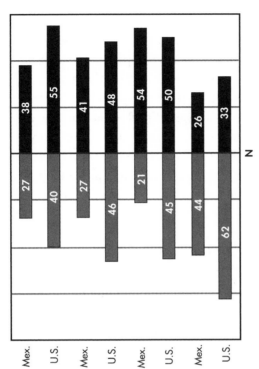

Fig. 7.5. Mexican and US Opinions on Responsibility for Common Problems (terms in the original source). *Source:* From Chicago Council on Foreign Relations, *Global Views 2004,* fig. 3 – 4, p. 29.

power "To establish a uniform Rule of Naturalization,"[71] only Congress can pass laws regulating immigration.[72] This also means that Congress can, if it wishes, pass laws with respect to noncitizens that would be unconstitutional if applied to US citizens. A minority of legal scholars has challenged the doctrine of plenary power in general. However, even a recent article that is sharply critical of the doctrine concludes: "Typically, although Congress's legislative power over many areas (e.g., patents, interstate commerce) is described by courts as 'plenary,' it is still subject to normal constitutional limitations. In contrast, courts have traditionally considered the power of the federal government over immigration to be nearly unlimited and the constitutional rights of immigrants to be extremely limited—in many cases, virtually nonexistent."[73] The author goes on to criticize his fellow legal scholars for producing what he describes as a "staggering" number of academic law articles about the plenary powers of Congress regarding immigration.[74]

Meanwhile, other critics argue from principles of international human rights that no government has the right to exercise such plenary power. Still others argue that the executive branch agencies share such plenary power with Congress.[75]

Nonetheless, on the basis of this long-standing principle of plenary congressional power in this area, both the judicial and executive branches traditionally have deferred to the legislative branch with respect to immigration law and policy. This renders the making of immigration policy very different in the United States than in most parliamentary democracies, in which the executive organs of government propose most legislation and also exercise administrative discretion with considerably less input from the legislature.

The role of the Congress in US immigration policy is one critical explanation of the gap between formal law and policy versus actual practice. The dynamics of campaign finance, interest group formation, and expanding professional lobbying activities over the past decades have greatly increased the impacts upon Congress of pressure groups of many types—economic, political, geographic, racial/ethnic/religious, and so on. Immigration issues have attracted a large volume of such lobbying, led by admittedly small but nonetheless well-organized and heavily financed groups.

The most visible are the many industry trade associations representing firms involved in labor-intensive fruit and vegetable agriculture[76] (not to be confused with the capital-intensive grain agriculture concentrated in the Midwest). Many of these trade associations are supported financially by large "corporate farming" firms (sometimes called "agribusiness") concentrated in California and the Southwest, firms that also pursue their own direct lobbying activities. These firms do not fit the conventional image of "farmers"; they are large, vertically integrated, industrial producers of labor-intensive food products, with operations covering thousands of acres and corporate headquarters often located in large cities, such as Los Angeles.

Beyond labor-intensive agriculture in the Southwest, there are other more widely spread employers of low-wage labor in industries such as hotels[77] and restaurants[78] (together often called the "hospitality" industry), nursery and landscaping firms, and some parts of the construction industry, mostly residential housing. Like low-wage agricultural employers, such firms undertake their own direct political activities, including lobbying and campaign finance, while also supporting industry associations that do the same.

Other groups also are engaged in very active lobbying efforts. Among the most notable are those representing some high-tech companies and ethnic and religious groups. More generally, the national trade association of immigration lawyers, the American Immigration Lawyers Association (AILA), has long been one of the most active and visible lobbying groups in the Washington politics of immigration.

Most of the groups just mentioned have direct and substantial economic interests in the nature of immigration law and enforcement. However, their interests focus on different aspects of immigration, with the low-wage employer groups focused upon unauthorized migration and temporary worker programs for low-skill workers, while the high-tech companies' focus is understandably upon more highly educated migrants.

Meanwhile, the interests of religious and ethnic groups are driven more by theological considerations or by identity with particular streams of migrants. While their interests diverge and their ideological perspectives often differ markedly, many of these groups have chosen to work together in otherwise unlikely lobbying coalitions that jointly promote the immigration goals of a broad range of interest groups.

There are also groups of a more-ideological complexion, for whom immigration policies do not relate to financial or theological or identity interests but instead to their values and preferences about government regulation of migration, the acceptability of government involvement in labor markets, the rights of individuals vis-à-vis government, and related matters. Here one can find equally strange bedfellows as among the other interest groups. For example, similar positions can be identified among libertarians of both the right and the left (for example, the Cato Institute and *The Wall Street Journal's* editorial page on the libertarian right, the American Civil Liberties Union on the libertarian left), among some traditional conservatives and liberals, and so on. Indeed US immigration policy advocates have taken advantage of these overlapping perspectives to construct unusual left-right lobbying coalitions that promote the positions they hold in common about immigration policy, even as the members of such coalitions continue to struggle energetically against one another on most other issues.

Consider for example the National Immigration Forum, a Washington-based advocacy organization established in 1982 (as the National Forum on Immigration and Refugees) and from its inception heavily financed by the Ford Foundation, one of the largest foundations in the world and generally seen as left of center in political terms. The National Immigration Forum's founder and first president was Rick Swartz, a liberal/progressive immigration lawyer and advocate who previously had been active in promoting refugee status for migrants from Haiti. During 1982 and 1983 the leaders of the forum described the organization as nonadvocacy, a "big tent" designed to build understanding among those holding differing views of immigration policy.[79] However they quickly transformed it into a coalition of religious, ethnic, employer, union, and other organizations ranging from the left to the right in conventional political terms but united in advocating and lobbying for more expansive immigration policies and excluding from forum membership groups that did not favor such positions. The National Immigration Forum now describes itself as "the leading immigrant advocacy organization in the country with a mission to advocate for the value of immigrants and immigration to the nation."[80] According to a laudatory 1996 article in *Wired* magazine, after he left the National Immigration Forum, Swartz established his own Washington lobbying and consulting firm and has made a rather prosperous career of creating and advising other left-right coalitions focused on highly lobbied Washington issues, such as the North American Free Trade Agreement (in support) and US farm subsidies (in opposition).[81]

As of 2011 the Board of Directors[82] of the forum includes, among others, members from the United Food and Commercial Workers International Union, which represents hundreds of thousands of workers in industries such as meatpacking, poultry processing, and food-processing sectors that have been prominently reported as exploiting migrant workers;[83] the Coalition for Humane Immigrant Rights of Los Angeles ("at the forefront in the fight for immigrant and refugee rights in Los Angeles and across the state and nation" [84]); Jeb Bush Jr., son of the former Republican governor of Florida and chairman of Florida Hispanic Outreach "SunPAC"[85]; the bishop of the Roman Catholic Diocese of Sacramento; the American Nursery & Landscape Association ("the national voice of the nursery and landscape industry"[86]); two board members from the immigration bar, a former president and general counsel of the American Immigration Lawyers Association, who now heads the immigration practice at the seven-hundred-lawyer firm of Duane Morris,[87] and a second immigration lawyer at the large Washington law firm and lobbying firm Greenberg Traurig.[88] (Until recently the board also included a vice president of the US Chamber of Commerce (Randel K. Johnson), who is responsible for the chamber's advocacy on labor, immigration, and employee benefits issues pending before Congress and the federal agencies. [89])

Finally, though the empirical evidence shows that the politics of immigration historically has not followed partisan lines, there have been signs of increasing partisanship in recent years, accompanied by claims of partisan advantage for each side, which have been invoked in rather puzzling ways. During the highly charged and ultimately unsuccessful legislative push for the "comprehensive immigration reform" proposals put forward by the bipartisan pair of Senators John McCain and Edward Kennedy in 2007, political strategists from *both* parties were claiming that *their* party would gain politically from the bill's very substantial expansion of immigration. The argument on each side was that its party would capture disproportionate support from those voters who backed expanded immigration and also from the increased numbers of immigrants themselves once they naturalize, yet they would not lose support from other voters. In reality, no one knew then, or could have known, how these electoral politics would have played out over the years. Yet one thing is sure: *Both* parties could not logically have achieved the partisan gains they were being promised by their own members. In the two-party American political system, if one party gains votes, the other party loses votes.

Members of Congress may be forgiven if they repeatedly conclude that on the volatile issues of immigration, they face a "lose-lose" situation. While numerous interest groups lobby energetically and expensively for increased volumes of immigration, public opinion appears to be substantially opposed. The unhappy choice for politicians seems to be: (1) antagonize organized and well-funded organizations that provide substantial sources of the campaign finance now needed for reelection (TV, radio, and so on); or (2) antagonize large numbers of voters whose votes they need for reelection. The choice often comes down to the balance of such elements in the particular member's district and constituents.

Given the cacophony and lose-lose game they face, congressional legislative responses have often taken on the contradictory character of symbolic toughness accompanied by hidden unenforceability. A popular symbol of "toughness" on unauthorized immigration is the so-called "border fence" along the two-thousand-mile (three-thousand-kilometer) US-Mexico border—actually not a fence but instead a set of physical barriers concentrated in high-density border regions, especially where US and Mexican cities are essentially contiguous (as in San Diego/Tijuana; El Paso/Ciudad Juárez; Laredo/Nuevo Laredo; and so on). Some of the same US politicians most vigorously demanding such border "hardening" have also more privately supported measures that make immigration enforcement almost impossible, such as the restrictions placed upon employers seeking credible identification documents for job applicants. Other US politicians publicly call for vigorous enforcement while privately criticizing enforcement agencies on many grounds, sometimes in response to complaints from interest groups in their congressional districts or among their other supporters.

The ambiguity of such approaches to the problem mirrors a more general ambivalence that pervades the US politics surrounding immigration policy.[90] As noted earlier, there is little support among the public for expansionary *policies* on immigration: Expansion of immigration is seen as posing threats to the coherence and unity of an American society that is already turbulent enough, or as presenting unfair competition for employment and housing. On the other hand, many of those opposed to expansion of immigration share the numerous American narratives that paint a highly positive and sometimes romantic picture of *immigrants* to the United States—hardworking, family oriented, salt of the earth—evoking collective memories of ancestral migrants that often are part of American family lore.[91]

The key distinction here is between the macro and micro levels. At the macro level Americans are generally opposed to policies favoring large-scale immigration, yet at the micro level they are favorably disposed to the individual immigrants and their families and sympathetic to the struggles they face.

This ambivalence leads to a well-known strategy among activist groups and among some journalists who cover the subject. Those seeking to restrain immigration tend to emphasize aggregate numbers, and their argued negative impacts on wages, employment, housing, criminality, education, and other statistical indicators. Meanwhile those seeking more expansive immigration policies focus more on individual migrants and their families, emphasizing the hardships they face and the successes they achieve. These strategies stretch even to the framing of questions for public-opinion surveys on the subject; the authorship and funding sources of such surveys often seems to determine their outcomes.

Recent Attempts at "Comprehensive Immigration Reform"

In 2006 a legislative effort aimed at comprehensive immigration reform began under the leadership of Democratic Senator Edward Kennedy of

Massachusetts and Republican Senator John McCain of Arizona (later nominated as Republican presidential candidate). The "comprehensive" nature of this Kennedy-McCain bill—later called the Hagel-Martinez bill after two other senators who took over its sponsorship, Chuck Hagel (Republican, Nebraska) and Mel Martinez (Republican, Florida)—was based on its claims to deal in one piece of legislation with all elements of past policy failures, rather than via piecemeal reform as had become common. Special attention was paid to the weaknesses of the prior major overhaul of US immigration policy, the Immigration Reform and Control Act (IRCA) of 1986, which it is interesting to note had also been described as "comprehensive."

Proponents of the 2006 bill and its 2007 successor argued that to finally fix the "broken" immigration system, it would be necessary to:

- Legalize a substantial fraction of the estimated 11–12 million unauthorized migrants resident in the United States ("bring them out of the shadows"; "clear the slate");
- Establish effective means of identifying who was authorized to work in the United States; and
- Add on to the current immigration system large legal temporary-worker programs favored by employers of unauthorized migrants.

It is not possible here to provide a full account of the politics that led to the ultimate failure of this comprehensive immigration reform. For our purposes it is interesting to note that the bill's sponsors did not provide any estimates of the total numbers of additional temporary and permanent visas that it would have made available. According to a senior staff member of the 2007 bill's cosponsor Senator Hagel,[92] there actually was no attempt by the sponsors to make such a quantitative estimate. Instead, their goal was to assemble a package of provisions favored by differing groups of senators, which together would coalesce into the sixty-vote majority in the Senate required to overcome an expected filibuster.

In the absence of numerical estimates provided by the bill's sponsors, a set of wildly differing projections was produced by a variety of sources both governmental and private. The various totals ranged from additional immigration numbers of 24 million over ten years to 66 million over twenty years.

A 2006 workshop that addressed the wide range of such numerical estimates concluded that they differed variously in their core assumptions, used different data sources, included or excluded different categories of immigrants and visas, included or excluded the proposed visa categories that were numerically unlimited, and differed in estimating either the number of visas that would be available or the numbers that would actually be used.[93] The Congressional Research Service concluded that some of the bill's provisions were sufficiently ambiguous or opaque as to make it impossible to offer a credible numerical estimate of how many visas would result from its passage.[94] Readers will be aware of developments in this field that unfolded after this book went to press in early 2013.

Summary and Conclusions

The three member countries of the North American Free Trade Agreement have been characterized by large disparities in their trajectories of fertility and migration. These differences are most notable between the neighboring countries of the United States and Mexico. In recent years their fertility rates have been tending toward convergence, but highly visible disparities have, if anything, increased in the volume, direction, and character of migration patterns between them. (It would be interesting, but beyond our remit, also to consider the relationships of NAFTA to migration between Mexico and Canada, although until recently the volumes of such migration have been modest and well controlled.)

Meanwhile, the story of movements across the two-thousand-mile border between Mexico and the United states is an ongoing one, full of political conflict, ideological and interest-group contestation, and violence related to smuggling and trafficking in drugs, humans, and weapons. These issues seem very unlikely to fade away and indeed may become more intense in the near future.

Above all, the subject of Mexico–United States migration shows how fundamentally demographic events can be framed by political forces. These migratory movements also illustrate the relative impotence of both US and Mexican authorities to control events on the ground, constrained as they are by domestic political forces in both countries. Parallel to the increasingly emotive national politics of immigration reform is a separate world of local politics, such as those that have appeared at the state level in the United States; increasingly it is at these lower levels where the most heated conflicts over immigration are being fought.[95]

All that we can say in conclusion is that the subject of undocumented or unauthorized immigration from Mexico to the United States is an increasingly emotive and polarizing phenomenon, perceived very differently by US elites and the US public. It is too a phenomenon that now has persisted for more than a half century, despite repeated promises by both Mexican and US national leaders that it will be resolved by new policies focused on trade, investment, or enforcement. Depending upon one's perspective, this demonstrates either the inherently uncontrollable nature of immigration or the effective control of national policy by interest-group politics. It also points to the difficulties that politicians in both countries face whenever they seek to find a solution to this divisive issue. Of one thing we can be certain: As the French say, *La lutte continue*—"the struggle goes on."

Conclusion

Putting the Politics Back In

The extensive literature on the first demographic transition, initiated during the 1920s and 1930s, sought to explain the fertility declines that began in Europe in the eighteenth century primarily by reference to economic development. The more-recent literature on the second demographic transition, which addressed the onset and persistence of very low fertility levels in the 1990s and after, has been heavily cultural in character. The explanatory power of both perspectives is limited by their relative inattention to political elements, as compared to economic or cultural trends, which in very different ways have brought radically different societies to historically unprecedented levels of low fertility today.

As we have noted earlier, politics is that network of power relationships extending from the family to the neighborhood to the village to the region to the nation state and beyond it. It is in these networks of unequal actors that the linkage among economic forces and cultural practices are negotiated.

One way in which politics can be configured usefully in discussions of fertility decisions is in terms of Beck's hypothesis of the "Risk Society." Derived from changes in norms about gender roles in Europe, this framework has uses in other contexts as well. Potential migrants from Mexico and Central America to the United States assess risks in multiple ways: The risks of remaining in Mexican agricultural regions long characterized by poverty and unable to compete with agricultural products imported from north of the US-Mexico border under NAFTA; the risks of crossing the border illegally, both of apprehension and of falling prey to violence or fraud perpetrated by frontier smuggler networks and reportedly by some Mexican police officers; the risks of living underground lives once past the border; the risks of losing their land rights and the support of their families at home over time.

Chinese villagers making decisions about their family size face risks of a different character but make their own assessments, which the "risk hypothesis" helps to illuminate. Village elders govern the decisions of individual couples under Communism, just as they have done for centuries in China, but for decades now there also has been a state framework promoting the one-child family. The risks of violating this norm are substantial, and they involve political discussions and pressures on many levels, extending from remote villages to Beijing, with multiple bureaucratic points on the way.

The political collapse of the Soviet Union and the Warsaw Pact presented risks to young adults in Russia and eastern Europe that carried with them very material implications for decisions about family formation and childbearing. Responses to low fertility rates in Russia have included both rhetorical and financial inducements from the state, but to understand the effects of such policies we need to take into account the uncertainty faced by a population that has gone from a planned to a market economy.

Using this kind of analysis of risk and perceptions of risk provides us with an alternative to more-mechanistic views, such as that economic growth leads directly to a decline in fertility rates, or that the state can easily influence couples to increase their family size.

A focus on risk has an additional advantage. It enables us to avoid treating culture as somehow existing separately from politics, as if notions of the division of labor within the family or maternity or childbearing change independently of the way structures of family or political power operate. Ignoring the demographic significance of politics, or relegating it to a residual variable, simply makes no sense in the world in which we live.

Twenty years ago, the Office of Population Research at Princeton University framed an ambitious project—to chart the course and character of Europe's fertility decline since the early stages of the European industrial revolution. In its component national studies, the Princeton demographers adopted innovative measurements of the components of fertility that were as rigorous as the limited historical data allowed. They also tried to develop a set of testable hypotheses that could help refine what was known as the "theory" of the demographic transition, a set of historical generalizations that sought to account for the shift from high fertility and high mortality before industrialization to low fertility and low mortality after it.

The results emerging from the project were positive, including development and publication of best-practice data and analyses on the demographic history of European states. But the results turned out to be negative with respect to being able to provide economic explanations of fertility change over time. Indeed, in the Spanish and Russian cases, the surprising historical patterns of fertility decline uncovered by the Princeton project suggested that the most powerful factors affecting the patterns of fertility decline were cultural (as measured by language patterns) rather than economic or social. Commonalities in fertility decline were more prominent in regions and provinces with linguistic similarities than in regions or provinces with similar levels of economic social development.

This empirical outcome related to cultural patterns was a surprise to the group of researchers engaged in the European Fertility Study—and powerful evidence of the virtues of subjecting theoretical claims to the test of empirical evidence. It was also perhaps a disappointment to some who hoped for quantitative economic or social variables to emerge as the harbinger or catalyst of fertility decline. But it opened a door to moving population studies away from a partnership exclusively with economists and sociologists and, instead, to a more inclusive joint effort in which economics and sociology would play important roles but would incorporate important insights offered by others, including historians, political scientists, linguists, and anthropologists.

This book is in the tradition of that shift toward a broader range of perspectives on the origins of fertility decline, in this case specifically to include the political dimensions. Our aim has been to provide evidence that not only economic, social, and cultural factors but also the politics and public policies of recent history can help us understand demographic trends in measurable and demonstrable ways. This is not to claim that economic, social, or cultural factors are irrelevant; to the contrary. We argue instead that the force of these drivers is real but mediated by political institutions on many levels. Politics is about power, and power starts right at home. Families are not undifferentiated units of decision makers but places of contestation. So are neighborhoods and villages; so too are cities and suburbs. All are sites of political conflict and creativity. Ignoring them makes no sense at all when we try to unravel the puzzle of the widening spread of very low fertility that first appeared during the 1930s primarily in western Europe, and now can be found in a staggering diversity of settings ranging across the world—in Canada, Spain, Italy, Greece, Russia, Iran, South India, China, South Korea, Japan—and many others.

Only by acknowledging the power of political forces can we hope to move the discussion of population trends away solely from matters of technical and bureaucratic expertise and toward a vital exchange with those who work in political science, history, and the humanities. We have noted that demography is too important a matter to be left to the demographers alone. To ignore or diminish the high value of the many important products of demographic research would be absurd, of course. Our aim instead is to urge others to join demographic researchers in a creative partnership, without which many observers are likely to remain puzzled and alarmed at recent demographic trends and the threatening futures that some see them as portending.

The paradox here is that the technologies of population projection developed by demographers are at once the most reliable methods for anticipating important trends over the short-to-medium future, and at the same time methods that are subject to inevitable uncertainties that become magnified the longer they are extended into increasingly hazy futures. The most recent demographic projections produced by the UN Population Division, on which part of the discussion in this volume are based, represent a significant improvement in available methods for incorporating such uncertainties into long-range projections, that is, those that stretch out beyond a decade or two.

Interpreted correctly, these increasingly sophisticated demographic projections offer valuable indications that the path of future fertility rates in low-fertility countries plausibly may be modestly upward, rather than the fertility "death spiral" feared by some commentators. Similarly, understanding of the changing significance of chronological age as healthy life spans extend into later years provides insights into the ways in which the fixed age boundaries of measures such as the "old-age dependency ratio" can be misleading indicators of actual "dependency." A fuller discussion of these issues may be found in appendix B. Meanwhile objective analyses of the demographic effects of international migration illuminate both the limitations and potentials of alternative policy approaches to such migration.

In all of these, politics and policies have significant roles to play— both in affecting the demographic shifts that are under way and in framing flexible and constructive adaptations to the demographic changes that do occur. Taken together, better understanding of the most plausible future trends in fertility, of the changing meaning of "age dependency," and of the impacts of immigration provide a guide for the perplexed. The alternative is naive acceptance of increasingly apocalyptic fears about what are likely to be gradual changes in future population size, age structure, and composition in most countries.

Informed analysis is always preferable to uninformed rhetoric, which was and remains ubiquitous in many discussions of low fertility. Putting the politics back into the public discussion of population issues is informed citizenship, no more and no less.

Appendix A
UN Projections of Total Fertility
Rates for Selected Countries

In mid-2010 the United Nations Population Division released a new series of long-range projections of the total fertility rate by country. These fertility projections are based upon a new methodology that builds upon past UN projection techniques but incorporates new approaches designed to address some of the limitations of previous efforts.

A full discussion of the UN's new methods is available in a White Paper published on the UN Web site in November 2009,[1] and in a 2011 publication in the journal *Demography*.[2] Like the earlier UN projections, the 2010 projections follow a model of fertility change over three phases:

1. High and stable fertility rates that generally prevail before the onset of fertility declines related to demographic transition.
2. Transition of high fertility rates to replacement levels of fertility or below, over an extended period of years or decades.

3. Low fertility rates following the end of the demographic transition, often below replacement but tending toward recovery and oscillations around replacement levels.[3]

The revised UN methodology employs for the first time a probabilistic model that addresses some of the limitations of past UN projection models. In brief, these are as follows:

- Past UN projection models have been deterministic and hence did not allow for assessment of the uncertainties that inevitably affect any forward projections.
- Past UN projections for a given country in which fertility had not yet declined to replacement levels have been based upon a choice made by UN analysts as to which future trajectory of fertility decline is most likely to apply. The selected trajectory had to be chosen from a set of only three model trajectories of fertility decline (known as "Fast/Slow," "Slow/Slow," and "Fast/Fast"). The choice for each country was based on observations or expert knowledge about that country. These projections are therefore not fully country-specific, especially since subsequent analysis showed that the three model trajectories did not capture a full range of past variations in fertility declines among countries.
- Since the 1990s UN demographic projections have assumed that all countries' fertility trajectories will converge toward an ultimate TFR level of 1.85. Countries in which fertility had already declined to below-replacement levels were assumed to follow the most recently observed trajectory for a further five to ten years, and then to experience a linear and slow fertility increase (only 0.05 children per woman every five years) until the TFR reached 1.85. For countries with very low TFRs this meant that the 1.85 level would not be reached by the end of the projection period for these projections, which was then 2050.[4]

- The "High" and "Low" projection variants in the past have been based upon a simple and rather arbitrary assumption that each would depart from the "Medium" variant level by plus or minus half a child, that is, a TFR that is +0.5 or −0.5 of the "Medium" TFR. According to this assumption, this range is held constant, although the UN experts understood that it should be expected to increase over time with the greater uncertainty that necessarily arises over the decades of the projection period. As such these projection variants illustrate the sensitivity and the cumulative effect on demographic components that +/−0.5 child might have.

The new probabilistic fertility projection method developed by the UN builds upon the long-standing deterministic model but is designed to reduce some of these deficiencies. It is based upon some one hundred thousand repetitive projections or simulations for each country, which allow the outcomes to be affected by random variations and the experience of other countries in the past at similar fertility levels (that is, faster or slower change). These numerous simulations are then used to calculate a median projection trajectory for each country, accompanied by a statistically based "prediction interval" (both 95 percent and 80 percent prediction intervals are provided) which can be used as upper and lower bounds. The 80 percent prediction intervals often correspond to the previous +/−0.5 child alternates that defined the "High" and "Low" variants (which is now centered around the median). The new projections also do not "force" all countries' fertility projections to converge to 1.85 but instead allow them to reach subreplacement levels and in the long run to converge and fluctuate around replacement level.

The graphs that follow provide the results of these new UN projection methods for the total fertility rates of countries discussed in this book. A word of explanation is in order to clarify further the nature and utility of these graphs.

First, the projections go out to the year 2100, whereas the earlier UN projections ended at 2050. We recommend however that readers focus primary attention upon the next few decades, that is, up to 2050, since ninety years is well beyond a credible range for demographic projections.

Second, the "observed TFR" in each national graph provides the best estimates of the actual fertility rates as measured by the TFR from 1950 to 2010.

Third, following the year 2010 the forward-looking graphs for each country provide a wide array of possible TFR trajectories in a graphic format that facilitates easy comparison. These include:

- An illustrative set of a sample of the one hundred thousand probabilistic projections calculated for each country. The cluster of faint and erratic lines provides useful graphic illustrations of the uncertainties that underlie the future as illustrated by such probabilistic projections.
- A median projection (the heavy solid line continuing from the estimated TFR for 2010), which might be considered the "best" projection trajectory that can be calculated from the large number of probabilistic projections simulated.[5]
- Estimated "prediction intervals" (PI), calculated statistically from the large number of probabilistic projections. The "PI 80" estimates (the heavy dashed lines above and below the median projection) provide an illustration of plausible upper and lower bounds among the many projection alternatives, excluding the 10th and 90th percentiles of the distribution of projection outcomes. The "PI 95" estimates (the dotted lines above and below the PI 80 lines) provide a wider range of uncertainty by excluding only the 2.5th and 97.5th percentiles.
- Finally, to facilitate comparison with its previous projection methodologies, the UN also graphs the $+/-0.5$ children assumptions that previously were used to define the "High" and "Low" variants (the light dot-dash lines).

How should these sophisticated UN projections of future fertility rates best be understood? The first and most important caveat is that they are projections, not forecasts, and like all projections are based upon assumptions. For each country the trajectory of past fertility rates has been calculated or estimated up to 2010, and then a range of plausible future trends has been calculated based on the key assumption that in the future most countries will follow paths of fertility change that have been modeled on the basis of previous empirical experience in other countries.

In short, these new projections are calculated under a probabilistic model designed to incorporate at least some of the uncertainties inherent in any forward-looking calculations. The fertility data used are the best available. The projection techniques are state-of-the-art. The projections provide a median summary of thousands of projection runs for each country, accompanied by two bands that encompass 80 and 95 percent of the multiple projection calculations.

However, the recently revised UN projections include a significant change in the assumed level of fertility to which all countries tend to converge. Instead of an end point of a total fertility rate of 1.85, which was assumed by the prior long-range "Medium" projections by the UN, the total fertility rates in the new projections are assumed to converge and fluctuate around the replacement level, that is, about 2.1 children per woman. This modified assumption can have important implications for numerical outcomes of the projections, especially so in the out-years of the projection period, that is, the last half of the twenty-first century. It also is an assumption that has raised some controversy among prominent demographers. The former director of the UN Population Division argues that "there appears to be little, if any, empirical or theoretical rationale for the widely cited UN projections to assume convergence to replacement level fertility." Instead he sees this assumption as "demographically convenient. . . . The assumption leads to population stabilization, thereby avoiding demographically and politically problematic outcomes."[6] He notes that the new UN projections, like those in the past, do provide higher and lower projection alternatives to the "median" projection. However it is common for journalists and policy makers to ignore the reality of a wide range of plausible projections and instead to embrace the single trajectory of the median projection (or the "Medium" variant in the previous projections). The professional dissonance about such matters, coupled with the rising uncertainties for the out-years in any long-term projection, provides further support for the recommendation that the primary focus in interpreting the UN projections should be upon the nearer-term projection periods, that is, up to about 2050.

None of this is to say that these (or any other) projections represent highly reliable forecasts of the future of fertility and population in 2050 or 2100. Nothing is or can be certain about the future—and especially about the long-term future. What these projections do represent, however, is the best available source of forward-looking assessments, of plausible futures about fertility rates, accompanied by informative bands of statistical uncertainty that appropriately become wider as the projection proceeds forward from the present. As noted earlier, the thick central line is the median projection that may be interpreted as the "best" projection trajectory. However, to minimize any undue certainty in interpretations of this median projection, it is surrounded by a "cloud" of faint projection lines reflecting a small sample of the array of probabilistic projections on which the median was based, and by upper and lower dashed and dotted lines reflecting the 80 and 95 percent prediction intervals in the hundred thousand independent projections undertaken for each country.

If we accept the median projection trajectory as reflecting the "best" forward look for each of the countries for which graphs are presented, we can see that the new UN projection techniques are suggesting that for countries in which fertility has already declined below replacement levels, there most likely will be a return over a period of decades to replacement fertility or something either just below or just above it. For countries such as India and Mexico, in which fertility rates have been declining but are not yet below replacement, the models suggest a continuation of fertility decline to levels somewhat below replacement by 2050, but nothing like the recent very low levels of the Spanish or Italian cases. Of course, these comments relate to the median; other trajectories such as those illustrated in the cloud of surrounding probabilistic projections in each graph are also entirely plausible.

The UN demographers are saying that, on a probabilistic projection model based on the best available data, the very low fertility rates being seen today in countries such as Japan or Germany are more likely than not to be a poor guide to fertility levels in 2050.

Nothing is certain, but the UN's careful and sophisticated modeling efforts suggest that high anxieties about sustained levels of very low fertility, or of declines to even lower levels, are misplaced—or put another way, informed discussion of fertility in the future should not be based upon extreme projections. These sober assessments are in stark contrast with many public pronouncements predicting extreme demographic outcomes.

These data suggest that the classic conceptualization of the "demographic transition" may continue to be useful, with the addition of a below-replacement "dip" in Europe at the end of the twentieth century, and in other regions in the first decades of the twenty-first century. Given the relatively slow pace of demographic change, a "dip" in this case may be understood to extend over a period of a few decades rather than a few years. Over the longer historical period of several centuries since the eighteenth century—the focus of the "demographic transition"—the overall pattern is still one of a shift from a demographic regime of high fertility / high mortality equilibrium to one of low fertility / low mortality equilibrium. The very low fertility of the period 1980–2000 or so in the developed world and of 1990–2010 in a number of Asian countries may turn out to represent, therefore, an exceptional "moment" in this overall replacement of one demographic regime by another. After all, the postwar baby boom of 1946–1965 was of similarly short duration. Inflections matter, but underlying patterns can persist nonetheless. On the other hand, it is also possible that a below-replacement demographic regime will become a common phenomenon, requiring a modification in the theory of the demographic transition. Only time will tell.

Interestingly, the bands of fertility projections above and below the median but within the "projection interval" lines in the new UN projections may be interpreted as the space where population policies can act in important ways. We have argued that fertility changes, alongside all demographic developments, have an important political dimension to them. The cloud of thousands of alternative projections produced by the UN offers a visual representation of the domain in which politics and policies may matter in significant ways. The availability of these probabilistic fertility projections does not, however, mean that the mix of factors influencing fertility decisions has become more stable. Uncertainty remains with us in this domain, whether we like it or not.

Perhaps the best way to characterize these data is to see them as describing plausible futures. They are plausible because they are based on empirical data on fertility trends over the past two to three decades. They represent the best that can be done in imagining the future of fertility levels. The assumption that leads most of the median lines to converge around the replacement level with an upward trend is precisely that: an assumption. It may turn out to be untrue. But in any event we have substantial reason to be skeptical about the injection of the language of fear into an already highly charged political environment on the basis of mathematical models that necessarily depend upon the assumptions on which they rest. This is the best demographers can do. The best all of us can do is to accept the inherent uncertainties and to avoid eclipsing reason by rhetoric.[7]

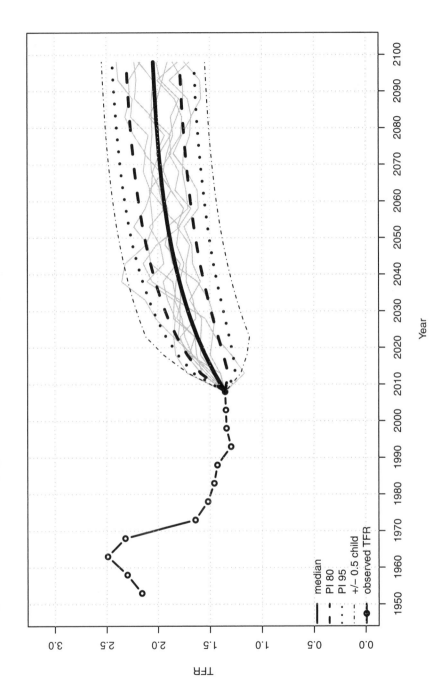

Fig. A.1. Germany: Observed and Projected Fertility, 1950–2100

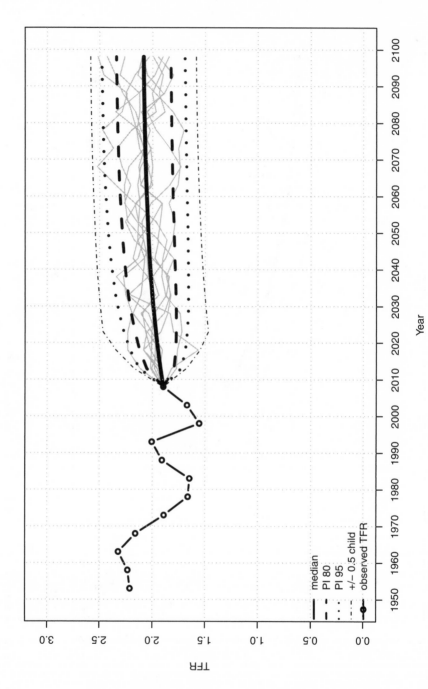

Fig. A.2. Sweden: Observed and Projected Fertility, 1950–2100

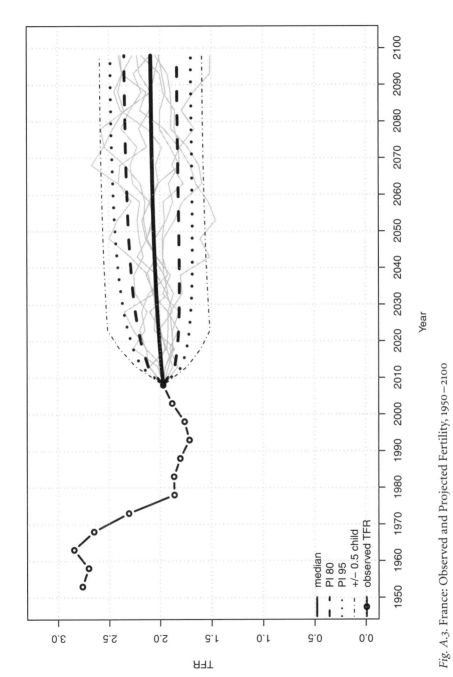

Fig. A.3. France: Observed and Projected Fertility, 1950–2100

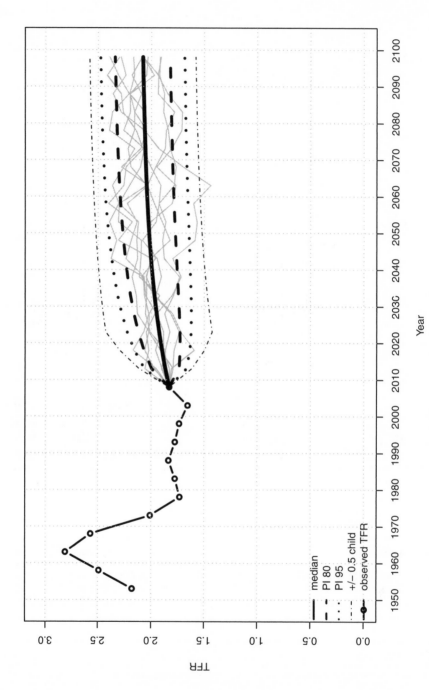

Fig. A.4. United Kingdom: Observed and Projected Fertility, 1950–2100

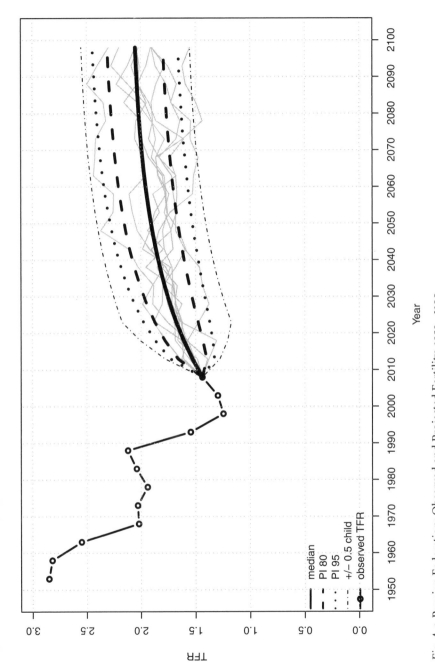

Fig. A.5. Russian Federation: Observed and Projected Fertility, 1950–2100

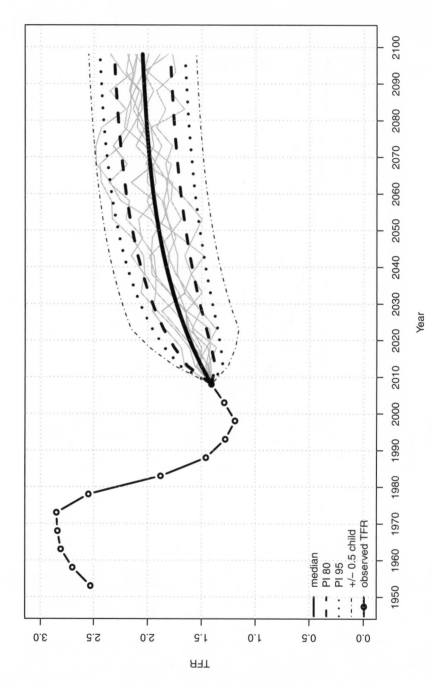

Fig. A.6. Spain: Observed and Projected Fertility, 1950–2100

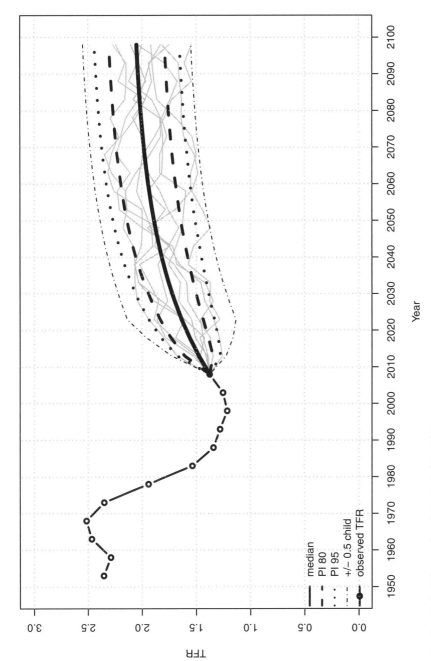

Fig. A.7. Italy: Observed and Projected Fertility, 1950–2100

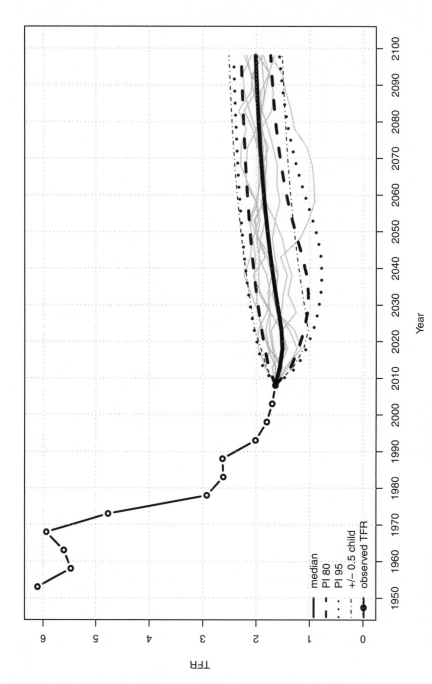

Fig. A.8. China: Observed and Projected Fertility, 1950−2100

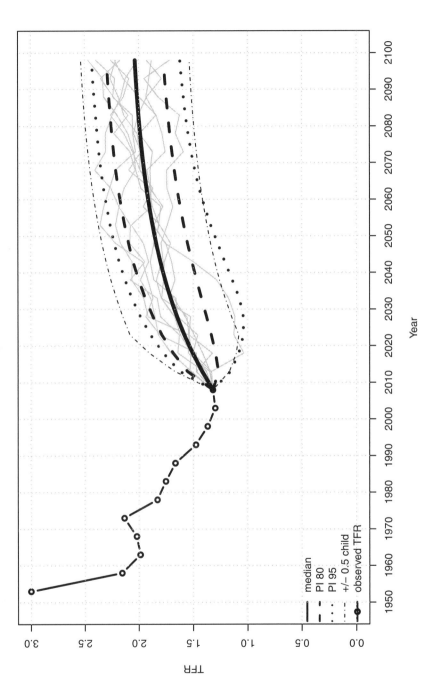

Fig. A.9. Japan: Observed and Projected Fertility, 1950–2100

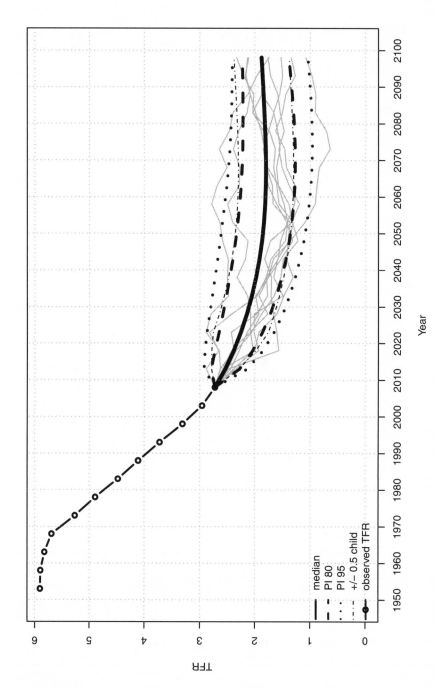

Fig. A.10. India: Observed and Projected Fertility, 1950–2100

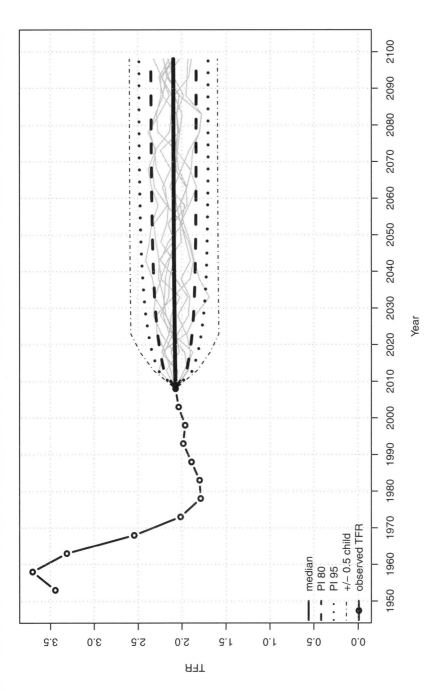

Fig. A.11. United States of America: Observed and Projected Fertility, 1950–2100

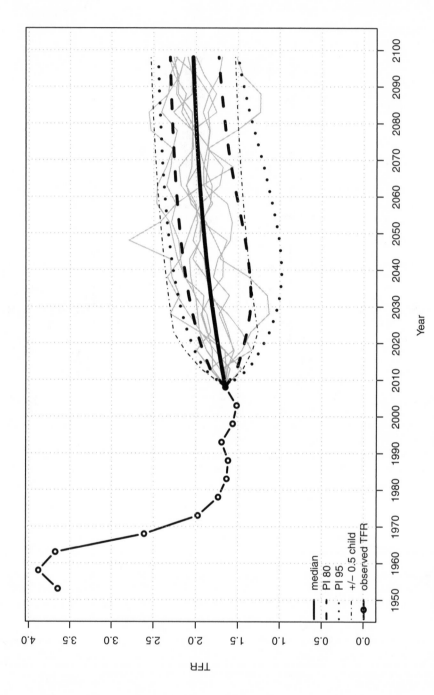

Fig. A.12. Canada: Observed and Projected Fertility, 1950–2100

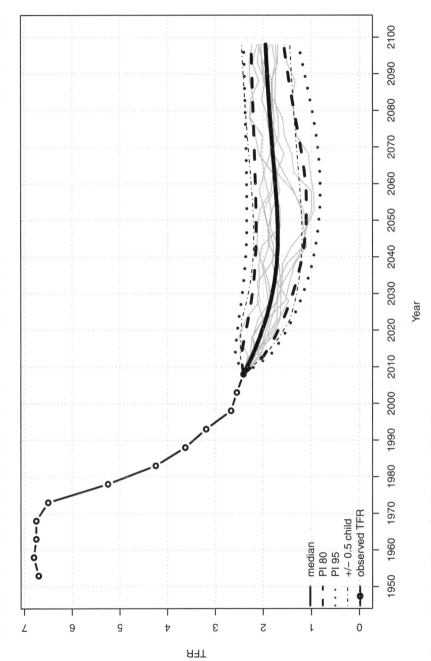

Fig. A.13. Mexico: Observed and Projected Fertility, 1950–2100

Appendix B

Effects of and Adaptations to Changing Demographic Composition: A User's Guide

Michael S. Teitelbaum

This appendix addresses some of the primary effects of low fertility upon demographic composition and of feasible adaptations to such changes.[1] These complex issues are essential elements in our understanding of the unfolding history of population trends and of the implications of possible future trends. This discussion is intended to inform and clarify the material we present in the various chapters of this book.

Political argument ranges widely in this field, and much of it seems immune to evidence and occasionally to reason itself. Policy makers in low-fertility countries have no such luxury. They face a sobering task. Theirs is the business of finding instruments to help a population and a polity adjust to a future that has few historical antecedents. On many of the concrete issues that emerge, such as those related to public pensions, health care, and immigration patterns, for instance, the policy decisions they make really do matter. They matter not only in the sense that they may have impacts upon the course of future demographic developments, but also as to whether they contribute to sensible adaptations to demographic change and to minimizing political conflicts and negative economic trends that may ensue. Let us consider, therefore, a number of ways in which we can understand the issues with which policy makers and other informed citizens in low-fertility countries struggle when they reflect on population change and the future well-being and prosperity of their people.

Population Dynamics:
Aggregate Growth and Changing Demographic Composition

Demographic forces have affected economic and political trends in the past, and in the future can be expected to continue to do so. Much of the emphasis has been upon the argued impacts of gross population size and growth rates upon the economy. It is true, of course, that growth or decline in a country's population might affect the aggregate size of its GDP, but this tells us rather little about the effects upon the economic well-being of that country's population or the stability of its political system and government. For example, rapid population growth might translate (other things being equal) into GDP increase via growth in aggregate demand and labor supply, but in a country with limited land and other resources, GDP per capita could at the same time decrease while economic inequalities could rise. Alternatively, a larger or denser population in a sparsely populated country or region with ample resources might facilitate efficiencies and economies of scale that would tend to raise both GDP and per capita economic well-being. The economic effects of population growth and decline therefore depend heavily upon the context in which they take place.

While the aggregate size and growth rate of a population can have significant effects, so too can changes in its demographic *composition* that are more subtle than size and growth. Among such changes, shifts in age composition that follow from sustained low fertility have rightly attracted the most attention in recent years. Other aspects of demographic composition may also prove important in some countries, including sex composition and cultural composition.

Age Composition

In countries with low mortality, it is the level of fertility that is usually the dominant driver in changing age composition.[2] Societies in which fertility recently has declined from previously high levels often experience a virtuous cycle known as the "demographic dividend." This is a time-limited and transitional window of opportunity that enables accelerated economic and human development.[3] During this transitional period there is an increase in the proportion of the population of "working age," which, if there is effective demand for such labor, increases both economic output per capita, tax revenues, and government savings. There is a parallel reduction in the "youth dependency ratio," which moderates growth in demand for government services, such as education, that would otherwise have increased more rapidly, thereby allowing governments to invest in productivity-enhancing measures, such as higher levels and higher quality of education. Families with fewer children also can save more, thereby adding to national savings or investing more of their own resources in their children's education and health and increasing their "quality," their future economic productivity, and their contribution to national economic advance.

Eventually, though, the proportion in older cohorts begins to rise as the young adult groups age. This subsequent shift in the age structure is often referred to as "demographic aging" or "population aging," a topic that has recently stimulated worries among economic pundits and politicians concerned about its argued negative effects on the economy. The primary concern is that demographic aging produces a rising tide of "aged dependents" who need to be supported by taxes paid by working-age cohorts that are growing less rapidly. Such concerns have often been exaggerated, and some treatments have been frankly alarmist. Part of this may be an unintentional effect of terminology: In English and other languages, applying an individual concept such as "aging" to upward shifts in the age structure of a large population tends to conflate the individual-level effects of aging with the collective attributes of a shift in the relative size of age cohorts ("demographic aging").

There is a long intellectual tradition of disputes about this phenomenon, in which frailty—national, societal, cultural—is attributed to this collective concept of "aging." It has been especially visible in French intellectual circles, going back to the nineteenth century when some attributed the national catastrophe of the Franco-Prussian War to

France's early fertility decline, coming before those of Germany and the United Kingdom—a perspective that we have elsewhere termed "strategic demography."[4] Later, French analysts, and especially a small number of intellectuals led by Alfred Sauvy,[5] pointed to the "demographic aging" that resulted from the early French fertility decline as a source of France's declining power and prosperity during the late-nineteenth and twentieth centuries. For example:

> The decline of the French Navy [during the later nineteenth century] was more severe than in other countries. Under the influence of population aging, the French Government and Parliament subsidized the Navy's sailing ships while other countries were adopting steam-powered craft.[6]

> The terrible failure of 1940, more moral than material, must be linked to this dangerous sclerosis. We saw all too often, during the occupation, old men leaning wearily towards the servile solution, at the time that young were taking part in the national impulse towards independence and liberty. This crucial effect of our senility, is it not a grave warning?[7]

> An aging society is characterized by "old people, living in old houses, ruminating about old ideas."[8]

Whatever the merits of these claims, the primary concern about rising *old-age dependency* is that it produces unsustainable increases in the costs of public pensions and health care—unsustainable because they must be supported by taxes paid by "working age" cohorts that are growing more slowly or declining, resulting in a lower ratio of productive workers per unproductive/dependent persons receiving pensions and health care from the state. These effects might be amplified by the rising costs of health care for which the elderly have greater need, coupled with smaller families' lesser ability to provide family-based elder care leading to more demand for state-supported care.

It also is common to hear forecasts of looming *labor shortages* in societies with low or very low fertility. These arise from gradual replacement of expanding "working age" cohorts with nongrowing or even smaller cohorts that predictably follow fertility declines.

Concerns have also been raised that demographic aging will lead to *shortages of capital* for investment. Such concerns are based upon the "life-cycle theory of consumption and saving" associated with Franco Modigliani and his colleagues, which asserts that growing cohorts at older ages, who as working-age adults had been the primary source of capital for investment, will begin to "dis-save" by spending down their savings to support their (nonproductive) retirement, which itself will be lengthened by increases in the number of years of life expectancy postretirement.[9]

Finally, additional concerns have been raised that demographic aging implies *reduced societal innovation and vigor.* The assumption here is that the characteristics of more "elderly" populations are similar to those of more-elderly individuals: less energetic, less nimble, less open to new ideas and technologies, generally less dynamic and more boring. The warnings expressed by Sauvy and his followers from the 1940s into the 1980s reflect such worries in evocative language.

All of these concerns contain some worthwhile insights that warrant thoughtful attention. There is no doubt at all that fertility declines imply gradual shifts in the proportion of a population in different age categories; the faster and lower fertility falls, the more rapid and substantial the shift in age composition. Fertility declines during the past half century have been more rapid, and sustained fertility rates lower, than during the previous century. This in turn implies that many societies are moving into uncharted demographic territory, especially with respect to age composition, and hence our understanding based upon demographic history provides only hazy insights into the future.

Yet all of the concerns just outlined also are themselves based on historical experiences that may not prove to be accurate guides to the future. One fundamental problem is that the meanings of chronological age in the future cannot be accurately inferred from the past. Yet we continue to define old-age dependency using unchanging age categories, notwithstanding ample evidence that the meanings of these categories also are changing relatively rapidly. Persons aged 65 and over are defined as "aged dependent," although this 65-year boundary was established in various countries during the 1930s, 1940s, and 1950s as the primary eligibility criterion for public pensions. Since then life expectancy at age 65 has risen substantially. Moreover the proportions of those over 65 who are really physically dependent have declined, as have the proportion of workforces engaged in heavy physical labor in low fertility countries. A countervailing trend is also important to recognize—that over the same period the real costs of health care have been increasing substantially.

In the face of these very substantial changes in the underlying realities, why have most discussions of old-age dependency continued to use the boundary age of 65 and over? In part this rigidity is due to the understandable desire to be able to compare age structures over time and across societies. In part it is due to vigorous political opposition to any proposed increases in the eligibility ages for public pensions. Yet we may be misleading ourselves by carefully calculating long-term trends in Old-Age Dependency Ratios (OADR) based upon age boundaries that are held constant even though we know that the underlying physical and medical boundaries are shifting in substantial ways.

Conventional measures of old-age dependency are based on the distribution of the population according to chronological age, that is, the number of years lived since birth. Sanderson and Scherbov conclude that chronological age provides measures of demographic aging that are comparable across nations and time but that they have "not reflected reality" in that "aging is not only about the fact that people in a population are, on average, older. It also means that these older people are healthier and have longer remaining life expectancies than their earlier counterparts."[10] As but one indicator, consider trends in life expectancy at age 65: In the period 1970–2002, life expectancy at age 65 increased about 1.6 years per decade in Australia, Italy, and western Germany, and by 2.3 years per decade in Japan.[11]

For this reason they believe that in the interest of understanding real trends in old-age dependency, measures based on chronological age should be accompanied by alternative measures based on a concept of "prospective age." This "assigns ages to people on the basis of their remaining life expectancies in a reference year, not on the number of years they have already lived," and leads to an additional indicator of old-age dependency they call the Prospective Old-Age Dependency Ratio

(POADR). Unlike the traditional OADR, this measure takes into account changes in life expectancy at older ages, replacing the unchanging boundary between "adulthood" and "old age" of 65 years (chronological age) used in the OADR to a potentially rising Old-Age Threshold, defined as the age at which remaining life expectancy first falls below 15 years. The Prospective Old-Age Dependency Ratio is calculated as the ratio of the number of people above this potentially changing Old-Age Threshold age to the number aged from 20 years up to this Old-Age Threshold age.

Put another way, the conventional version of the Old-Age Dependency Ratio (OADR) is defined as the ratio of persons 65 and older to persons 20–64, that is:

$$\text{OADR} = \frac{\text{persons 65 and over}}{\text{persons 20–64}}$$

whereas their Prospective Old-Age Dependency Ratio (POADR) sets the boundaries of the categories at the "Old-Age Threshold," that is, the age at which remaining life expectancy becomes less than 15 years:

$$\text{POADR} = \frac{\text{persons older than the Old-Age Threshold}}{\text{persons aged from 20 upto the Old-Age Threshold}}$$

If the beginning of "old age" is thus defined as when remaining life expectancy drops below 15 years rather than the constant of 65 years, the resulting alternative ratio of "dependency" can be quite different depending on the mortality rates in different countries. For more-developed regions, the OADR increases from 25.1 to 47.0 between 2005 and 2045, but the POADR increases from 18.2 to 25.7. Both increase over the projection period, but the conventional indicator increases by 87 percent while the prospective indicator increases by 41 percent.[12]

One appropriate concern with using remaining life expectancy rather than the fixed chronological age of 65 is that increasing life expectancies at older ages might be accompanied by increasing disabilities and hence would not accurately reflect additional years of potential productivity. In a 2011 working paper, Sanderson and Scherbov go on to consider this possibility by a separate adjustment of the conventional old-age dependency ratio ("Adult Disability Dependency Ratio"), which takes severe disabilities into account. Their analysis suggests that "life expectancies without disabilities at age 65 in high income OECD countries are likely to increase by around 2.7 years between 2005–10 and 2045–50. Proportions of 60+ populations with disabilities are likely to be only marginally higher in 2045–50 than in 2005–10. We also show that the speed of increase of the Adult Disability Dependency Ratio is around one-fifth as fast as the conventional old age dependency ratio."[13]

These suggested additions to our measures of old-age dependency warrant further analysis and testing before they can viewed as robust and credible. However, such analyses may provide useful insights into the ways in which conventional measures of old-age dependency may be insensitive to real changes in "real" dependency, and in this way may distort our understanding of the real impacts of demographic aging.

OTHER CONCERNS ABOUT DEMOGRAPHIC AGING

Although demographic aging and its implications have been the primary concern of those expressing alarm about the effects of low fertility, some have also expressed worries about impending shortages of labor, shortages of capital, and waning societal vigor and innovativeness. Each of these concerns deserves at least brief consideration.

SHORTAGES OF LABOR

There are concerns that sustained low fertility will inevitably lead to labor shortages. Indeed, it is common to hear employers who find it increasingly difficult to recruit at the levels of remuneration they are used to offering describing these experiences as evidence of labor shortages.

In neoclassical economics, rising wages are understood as part of the normal operation of market forces. True labor shortages can occur over the long term only in special cases, since labor markets normally would adjust to any short-term insufficiencies in labor supply with rises in wages, and these in turn would lead to more labor-force participation, capital investment in labor-saving technologies that would not be warranted if wages were lower, and resulting rises in productivity. It is evident that most low-fertility societies have large reserve labor forces, that is, the large unemployed and underemployed populations in much of Europe and the United States; the underemployed in China; countries in which large fractions retire in their fifties or early sixties; and countries (for example, Japan) still experiencing low female labor-force participation. How long such adjustments would take is a matter of dispute. With respect to unemployment, Keynes's critique of the neoclassical school is that adaptation may take a very long time indeed, and that in the long term we are all dead.

CAPITAL SHORTAGES

Some argue that aging populations save less and hence lead to shortages of the investment capital needed for increasing economic prosperity. These views often rely upon the "life cycle model of saving," in which individuals behave rationally by saving most heavily during their prime income-earning ages, knowing that they will "dis-save" when they retire and become "dependent."

The assumptions of the life cycle model of savings are based upon theoretical interpretations that have increasingly come into conflict with empirical evidence, especially in Europe and Japan. This departure of actual behavior from theory may be driven by higher-than-anticipated interest in intergenerational bequests, which seem to account for between 50 and 80 percent of the total wealth accumulation of individuals and families—at the higher end of this range in western Europe and Japan and at the lower in the United States.[14] In addition there are some indications that the life cycle model of savings at different ages does not seem to operate in the same way in the Asian countries that are experiencing the most rapid increases in the proportions 65 and over, such as Japan.[15]

Likely saving and "dis-saving" behavior among the "aged" of the future (however we define them) are very difficult to anticipate. As remaining life expectancy is extended, those entering into the aged category may experience strong incentives to work longer than earlier generations, to save more, and even to continue to save (or to "dis-save" at a slower rate than in the past) after retirement. Once again we find ourselves in uncharted territory as to the impact of unprecedented demographic patterns.

Though Alfred Sauvy's aphorism of "old people, living in old houses, ruminating about old ideas" offers a memorable portrayal of a society experiencing demographic aging, there actually is little evidence to support the notion that societies with "older" age compositions are less vigorous and innovative. France's relative military and economic decline in the nineteenth century had more to do with political and military developments than with French demography. There are numerous empirical examples of countries with high median ages but effective political and economic leadership that have been both innovative and successful in economic terms. Obvious examples would include Germany, Sweden, Norway, and Switzerland. The danger here is unwarranted elision from the individual to the collective level—ascribing characteristics arguably common among older individuals to societies with "older" age compositions.

Some Real Challenges

Overall, then, considerable skepticism is in order in assessing casual claims about the inevitability of negative effects resulting from the demographic aging that results from fertility declines. Yet demographic aging does pose some real challenges.

PENSION SYSTEMS

The most obvious of these relate to so-called Pay-As-You-Earn (PAYE) public pensions systems that depend upon financial transfers from the working population to those in retirement. As the ratio declines of workers paying taxes to support such pension systems to retirees receiving pension payments, the tax burdens upon the former can become very large—other things being equal. A second obvious example is anticipated increases in expenditures on health care, which is more heavily used by older people than by younger.

However "other things" are not fixed and constant, but instead are subject to change and are much affected by politics and policy. For PAYE pension systems, the effects of demographic aging will predictably be far more powerful in countries with policies favoring pension income-replacement rates that are high, ages for pension eligibility that are low relative to remaining life expectancy, and limited encouragement of alternative sources of retirement income.

Among countries with low fertility rates, there is much variation along these lines. One analysis concludes that the public pension systems of continental Europe are most vulnerable to the impacts of demographic aging, especially in countries such as France, Germany, and Italy. Meanwhile different pension policies in other countries, such as the United States, United Kingdom, and Canada have made them less vulnerable to demographic aging trends, primarily because public pension benefits are less generous (especially for those with higher earnings), require higher ages for pension eligibility, and include incentives that result in retirees having other sources of retirement income.[16] For health-care expenditures, the larger challenges affect a different set of countries, especially those in which policies to contain health-care costs have been weak. The most notable of these is the United States, which has so far failed to embrace effective cost-containment measures for its exceptionally expensive health-care system.

Political leaders face strong opposition to modifying the terms of public pension provision, as may be seen in recent controversies in France, Greece, and elsewhere, and to imposing cost-containment upon health care, as may be seen in the fractious and decades-old debate over health-care reform in the United States. For this reason policy action to modify social institutions such as pensionable age, pension replacement rates, and health-care provision often have lagged well behind increases in remaining life expectancies. In countries in which the politics lead to policy stalemate or overly sluggish adjustments, there will almost certainly be serious problems as the proportions of the "aged dependent" increase.

SEX COMPOSITION

Another shift in population composition—in the male/female ratio at different ages—is visibly underway in a few important countries and hence warrants at least brief mention here. The countries involved are mostly Asian, and include, for example, China, South Korea, and India. All show evidence of strong cultural preferences among parents for sons as compared with daughters. If fertility rates are low and these son preferences are acted upon, the result can be unusually high ratios of male to female births. As these cohorts of newborns age into young adulthood over a period of two decades, there can be significant "marriage squeezes," in which the number of males seeking wives exceeds the number of women seeking husbands, at least at conventional ages of marriage for males and females that are themselves culturally defined.[17]

A number of social adaptations are possible in response to such marriage squeezes. These include importation of brides (which has already occurred in rural South Korea); expansion of conventional age differentials between grooms and brides, as men defer marriage and seek brides from younger cohorts; expanded proportions of single-headed households; expanded numbers of young males involved in sex-related crimes and prostitution markets;[18] or substantial numbers of disgruntled young unmarried males who seek to emigrate or are subject to recruitment for violent or otherwise destabilizing activities. It is also possible that, as has already been seen in South Korea, there will be a weakening over time of the culturally defined son preferences that currently are so apparent in the fertility data for other Asian countries, such as China and India.

CULTURAL COMPOSITION

There are many countries with long-standing tensions and competition among culturally defined groups. In such settings fertility declines can become politically volatile if they are more rapid among some groups than others and therefore can result in significant shifts in the distribution of such groups in the population. A list of such categories might include:

- Nationality;
- Language;
- Race;
- Ethnicity;
- Clans, tribes, castes;
- Religion (including sectarian divisions within religions, such as Sunni and Shia in Islam).

The existential fears that may result can translate into political and economic instability. The salience of such differential declines in fertility depends heavily upon the particularities of national histories and ideologies, along with the way such issues are reflected in political discourse. A list of elements that may exacerbate such tensions include:

- A history of external rule by an empire;
- Historical conflicts along lines of religion, for example, in the Balkans, Kashmir;
- Conflicts among divergent sects of the same religious group (for example, Sunni, Shia);
- Political domination by minority groups (for example, in Syria, Bahrain, Rwanda, Burundi, Lebanon);
- A history of slavery, indentured labor, racism (for example, in Sri Lanka, Uganda, United States);
- Historical or contemporary conflicts with neighboring countries that have mixed ethnic, religious, or national populations (for example, in Kosovo, Greece/Turkey/Cyprus, Israel, Iran/Iraq/Syria);
- High levels of cultural homogeneity and national solidarity (for example, in Japan, South Korea, China);
- High levels of cultural heterogeneity coupled with a history of conflictual and separatist tendencies (for example, in India, Belgium, Afghanistan, former USSR);
- Cultural/political ideology that is exclusive (for example, the German *Volk*) versus inclusive (for example, the French *citoyen*); related to this are legal principals based upon *jus soli* or *jus sanguinis*;

- A political history of class consciousness or populism;
- Monarchical/hereditary rule seen as illegitimate by significant portions of the population.

Under some circumstances of long-standing competition and tension among such groups, sustained differentials in demographic growth, and/or international influxes that increase the size of certain groups, may lead to changes in demographic composition that are politically salient and that tend toward political instability. There are obvious examples of this phenomenon, such as in Lebanon, Israel, Afghanistan, and in many countries of sub-Saharan Africa. Public opinion about such compositional shifts may also vary based on whether relative demographic growth or decline is due to different rates of indigenous growth or to international migration. It is worth noting, however, that some intellectual perspectives tend to ignore or minimize the importance of differences among cultural groups, as well as the significance of whether increments to them are imported or homegrown. This perspective, visible in some writings in economics, is overly abstract and rationalistic; it ignores the often irrational but passionate realities of competition along cultural lines that prevail in many settings.

The conclusion that follows from this discussion is that *demography is not destiny*, and that *policy responses to demographic change can matter a great deal*. Changes in demographic composition per se may not pose huge risks to future economic and political prospects, but policies that ignore or fail to adapt to these trends do. Once again, real understanding of the implications of low fertility requires that these political and policy elements be included in the discussion.

Notes

ONE Globalization and Demography

1. Jagdish Bhagwati, *In Defense of Globalization* (Oxford and New York: Oxford University Press, 2004).

2. Barbara Adam, Ulrich Beck, and Joost van Loon, *The Risk Society and Beyond* (London: Sage, 2000), pp. 6–8.

3. Angus Maddison, *The World Economy: A Millennial Perspective* (Paris: OECD, 2001), pp. 95–100.

4. World Trade Organization, *Understanding the WTO: The GATT Years From Havana to Marrakesh* (Geneva: World Trade Organization, 2009); available online at http://www.wto.org/English/thewto_e/whatis_e/tif_e/fact4_e.htm.

5. Ibid.

6. Source: United Nations, *The Millennium Report: Globalization*, http://www.un.org/cyberschoolbus/briefing/globalization/. The UN source cited here states "more than US$1.5 billion" (for the second item in the list) but this is evidently a typographical error that should have read "US$1.5 trillion"; as written it would have represented a 90 percent decline from 1973 to the present. Other sources estimate daily foreign exchange turnover at $1.9 trillion (the *Economist*) to nearly $4.0 trillion (the Bank for International Settlements). See *International Business Times*, "What is Foreign Exchange (Forex)?" 11 February, 2012; available online at http://au.ibtimes.com/articles/110821/20110210/what-is-foreign-exchange-currency-conversion-financial-markets-forex-foreign-exchange-markets.htm.

7. Office of Immigration Statistics, Department of Homeland Security, *Yearbook of Immigration Statistics: 2008* (Washington, DC: Department of Homeland Security, 2009), table 1; available online at http://www.dhs.gov/ximgtn/statistics/publications/

LPR08.shtm. See also Adam McKeown, "Global Migration, 1846–1940," *Journal of World History* 15, no. 2 (June 2004), pp. 155–89.

8. United Nations, Department of Economic and Social Affairs, Population Division, *International Migration Report 2006: A Global Assessment* (New York: United Nations, 2009), p. 1, table 3; available online at http://www.un.org/esa/population/publications/2006_MigrationRep/report.htm.

9. Hania Zlotnik, "International Migration and Development," 65th session of the United Nations General Assembly, Ninth Coordination Meeting on International Migration, New York, 17–18 February 2011 (New York: Population Division, UN Department of Social and Economic Affairs, 2011); available online at http://www.un.org/esa/population/meetings/ninthcoord2011/zlotnik-ittmig65ga.pdf.

10. We place the term within quotation marks, since even "dramatic" change in demography is still rather slow and gradual compared with economic or political change.

11. For a full discussion, see Michael S. Teitelbaum and Jay Winter, *The Fear of Population Decline* (Orlando, FL, and London: Academic Press, 1985), chap. 3.

12. Population Division, Department of Economic and Social Affairs, United Nations Secretariat, *Partnership and Reproductive Behaviour in Low-Fertility Countries*, revised version for the Web, May 2003, ESA/P/WP. 177, p. 1, table 1; available online at http://eww.un.org/esa/population/publications/reprobehavior/partrepro.pdf. Note: The tabulations exclude small countries with populations of less than 150,000.

13. Joshua R. Goldstein, Tomáš Sobotka, Alva Jasilioniene, "The End of 'Lowest-Low'" Fertility?" *Population and Development Review* 35, no. 4 (December 2009), table 1 and fig. 2, pp. 669–70.

14. This count excludes small countries with populations of less than one million and countries with low-quality data on births and population; it includes east and west Germany and Hong Kong as separate countries. See also Hans-Peter Kohler, F. C. Billari, and J. A. Ortega, "The emergences of lowest-low fertility in Europe during the 1990s," *Population and Development Review* 28, no. 4, 2002, pp. 641–80.

15. Commission of the European Communities, *Communication from the Commission: Green Paper, "Confronting the Demographic Challenge: A New Solidarity between the Generations,"* doc. no. COM (2005) 94 final, Brussels, 16.3.2005; available online at http://eur-lex.europa.eu/LexUriServ/site/en/com/2005/com2005_0094en01.pdf.

16. These ideas are most closely associated with Gary Becker. See Gary S. Becker, "The Economic Way of Looking at Life," Nobel Prize Lecture, 9 December 1992; available online at http://nobelprize.org/nobel_prizes/economics/laureates/1992/becker-lecture.pdf.

17. Gary S. Becker and H. G. Lewis, "On the Interaction between the Quantity and Quality of Children," *Journal of Political Economy* 81, no. 2 (1973), pp. S279–S288.

18. See Dirk J. van de Kaa, "The Idea of a Second Demographic Transition in Industrialized Countries," paper presented at the Sixth Welfare Policy Seminar of the National Institute of Population and Social Security, Tokyo, Japan, 29 January 2002.

19. Ibid., pp. 1–2.

20. Ibid., fig. 2, pp. 9–10.

21. Dirk J. van de Kaa, 2001, "Second Demographic Transition," in *International Encyclopedia of the Social and Behavioral Sciences*, vol. 5, p. 3487.

22. Goldstein, Sobotka, and Jasilioniene, "End of 'Lowest-Low' Fertility?" pp. 687–91.

23. Commission of the European Communities, *Communication from the Commission: Green Paper*, pp. 10–11.

24. Ibid., p. 5.

25. Gary S. Becker, *A Treatise on the Family* (Cambridge, MA: Harvard University Press, 1981), pp. 149–50.

26. Van de Kaa, "Idea of a Second Demographic Transition," pp. 30–31.

27. Goldstein, Sobotka, and Jasilioniene, "End of 'Lowest-Low' Fertility?" p. 685.

28. Commission of the European Communities, *Communication from the Commission: Green Paper*, p. 7.

29. Ibid., pp. 6, 10.

30. United Nations Population Division, Department of Economic and Social Affairs, *Replacement Migration: Is It a Solution to Declining and Ageing Populations?* (New York: United Nations, 2000).

31. Ibid., Executive Summary, p. 4.

32. Ibid., tables IV.4 and IV.7.

33. "Migration de remplacement: une solution aux populations en declin et viellissantes" *Le Monde*, 6 January 2000.

34. "Le rapport qui alarme l'Europe," *Le Figaro*, 10 January 2000.

35. For a fuller discussion of the report and the garbled reactions to it, see Michael S. Teitelbaum, "The Media Marketplace for Garbled Demography," *Population and Development Review* 30, no. 2 (June 2004), pp. 317–27.

36. Teitelbaum and Winter, *Fear of Population Decline*, chap. 2.

37. Kelly M. Greenhill, *Weapons of Mass Migration: Forced Displacement, Coercion, and Foreign Policy* (Ithaca, NY, and London: Cornell University Press, 2010, p. 2.

38. For the full text of the convention and its associated protocol, see United Nations High Commissioner for Refugees, *Convention and Protocol relating to the Status of Refugees*, http://www.unhcr.org/protect/PROTECTION/3b66c2aa10.pdf.

39. Greenhill, *Weapons of Mass Migration*, p. 2.

40. United States Conference of Catholic Bishops, Inc., and Conferencia del Episcopado Mexicano, "Strangers No Longer: Together on the Journey of Hope," Washington, DC: US Conference of Catholic Bishops, 22 January 2003, paras. 33–39; available online at http://www.usccb.org/issues-and-action/human-life-and-dignity/immigration/strangers-no-longer-together-on-the-journey-of-hope.cfm.

41. Statement of Zeyno Baran, director, International Security and Energy Programs, The Nixon Center, in *Uzbekistan: The Key to Success in Central Asia?* Hearing before the Subcommittee on the Middle East and Central Asia, Committee on Inter-

national Relations, US House Of Representatives, 108th Cong., 2nd sess. (15 June 2004), serial no. 108–126, 94–278, pdf, p. 73; available online at http://commdocs.house.gov/ committees/intlrel/hfa94278.000/hfa94278_of.htm.

TWO European Population

1. In this context, Beck's use of the English word *"reflexive"* injects some confusion into the discussion. One of the several meanings of the word *reflexive* is behavior that is "habitual and unthinking," as in neurological "reflexes" that produce responses to stimuli without involvement of the brain. This is, of course, the very opposite of what Beck has in mind; his focus is on knowledge enabling people to "reflect" upon their circumstances and the risks surrounding it. The ambiguity here may be due to translation of the original German to English. We will stay with Beck's usage of "reflexive," and keep it always in quotation marks. A. Giddens and C. Pierson, *Conversations with Anthony Giddens. Making Sense of Modernity* (Cambridge, UK: Polity, 1998), pp. 103–5; for the full formulation of Beck's position, see Ulrich Beck, *Risk Society: Towards a New Modernity* (London: Sage Publications, 1992).

2. Svetlana Boym, *The Future of Nostalgia* (Cambridge, MA: Harvard University Press, 2002), p. 101.

3. Giddens and Pierson, *Conversations with Anthony Giddens*, p. 105. One possible exception to Giddens's claim is Islamic society, where divorce is legally recognized.

4. Christopher Lasch, *Haven in a Heartless World: The Family Besieged* (New York: Basic Books, 1977).

5. Ulrich Beck, *World Risk Society* (Cambridge, UK: Polity, 1999), pp. 116–18.

6. Nassim Nicholas Taleb, *The Black Swan: The Impact of the Highly Improbable* (New York: Random House, 2007).

7. Anthony Giddens, "Risk and Responsibility," *Modern Law Review 62*, no. 1 (1999), pp. 1–10; Ulrich Beck, *Risk Society: Towards a New Modernity* (New York: Sage, 1992, Eng. ed.).

8. Nicholas Eberstadt, *Russia's Peacetime Demographic Crisis: Dimensions, Causes, Implications*, NBR project report (Washington, DC: The National Bureau of Asian Research, May 2010), p. 45.

9. Murray Feshbach, "Dead Souls," *Atlantic Monthly*, January 1999, pp. 26–27; available online at http://www.theatlantic.com/past/docs/issues/99jan/deadsoul.htm.

10. Ibid.

11. Wilson Center News, "Scholar Predicts Serious Population Decline in Russia: Spotlight on Wilson Center Senior Scholar Murray Feshbach," 29 January 2004; available online at http://www.wilsoncenter.org/index.cfm?fuseaction=news.item&news _id=56906

12. Murray Feshbach, "Behind the Bluster, Russia Is Collapsing," *Washington Post*, 5 October 2008; available online at http://www.washingtonpost.com/wp-dyn/ content/article/2008/10/03/AR2008100301976.html.

13. Eberstadt, *Russia's Peacetime Demographic Crisis*, pp. 14, 16, 20.

14. Ibid., p. 19.

15. Ibid., pp. 15, 19.

16. Nicholas Eberstadt, "Russia, the Sick Man of Europe," *Public Interest* 158 (Winter 2005), pp. 3–20.

17. Nick Eberstadt, "Drunken Nation: Russia's Depopulation Bomb," *World Affairs* (Spring 2009); available online at http://www.worldaffairsjournal.org/articles/2009 -Spring/full-Eberstadt.html.

18. Feshbach, "Behind the Bluster."

19. Feshbach, "Dead Souls."

20. "Natural Population Decline in Russia Down by 31% in 2009—Putin," *Ria Novosti*, 16 February 2010; available online at http://en.rian.ru/russia/20100216/157906438 .html.

21. "Demographic Crisis a Mega-Project for Govt.—Medvedev," *Ria Novosti*, 15 May 2006; available online at http://en.rian.ru/russia/20060515/48110242.html.

22. Ansley J. Coale, Barbara A. Anderson, Erna Härm, *Human Fertility in Russia since the Nineteenth Century* (Princeton, NJ: Princeton University Press, 1979).

23. Judy Dempsey, "German Politician Makes Anti-Immigrant Remarks," *New York Times*, 12 October 2010.

24. Michael Woodhead, "All Jews Share a Certain Gene?" *Daily Mail*, 30 August 2010.

25. "German Central Banker Condemned for 'Racist' Book," BBC News Europe, 30 August 2010, http:// www.bbc.co.uk/news/world-europe-11131937.

26. Melissa Eddy, "Thilo Sarrazin, German Banker, to Quit after Remarks about Jews, Muslims," *Huffington Post News*, 9 September 2010; available online at http://www .huffingtonpost.com/2010/09/09/thilo-sarrazin-german-cen_n_711358.html.

27. Charles S. Maier, *The Unmasterable Past: History, Holocaust, and German National Identity* (Cambridge, MA: Harvard University Press, 1988).

28. Matthew Weaver, "Angela Merkel: German Multiculturalism Has 'Utterly Failed,'" *Guardian*, 17 October 2010.

29. Judy Dempsey, "Anti-Foreigner Attitudes Surge in Germany," *New York Times*, October 13, 2010.

30. Klaus-Dietrich Bedau, "Population Trends, Employment Levels, Economic Performance, and Income Evolution in East and West Germany since Unification," *Journal of Income Distribution* 8, no. 2 (January 1998), pp. 207–23.

31. John C. Caldwell and Thomas Schindlmayr, "Explanations of the Fertility Crisis in Modern Societies: A Search for Commonalities," *Population Studies* 62, no. 3 (2003), table 1, p. 242.

32. "European Birth Rates Data: What Is Happening to Germany?" *Guardian* 19, May 2010; available online at http://www.guardian.co.uk/news/datablog/2010/may/19/ european-birth-rates-data-germany; data cited from Eurostat at: http://epp.eurostat.ec .europa.eu/tgm/table.do?tab=table&init=1&plugin=0&language=en&pcode=tps00112.

33. European Commission, Eurostat, *Europe in Figures: Eurostat Yearbook 2010* (Luxembourg: European Union, 2011), fig. 2.14, p. 174; available online at http://epp

.eurostat.ec.europa.eu/cache/ITY_OFFPUB/KS-CD-10–220/EN/KS-CD-10–220 -EN.PDF.

34. European Commission, Eurostat, "Population at 1 January," 2000–2011; available online at http://epp.eurostat.ec.europa.eu/tgm/table.do?tab=table&init=1&langua ge=en&pcode=tps00001&plugin=1.

35. European Commission, Eurostat, *Europe in Figures*, fig. 2.14, p. 174.

36. European Commission, Eurostat, "Population at 1 January," 2000–2011.

37. Eurostat, "Proportion of Live Births Outside of Marriage," 1997–2008; available online at http://epp.eurostat.ec.europa.eu/portal/page/portal/statistics/search _database.

38. Peter McDonald, "Sustaining Fertility through Public Policy: The Range of Options," *Population 62*, no. 3 (2002), pp. 417–66; Ron Lesthaeghe and Paul Willems, "Is Low Fertility a Temporary Phenomenon in the European Union?" *Population and Development Review 25*, no. 2 (1999), pp. 211–28; Tomas Frejka and John Ross, "Paths to Sub-Replacement Fertility: The Empirical Evidence," in *Global Fertility Transition*, ed. R. A. Bulatao and J. B. Casterline (New York: Population Council, 2001), pp. 213–54; Paul Demeny, "Replacement Level Fertility: The Implausible Endpoint of the Demographic Transition," *The Continuing Demographic Transition*, ed. G. W. Jones et al. (Oxford: Clarendon Press, 1997), pp. 94–110.

39. For an "aperitif," try this: Gerhard Heilig, Thomas Büttner, and Wolfgang Lutz, "Germany's Population: Turbulent Past, Uncertain Future," *Population Bulletin* 40, no. 4 (1990), pp. 1–46.

40. Michael S. Teitelbaum and Jay Winter, *The Fear of Population Decline* (Orlando, FL, and London: Academic Books, 1985), chap. 3.

41. Norman B. Ryder, "The Future of American Fertility," *Social Problems 26*, no. 3 (1979), pp. 359–70.

42. John C. Caldwell, *Theory of Fertility Decline* (London: Academic Press, 1982), pp. 233–66.

43. Philippe Ariès, "Two Successive Motivations for the Declining Birth Rate in the West," *Population and Development Review 6*, no. 4 (1980), pp. 645–50, esp. 650.

44. Caldwell and Schindlmayr, "Explanations of the Fertility Crisis," p. 245.

45. Ibid., pp. 245–46.

46. John Bongaarts and G. Feeney, "On the Quantum and Tempo of Fertility," *Population and Development Review* 24, no. 2 (1998), pp. 271–91; A. Berrington, "Perpetual Postponers? Women's, Men's and Couples' Fertility Intentions and Subsequent Fertility Behaviour," *Population Trends* 117 (Autumn 2004), pp. 9–19. See also T. Sobotka, H.-P. Kohler, and F. C. Billari, "The Increase in Late Childbearing in Europe, Japan, and the United States," paper presented at the 2007 annual meeting of the Population Association of America, New York, 29–31 March 2007; and T. Sobotka and M. R. Testa, "Childlessness Attitudes and Intentions in Europe," in *People, Population Change and Policies: Lessons from the Population Policy Acceptance Study*, ed. C. Höhn, D. Avramov, and I. Kotowska, vol. 1, European Studies of Population series 16/1 (Frankfurt: Springer-Verlag, 2008).

47. Anne H. Gauthier, "Family Policies in Industrialized Countries: Is There Convergence?" *Population* 62, no. 3 (2002), pp. 447–75.

48. David S. Reher, "Family Ties in Western Europe: Persistent Contrasts," *Population and Development Review* 24, no. 2 (1998), pp. 203–34.

49. Patricia Ehrkamp and Helga Leitner, "Beyond National Citizenship: Turkish Immigrants and the (Re)construction of Citizenship in Germany," *www2.fiu.edu/~tcs/summer/readings-hl.doc*.

50. David Lowenthal, *The Past Is a Foreign Country* (Cambridge: Cambridge University Press, 1985).

51. Marià-José Gonzàlez and Teresa Jurado-Guerrero, "Remaining Childless in Affluent Economies: A Comparison of France, West Germany, Italy and Spain, 1994–2001," *European Journal of Population* 22 (2006), pp. 317–52.

52. Alicia Adsera , "Where Are the Babies? Labor Market Conditions and Fertility in Europe," *European Journal of Population* 26 (2010), pp. 19–32.

53. David Kertzer, Michael White, Laura Bernhardi, and Giuseppi Gabrielli, "Italy's Path to Very Low Fertility: The Adequacy of Economic and Second Demographic Transition Theories," *European Journal of Population* 25 (2009), pp. 90–93.

54. Ibid., p. 95.

55. Jan M. Hoem, "Preface: Childbearing Trends and Policies in Europe," *Demographic Research* 19, no. 1 (2008), pp. 1–4.

56. Kertzer et al., "Italy's Path," pp. 99–123.

57. For the history of the phrase "socialism of the fools," see Richard J. Evans, *The Coming of the Third Reich* (London: Penguin, 2005), p. 496.

58. Mary Daly and Sara Clavero, "Contemporary Family Policy in Ireland and Europe," http://www.welfare.ie/EN/Policy/ResearchSurveysAndStatistics/Families ResearchProgramme/Documents/cfpreport.pdf.

59. For a discussion, see Teitelbaum and Winter, *Fear of Population Decline*, especially chaps. 2 and 3.

60. Anne H. Gauthier, *The State and the Family: A Comparative Analysis of Family Policies in Industrialized Countries* (Oxford: Clarendon Press, 1996); Anne Gauthier, "Historical Trends in State Support for Families in Europe (Post-1945)," *Children and Youth Services Review* 21, no.11/12 (1999), pp. 937–65.

61. Daly and Clavero, "Contemporary Family Policy," p. 156.

62. Ibid., pp. 156ff.

63. Ibid., p. 159.

THREE   Islam in Europe

1. James Kirkup, "Tory Chief Baroness Warsi Attacks 'Bigotry' against Muslims," *Daily Telegraph*, 20 January 2011.

2. The Runnymede Trust, *Islamophobia: A Challenge for Us All* (London: Runnymede Trust, 1997). See also Robin Richardson, ed., *Islamophobia: Issues, Challenges and Action. A Report by the Commission on British Muslims and Islamophobia* (Stoke on Trent, UK: Trentham Books, 2004), pp. v–viii.

3. Richard Stone, foreword to Richardson, *Islamophobia*, p. vii. The earlier report was titled *A Very Light Sleeper* (London: Runnymede Trust, 1992).

4. Richardson, *Islamophobia*, p. vi. Herewith a list of the members who wrote the 1997 Runnymede Trust report:

- Professor Gordon Conway, vice-chancellor, University of Sussex
- Maqsood Ahmad, then director of Kirklees Racial Equality Council
- Professor Akbar Ahmed, then fellow of Selwyn College, Cambridge
- Dr. Zaki Badawi, principal of the Muslim College, London
- Rt. Rev. Richard Chartres, Bishop of London
- Ian Hargreaves, then editor of the *New Statesman* and later professor of media studies at the University of Cardiff
- Dr. Philip Lewis, then adviser on interfaith issues to the bishop of Bradford and lecturer in religious studies at the University of Leeds and now lecturer in peace studies at the University of Bradford
- Zahida Manzoor, chair of the Bradford Health Authority
- Rabbi Julia Neuberger, later chief executive of the King's Fund
- Trevor Phillips, chair of the Runnymede Trust and later vice-chair of the Greater London Authority and chair of the Commission for Racial Equality
- Dr. Sebastian Poulter, reader in law at the University of Southampton
- Usha Prashar, civil service commissioner
- Hamid Qureshi, then director of the Lancashire Council of Mosques
- Nasreen Rehman, trustee of the Runnymede Trust
- Saba Risaluddin, director of the Calamus Foundation
- Imam Dr. Abduljalil Sajid, chair of the Muslim Council for Religious and Racial Harmony, UK
- Dr. Richard Stone, chair of the Jewish Council for Racial Equality
- Rev. John Webber, adviser on interfaith issues to the bishop of Stepney

5. See Richardson, *Islamophobia*, p. vi, for a list of the members of the 2004 report:

- Dr. Richard Stone, chair of the Uniting Britain Trust and the Jewish Council for Racial Equality
- Solma Ahmed, adviser to the government's Community Housing Task Force
- Yousif Al-Khoei, director of the Al-Khoie Foundation
- Dr. Kate Gavron, vice-chair of the Runnymede Trust
- Professor Ian Hargreaves, professor of media studies at the University of Cardiff
- Khalida Khan, director of the An-Nisa Society, London

- Dr. Philip Lewis, lecturer in peace studies at the University of Bradford
- Robin Richardson, codirector of the Insted Consultancy
- Imam Dr. Abduljalil Sajid, chair of the Muslim Council for Religious and Racial Harmony, UK
- Anil Singh, director of the Manningham Housing Association, Bradford
- Selina Ullah, senior manager Bradford Community Health Trust
- Rev. John Webber, adviser on inter-faith issues to the bishop of Stepney
- Talha Wadee, formerly director of the Lancashire Council of Mosques
- Pranlal Sheth, a trustee of the Uniting Britain Trust and of the Runnymede Trust, formerly a member of the Runnymede Trust Commission until his death in 2003

6. Ibid., p. 12.

7. American Psychiatric Association, "Healthy Minds, Healthy Lives," http://healthyminds.org/Main-Topic/Phobias.aspx.

8. Peter O'Brien, "Islam, Liberalism, and Xenophobia in Europe," in *Islam: Portability and Exportability*, ed. Samy S. Sayd, G. E. von Grunebaum Center for Near East Studies, UCLA, paper 6, 2008, pp. 63–65.

9. Abdoolkarim Vakil, "Is the Islam in Islamophobia the Same as the Islam in Anti-Islam; or, When Is It Islamophobia Time?" unpublished ms, King's College, University of London, UK, pp. 78–81; available online at http://www.ces.uc.pt/e-cadernos/media/ecadernos3/vakil.pdf.

10. UN news release, 7 December 2004.

11. "Is America Islamophobic?" front cover, *Time*, 30 August 2010.

12. Le loi #2004–228, du 15 mars 2004, *En application du principe de laïcité, le port de signes ou de tenues manifestant une appartenance religieuse dans les écoles, collèges et lycées publics.*

13. "French Girls Expelled over Veils," BBC, 20 October 2004.

14. "Sarkozy Stirs French Burka Debate," BBC News, 22 June 2009; Elaine Ganley, "France Moves Closer to Banning Full Muslim Veil," AP, 15 January 2010.

15. "Sarkozy Backs off Ban of Muslim Veil, Calls It 'Unworkable,'" *The Raw Story*, 16 January 2010; John Vinocur, "France Fails to Talk about the Real Issue," *New York Times*, 19 January 2010.

16. "French Veil Ban Clears Last Legal Hurdle," BBC News Europe, 7 October 2010; available online at http://www.bbc.co.uk/news/world-europe-11496459.

17. Ibid.

18. Steven Erlander, "For a French Imam, Islam's True Enemy Is Radicalism," *New York Times*, 13 February 2010.

19. Ibid.

20. Bronwyn Winter, "Secularism Aboard the *Titanic*: Feminists and the Debate over the Hijab in France," *Feminist Studies* 32, no. 2 (Summer 2006), pp. 279–98.

21. Note that at this writing this legislation still may be subjected to legal challenge at the European Court on Human Rights.

22. Ian Buruma, *Murder in Amsterdam: The Death of Theo van Gogh and the Limits of Tolerance* (New York: Penguin, 2007).

23. Ibid., p. 223.

24. "Profile: Geert Wilders," *BBC News*, 15 October 2009; available online at http://news.bbc.co.uk/2/hi/7314636.stm.

25. Patrick Grant, "Osama, Theo and the Agreement," *Fortnight* 433 (February 2005), pp. 18–19.

26. Peter J. Katzenstein and Timothy A. Byrnes, "Transnational Religion in an Expanding Europe," *Perspectives on Politics* 4, no. 4 (December 2006), pp. 679–94.

27. Michael S. Teitelbaum and Jay Winter, *A Question of Numbers: High Migration, Low Fertility, and the Politics of a National Identity* (New York: Hill and Wang, Farrar, Straus, Giroux, 1998), p. 49.

28. "Danish Police Shoot Man Trying to Enter Mohammed Cartoonist's Home," *Daily Telegraph*, 2 January 2010.

29. The phrase comes from Voltaire's *Candide* and reads as follows: "*Cans ce pays-ci, il est bon de tuer de temps en temps un amiral pour encourager les autres*" ("In England, it is good from time to time to kill an admiral to send a message to the others").

30. "Three Killed as Pakistan Cartoon Protests Escalate," *MSNBC*, 15 February 2006.

31. Swiss People's Party campaign poster, "For More Security," from "Proposed Swiss Immigration Laws Show Rise of New Racism and Xenophobia," *Mail on Line*, 7 September 2007, http://www.dailymail.co.uk/news/article-480493/Proposed-Swiss-immigration-laws-rise-new-racism-xenophobia.html.

32. Emmanuel Sivan, "The West's 'Principle of Height,'" *Ha'aretz*, 22 January 2010.

33. Matthew Weaver, "Swiss Far Right Forces Vote on Minaret Ban," *Guardian*, 8 July 2008.

34. Swiss People's Party campaign poster, "Vote Yes to Ban Minarets," From Michael Kimmelman, "When Fear Turns Graphic," *New York Times*, 17 January 2010.

35. John Esposito, "Islamophobia Comes to Switzerland," *Washington Post*, 2 December 2009; see also Dominique Haller, "A Swiss Perspective on the Minaret Ban," *Inside Islam: Dialogues and Debates*, University of Wisconsin at Madison, 10 December 2009; available online at http://insideislam.wisc.edu/index.php/archives/4118; Ian Trainor, "Islamophobia: Swiss Far Right Seeks Vote on Minarets Ban," *Guardian*, 9 July 2008; *http://www.guardian.co.uk/world/2008/jul/09/religion.islam*.

36. "Swiss Vote to Ban Minaret Construction," CNN, 29 November 2009; available online at http://edition.cnn.com/2009/WORLD/europe/11/29/switzerland.minaret.referendum/index.html.

37. See, for example, Teitelbaum and Winter, *A Question of Numbers*, pp. 138–53.

38. Jean-Paul Sartre, *Anti-Semite and Jew* (Boston: Beacon Press, 1950).

39. Albert Hirschman, *The Rhetoric of Reaction* (New York: Basic Books, 1980).

40. Teitelbaum and Winter, *The Fear of Population Decline* (Orlando, FL, and London: Academic Press, 1985).

41. "Al-Qaddafi: Islam Taking over Europe—Victory within a Few Decades," Al Jazeera TV. 10 April 2006; available online at http://www.youtube.com/watch?v =i7ympF_grrA.

42. Cited in Christopher Caldwell, *Reflections on the Revolution in Europe: Immigration, Islam, and the West* (New York: Doubleday, 2009), p. 305, and in an article Caldwell wrote in the *Financial Times*, "A Partnership, If Only in Spirit," 2–3 December 2006.

43. Ian Fisher and Sabrine Tavernise, "Pope Backs Turkey's Bid to Join European Union," *New York Times*, 29 November 20.

44. James V. Schall, *The Regensburg Lecture* (South Bend, IN: St. Augustine's Press, 2007).

45. Thomas Hammarberg, commissioner for human rights of the Council of Europe, news release, June 2008.

46. Council of Europe, European Commission against Racism and Intolerance, "General Policy Recommendation No. 5: Combating Intolerance and Discrimination against Muslims," Strasbourg, 27 April 2000; available online at http://www.coe.int/t/dghl/monitoring/ecri/activities/GPR/EN/Recommendation_N5/Recommendation_5_en.asp#TopOfPage.

47. "Muslims Are Discriminated Against in Europe," Commissioner for Human Rights, Viewpoints, 2007, http://www.coe.int/t/commissioner/Viewpoints/070122 _en.asp.

48. European Monitoring Centre on Racism and Xenophobia, "Migrants, Minorities and Housing: Exclusion, Discrimination and Anti-Discrimination in 15 Member States of the European Union," 19 May 2008, http://www.libertysecurity.org/auteur655 .html.

49. Human Rights First, "2008 Hate Crime Survey: The Facets of Anti-Muslim Violence," http://www.humanrightsfirst.org/pdf/FD-081103-hate-crime-survey-2008 .pdf.

50. Human Rights First, "Violence against Muslims," using data on the fifty-six nations in the OECD, http://www.humanrightsfirst.org/media/disc/2009/alert/480/ index.htm.

51. Caldwell, *Reflections on the Revolution in Europe*, pp. (in order of examples) 21, 111, 222, 327, 349.

52. Bat Ye'or, *Eurabia: The Euro-Arab Axis* (Madison, NJ: Fairleigh Dickinson University Press, 2005).

53. Oriana Fallaci, *The Rage and the Pride* (New York: Rizzoli, 2002).

54. Melanie Phillips, *Londonistan* (New York: Encounter Books, 2006).

55. Bernard Lewis, *Europe and Islam* (Washington, DC: AEI Press, 2007).

56. Teitelbaum and Winter, *Fear of Population Decline*, chap. 2.

57. Steven Erlanger and Scott Shane, "Oslo Suspect Wrote of Fear of Islam and Plan for War," *New York Times*, 23 July 2011.

58. The violence sparked by the 2012 film *Innocence of Muslims* presented another ugly manifestation of the conflicts discussed in this chapter. There will be others.

FOUR   The China Trajectory

1. United Nations, Department of Economic and Social Affairs, Population Division, *World Population Prospects: The 2004 Revision*; available online at http://esa.un.org/unpp/p2kodata.asp.

2. United Nations, Department of Economic and Social Affairs, Population Division, *World Population Prospects: The 2008 Revision*; available online at http://esa.un.org/unpp.

3. Chen and Coale estimate Chinese total fertility in 1970 to have been 5.75 for all of China, and 3.22 and 6.31 for urban and rural areas respectively. S. Chen and Ansley Coale, *Chinese Provincial Fertility Data, 1940–1990* (Beijing: Zhongguo renkou chubanshe, 1993), p. 215. Reprinted in Isabelle Attané, "Chinese Fertility on the Eve of the 21st Century: Fact and Uncertainty," *Population: An English Selection*, vol. 13, no. 2, (2001), table A1, p. 95.

4. Attané, "Chinese Fertility," p. 79.

5. Ibid.

6. Sun Muhan, *Zhongguo jihua shengyu shigao* (A Draft History of Chinese Family Planning) (Beijing: Beifang funu ertong chubanshe, 1987), p. 66, cited in James Z. Lee and Feng Wang, *One Quarter of Humanity: Malthusian Mythology and Chinese Realities* (Cambridge, MA, and London: Harvard University Press, 1999), p. 191, fn 37.

7. Jonathan D. Spence, *The Search for Modern China*, 2nd ed. (New York and London: W. W. Norton, 1990), p. 649.

8. Ibid., p. 518.

9. Population Estimates Program, Population Division, US Census Bureau, "Historical National Population Estimates: July 1, 1900 to July 1, 1999," http://www.census.gov/population/estimates/nation/popclockest.txt.

10. Peng Xizhe, "Major Determinants of China's Fertility Transition," *China Quarterly* 117 (1989), pp. 1–37, especially p. 2.

11. Spence, *Search for Modern China*, p. 649.

12. Peng Xizhe, "Major Determinants," p. 5, cites one 1958 report that contraceptive supplies at that time were sufficient to meet the needs of only 2.2 percent of reproductive age couples.

13. Malcolm Potts, "China's One Child Policy," *British Medical Journal* 333 (19 August 2006), pp. 361–62.

14. Spence, *Search for Modern China*, p. 649.

15. See Yves Blayo, *Des politiques démographiques en Chine* (Paris: Presses universitaires de France, Institut national d'études démographiques, 1997).

16. Spence, *Search for Modern China*, pp. 548–49.

17. Ibid., pp. 549–50.

18. Quoted in ibid., p. 552.

19. Ibid., p. 551–52.

20. John Robottom, *Twentieth Century China* (New York: Putnam, 1971), p. 430.

21. One widely cited estimate, of thirty million excess deaths, is in Judith Banister, *China's Changing Population* (Stanford: Stanford University Press, 1987).

22. Spence, *Search for Modern China*, p. 575.

23. Dudley L. Poston Jr., "Social and Economic Development and the Fertility Transitions in Mainland China and Taiwan," *Population and Development Review* 26, supp.: *Population and Economic Change in East Asia*, (2000), p. 41.

24. Peng Xizhe, "Major Determinants," p. 2.

25. Chen and Coale, "Chinese Provincial Fertility Data," table A1.

26. Blayo, *Des politiques démographiques en Chine*, pp. 155–66.

27. Chen and Coale, "Chinese Provincial Fertility Data," table A1.

28. Zhongwei Zhao, "Deliberate Birth Control under a High-Fertility Regime: Reproductive Behavior in China Before 1970," *Population and Development Review* 23, no. 4. (December 1997), p. 753.

29. Edwin A. Winckler, "Chinese Reproductive Policy at the Turn of the Millennium: Dynamic Stability," *Population and Development Review* 28, no. 3 (September 2002), p. 381.

30. United Nations, *Proceedings of the World Population Conference* (New York: United Nations, 1974), vol. 3, p. 223.

31. Spence, *Search for Modern China*, p. 590.

32. US Department of State, Bureau of Democracy, Human Rights and Labor, Office of Country Reports and Asylum Affairs, "China Profile of Asylum Claims and Country Conditions," Washington, DC, May 2007, paras. 83–92; available online at http://www.cdjp.org/gb/fileupload/China_May_2007.pdf.

33. For more detail, see US Department of State, "China Profile," especially paras. 83–95.

34. Attané, "Chinese Fertility," p. 85.

35. United Nations General Assembly, "The Universal Declaration of Human Rights," Paris, 10 December 1948, article 16; available online at http://www.un.org/en/documents/udhr/index.shtml.

36. Proclamation of Teheran, "Final Act of the International Conference on Human Rights, Teheran, 22 April–13 May 1968," UN Doc. A/CONF. 32/41 at 3 (1968).

37. United Nations, World Population Conference, "World Population Plan of Action," Principle 14f, Bucharest, 1974.

38. For one perspective, by an opponent of this US policy, see Susan A. Cohen, "The United States and the United Nations Population Fund: A Rocky Relationship," *The Guttmacher Report on Public Policy* (New York: Alan Guttmacher Institute, 1999);available online at http://www.guttmacher.org/pubs/tgr/02/1/gr020101.pdf.

39. Michael S. Teitelbaum, "Fertility Effects of the Abolition of Legalized Abortion in Romania," *Population Studies* 26 (November 1972), pp. 405–17.

40. Karen Hardee-Cleveland and Judith Banister, "Fertility Policy and Implementation in China, 1986–88," *Population and Development Review* 14 (1988), pp. 245–86. For a more general discussion, see Judith Banister, *China's Changing Population*, 1987.

41. United Nations, World Population Conference, "World Population Plan of Action," Principle 14f, Bucharest, 1974, http://www.unfpa.org/6billion/populationissues/rh.htm.

42. Lee and Wang, *One Quarter of Humanity*, pp. 7–13.

43. Edwin A. Winckler, "Chinese Reproductive Policy at the Turn of the Millennium: Dynamic Stability," *Population and Development Review* 28, no. 3. (September 2002), pp. 382.

44. Ibid., p. 393.

45. Ibid., p. 383.

46. Ibid., pp. 391–92.

47. Ibid., pp. 393–96.

48. Ibid., pp. 397–98.

49. "Crisis Looms as China's Population Growth Rate Slows," *People's Daily Online*, 29 April 2011, http://english.people.com.cn/90001/90776/90785/7365367.html#.

50. Zhongwei Zhao, "Deliberate Birth Control," pp. 749–54.

51. Thomas R. Malthus, *An Essay on the Principle of Population* (London: John Murray, 1826), p. 214; cited in Zhongwei Zhao, "Deliberate Birth Control," p. 752.

52. Daniel Goodkind, "Marriage Squeeze in China: Historical Legacies, Surprising Findings," paper prepared for the 2006 annual meeting of the Population Association of America, Los Angeles, March 30–April 1, p. 2.; available online at http://paa2006.princeton.edu/download.aspx?submissionId=60652.

53. Spence, *Search for Modern China*," p. 590.

54. Monica Das Gupta, "Explaining Asia's "Missing Women,'" *Population and Development Review* 31 (September 2005): pp. 529–35.

55. Ansley J. Coale, "Five Decades of Missing Females in China," *Proceedings of the American Philosophical Society* 140, no. 4 (1996), pp. 421–50.

56. Sten Johansson and Ola Nygren "The Missing Girls of China: A New Demographic Account," *Population and Development Review* 17 (March 1991), pp. 35–51.

57. Ibid., pp. 45–46.

58. Emily Oster, "Hepatitis B and the Case of the Missing Women" *Journal of Political Economy* 113, no.6 (December 2005), pp. 1163–1216.

59. Banister, Judith, "Shortage of Girls in China Today," *Journal of Population Research* 21, no. 1 (May 2004), pp. 19–45.

60. Ibid., p. 21.

61. Ibid., p. 26.

62. Ibid.

63. Ibid., p. 23.

64. Quoted in Jim Abrams, "U.S.: One-Child Abuses Rampant in China," Associated Press, 14 December 2004, filed 12:58 P.M.

65. United Kingdom, Parliament, House of Lords, "Human Rights in China and Tibet," 18 December 1996, Hansard House of Lords, Columns 1571–1593; available online at http://www.publications.parliament.uk/pa/ld199697/ldhansrd/vo961218/text/61218-08.htm.

66. Lee and Wang, *One Quarter of Humanity*, p. 7. See also William Lavely and R. Bin Wong, "Revising the Malthusian Narrative: The Comparative Study of Population Dynamics in Late Imperial China," *Journal of Asian Studies* 57 (1998), pp. 714–48.

67. "Crisis Looms as China's Population Growth Rate Slows."

68. United Nations, Department of Economic and Social Affairs, Population Division, *World Population Prospects: The 2008 Revision*, April 30, 2011, 11:47:39 A.M.

69. Zachary Zimmer, and Julia Kwong, "Family Size and Support of Older Adults in Urban and Rural China: Current Efforts and Future Implications," *Demography* 40, no. 1 (February 2003), p. 41.

70. "Social Security in China: Government White Paper," Sections I, X, and Conclusions, in Information Office, State Council, "China's Social Security and Its Policy," Beijing, September 2004; translated into English in *Population and Development Review* 31, no. 1 (March 2005), p. 186.

71. Ibid.

72. Estimated from United Nations, Department of Economic and Social Affairs, Population Division, *World Urbanization Prospects: The 2009 Revision*, file 3: Urban Population by Major Area, Region, and Country, 1950–2050, Saturday, 30 April 2011, 12:02:56 P.M., POP/DB/WUP/Rev.2009/1/F3; http://esa.un.org/wup2009/unup/.

73. "Social Security in China," p. 188.

74. Winckler, "Chinese Reproductive Policy," p. 396.

75. Zai Liang and Zhongdong Ma, "China's Floating Population: New Evidence from the 2000 Census," *Population and Development Review* 30, no. 3 (September 2004), pp. 467, 484.

76. Ibid., pp. 470–71.

77. Ibid., p. 475.

78. "Crisis Looms as China's Population Growth Rate Slows."

79. "Social Security in China," p. 188.

80. Ibid.

FIVE   Population and Politics in India

1. United Nations, Department of Economic and Social Affairs, Population Division, *World Population Prospects: The 2010 Revision*, http://esa.un.org/unpd/wpp/index.htm.

2. Ibid.

3. United States Census Bureau, Population Estimates, Comparison of Preliminary Population Estimates and Census Counts, http://www.census.gov/popest/eval-estimates/eval-est2010.html.

4. Eurostat, "EU27 Population 501 Million at 1 January 2010," news release 110/2010, 27 July 2010; available online at http://epp.eurostat.ec.europa.eu/cache/ITY_PUBLIC/3-27072010-AP/EN/3-27072010-AP-EN.PDF.

5. United Nations, Department of Economic and Social Affairs, Population Division, *World Population Prospects: The 2010 Revision.*

6. Davidson R. Gwatkin, "Political Will and Family Planning: The Implications of India's Emergency Experience," *Population and Development Review* vol. 5, no. 1 (March 1979), p. 34. See also Rosanna Ledbetter, "Thirty Years of Family Planning in India," *Asian Survey* 24, no. 7 (July 1984), p. 736.

7. United Nations, Department of Economic and Social Affairs, Population Division, *World Population Prospects: The 2010 Revision.*

8. Jacques Véron, "The Demography of South Asia from the 1950s to the 2000s: A Summary of Changes and a Statistical Assessment," *Population* (English ed.) 63, no.1, (2008), pp. 9–90, table A.6.

9. Ibid., table A.7.

10. All projection estimates are based upon United Nations, Department of Economic and Social Affairs, Population Division, *World Population Prospects: The 2010 Revision.*

11. For a discussion of the probabilistic projection methods used in the 2010 UN demographic projections, see appendix A.

12. For a fuller discussion, see Neil DeVotta, "Demography and Communalism in India," *Journal of International Affairs* 56, no. 1 (Fall 2002), pp. 53–70.

13. Sudhir Laxman Hendre, *Hindus and Family Planning: A Socio-Political Demography* (Bombay, Supraja Prakashan, 1971), p. 45; quoted in De Votta, "Demography and Communalism," p. 64.

14. DeVotta, "Demography and Communalism," p. 53.

15. V. A. Pai Panandiker and P. K. Umashankar, "Fertility Control and Politics in India," *Population and Development Review* 20, supp.: *The New Politics of Population: Conflict and Consensus in Family Planning* (1994), p. 93.

16. Panandiker and Umashankar, "Fertility Control," pp. 92–93.

17. "Caste and Status," in *India: A Country Study,* ed. James Heitzman and Robert L. Worden (Washington, DC: GPO for the Library of Congress, 1995); available online at http://countrystudies.us/india/89.htm.

18. See Vani K. Borooah, "The Politics of Demography: a Study of Inter-Community Fertility Differences in India," *European Journal of Political Economy* 20 (2004), pp. 551–78.

19. DeVotta, "Demography and Communalism," pp. 57, 59.

20. Shaohua Chen and Martin Ravallion, *The Developing World Is Poorer Than We Thought, but No Less Successful in the Fight against Poverty,* Development Research Group, Policy Research Working Paper 4703 (Washington, DC: World Bank, August 2008), tables 6–8, pp. 32–39.

21. PPP is a conversion rate for a given currency into a reference currency designed to adjust for differences in actual purchasing power related to commodities.

The Development Data Group of the World Bank estimates PPPs from price surveys conducted by the International Comparison Program. For a description of the methodologies used, see World Bank, *Global Purchasing Power Parities and Real Expenditures 2005* (Washington DC: World Bank, 2008), appendix G; www.worldbank.org/data/icp.

22. The World Bank also provides comparable data for definitions of US$ 1.00 and US$ 2.00 per day. For the one dollar a year category 1981, the data show nearly 300 million Indians, about 42 percent of the country's population, in this category. If the higher poverty line of US$2.00 per day is used, these 1981 numbers are of course larger — 609 million, or nearly 87 percent of the population. Chen and Ravallion, *Developing World*, tables 7–8, pp. 33–36.

23. Economic and Social Commission for Asia and the Pacific (ESCAP), Statistics Division, Data Centre, Annual Data; available online at http://www.unescap.org/stat/data/swweb/DataExplorer.aspx. See also ESCAP, Statistical Yearbook for Asia and Pacific, section 16, table 16.1; available online at http://www.unescap.org/stat/data/syb2009/16-Economic-growth.asp.

24. Economic and Social Commission for Asia and the Pacific (ESCAP), Statistics Division, Data Centre, Annual Data, http://www.unescap.org/stat/data/swweb/Data Explorer.aspx.

25. Chen and Ravallion, *Developing World*, tables 7–8, pp. 33–36.

26. McKinsey Global Institute, *The "Bird of Gold": The Rise of India's Consumer Market* (McKinsey & Co., May 2007), p. 46; available online at http://mckinsey.com/mgi/publications/india_consumer_market/index.asp. While it notes that there is no real agreement as to what constitutes "middle class" in India, it defines "middle class" as those with household earnings of between two hundred thousand and one million rupees, which it converts to US$4,400–$22,000 per year—and then to a PPP equivalent of $23,000–$118,000.

27. Ibid., p. 46.

28. Ibid., p. 48.

29. M. S. Ahluwalia, "Economic Performance of States in Post-Reforms Period," *Economic and Political Weekly* (6 May 2000), pp. 1637–38. Ahluwalia's analysis is based on data from fourteen major states accounting for 95 percent of the population. He excludes from his analysis the small-population states of the northeast and other special-category states, such as Delhi, with its concentration of central government employees.

30. Ibid., p. 1638.

31. Michelle Baddeley, Kirsty McNay, and Robert Cassen, "Divergence in India: Income Differentials at the State Level, 1970–97," *Journal of Development Studies* 42, no. 6 (August 2006) pp. 1000–22.

32. Alaka Malwade Basu, *Culture, the Status of Women, and Demographic Behavior* (Oxford: Clarendon Press, 1992), pp. 22, 220–35.

33. See, for example, John Cleland, Chris Scott, and David Whitelegge, eds., *The World Fertility Survey: An Assessment* (New York and Oxford: Oxford University Press, 1987), pp. 721, 741–42. On the term *slum*, see p. 29.

34. John C. Caldwell, P. H. Reddy, and Pat Caldwell, *The Causes of Demographic Change: Experimental Research in South India* (Madison, WI: University of Wisconsin Press, 1988), p. 49.

35. Ledbetter, "Thirty Years of Family Planning," p. 736. See also Gwatkin, "Political Will and Family Planning," p. 34.

36. Gunnar Myrdal, *Asian Drama: An Inquiry into the Poverty of Nations* (New York: Pantheon, 1968), p. 66. Also quoted in Gwatkin, "Political Will and Family Planning," p. 36.

37. Robert L. Hardgrave Jr., "The Congress in India—Crisis and Split," *Asian Survey* 10, no. 3 (March 1970), pp. 256–62.

38. Myron Weiner, "Political Evolution—Party Bureaucracy and Institutions," in *India: A Rising Middle Power*, ed. John W. Mellor (Boulder, CO: Westview Press, 1979), p. 32.

39. United Nations, Department of Economic and Social Affairs, Population Division, *Population, Resources, Environment and Development: The 2005 Revision*; available online at http://unstats.un.org/pop/dVariables/DRetrieval.aspx.

40. The ruling was based upon relatively minor infractions, allegedly prompting *The Times* (London) to portray it as "firing the Prime Minister for a traffic ticket." Multiple online sources cite this quotation, but the original source has eluded us.

41. P. N. Dhar, *Indira Gandhi, the "Emergency," and Indian Democracy*, (New Delhi and New York : Oxford University Press, 2000). See also, "The Rise of Indira Gandhi" in Library of Congress, Country Studies, India, http://lcweb2.loc.gov/cgi-bin/query/r?frd/cstdy:@field(DOCID+in0029).

42. Gwatkin, "Political Will and Family Planning," p. 35.

43. Panandiker and Umashankar, "Fertility Control," p. 89, citing Shah Commission of Inquiry, *Third and Final Report* (New Delhi: Ministry of Home Affairs, 1978).

44. Ibid., p. 90, quoting Shah Commission, p. 154.

45. Gwatkin, "Political Will and Family Planning," pp. 37–38.

46. Matthew Connelly, *Fatal Misconception: The Struggle to Control World Population*, (Cambridge, MA, and London: Belknap Press of Harvard University Press, 2008), p. 300.

47. Ibid., p. 302.

48. Ibid., p. 310.

49. Ibid., pp. 321–23.

50. Ibid., pp. 322–323.

51. Ibid., p. 323.

52. Gwatkin, "Political Will and Family Planning," pp. 38–39.

53. Ibid.

54. Maharashtra Legislative Assembly, *Maharashtra Family (Restriction of Size) Bill, 1976*, bill no. 25 of 1976, Maharashtra, India.

55. Gwatkin, "Political Will and Family Planning," pp. 38–39.

56. Panandiker and Umashankar, "Fertility Control," p. 96.

57. Ibid.

58. Shah Commission, *Third and Final Report*, cited in Panandiker and Umashankar, "Fertility Control, p. 91. See also Gwatkin, "Political Will and Family Planning," pp. 48–49.

59. Library of Congress, Country Studies, India.

60. Gwatkin, "Political Will and Family Planning," p. 44.

61. Ibid., pp. 44–46.

62. Ibid., pp. 45–46.

63. Ibid., p. 48.

64. Ibid., p. 51.

65. Marika Vicziany, "Coercion in a Soft State: The Family Planning Program of India: Part 1: The Myth of Voluntarism," *Pacific Affairs* 55, no. 3 (Autumn 1982), pp. 373–402; Marika Vicziany, "Coercion in a Soft state: The Family Planning Program of India: Part 2: The Sources of Coercion," *Pacific Affairs* 55, no. 4 (Winter 1982–1983), pp. 557–92.

66. Vicziany, "Coercion in a Soft State: Part 1," p. 374.

67. Vicziany, "Coercion in a Soft State: Part 2," p. 581.

68. Ibid., p. 558.

69. Ibid., p. 577.

70. Vicziany, "Coercion in a Soft State, Part 1," p. 378.

71. Vicziany, "Coercion in a Soft State, Part 2," pp. 575–80. See also Gunnar Myrdal, *Asian Drama, p. 896.*

72. Panandiker and Umashankar, "Fertility Control," p. 91–92.

73. Ibid., p. 102.

74. Ibid., p. 101.

75. For a detailed discussion of this phenomenon, see Michael S. Teitelbaum and Jay Winter, *The Fear of Population Decline* (Orlando, FL, and London: Academic Press, 1985), esp. pp. 17–52.

76. Gwatkin, "Political Will and Family Planning," p. 33.

77. A. Dharmalingam and S. Philip Morgan, "Pervasive Muslim-Hindu Fertility Differences in India," *Demography* 41, no. 3. (August 2004), p. 543.

78. Dinesh C. Sharma, "Indian Policy Aims for Stable Population by 2045," *Lancet* 355 (26 February 2000), p. 734.

79. P. Sadasivan Nair, "Understanding Below-Replacement Fertility in Kerala, India," *Journal of Health, Population and Nutrition* 28, no. 4 (2010), pp. 405–6.

80. Ibid., p. 406.

81. Ibid., p. 407.

82. Ibid.

83. For a highly critical description of these vasectomy camps, see Vicziany, "Coercion in a Soft State: Part 2," pp. 576–80.

84. Gwatkin, "Political Will and Family Planning," p. 33.

85. Biju Govind, "GCC Residency Cap May Force Lakhs to Return," *Hindu*, 19 August 2008; available online at http://www.hindu.com/2008/08/19/stories/2008 081954710500.htm.

86. S. Irudaya Rajan and K. C. Zachariah, "Remittances and Its Impact on the Kerala Economy and Society," paper presented at a conference on "International Migration, Multi-Local Livelihoods and Human Security: Perspectives from Europe, Asia and Africa," 30 and 31 August 2007, Institute of Social Studies, The Netherlands. Copy in our possession. Home page for Center for Development Studies: www.cds.edu.

87. Rajan and Zachariah, "Remittances."

88. Ibid.

six   Japan

1. Government of Japan, Ministry of Internal Affairs and Communications, Statistics Bureau, Director-General for Policy Planning (Statistical Standards) and Statistical Research and Training Institute, Statistical Handbook of Japan, chap. 2: "Population," table 2.4; available online at http://www.stat.go.jp/english/data/handbook/c02cont.htm#cha2_2.

2. David McNeill, "More Foreigners Needed, but Not Particularly Wanted," *South China Morning Post*, 13 April 2006, p 13.

3. Linda Sieg, "'Birth-Giving Machine' Gaffe Hits Nerve in Japan," Reuters, 2 February 2007; available online at http://www.reuters.com/article/2007/02/02/us-japan-politics-idUST16444120070202.

4. Thanks are due to Fabian Drixler, Sheldon Garon, and Sawako Shirahase for their time and advice on this subject.

5. Irene B. Taeuber and Frank W. Notestein, "The Changing Fertility of the Japanese," *Population Studies* 1, no. 1 (June 1947), p. 16.

6. John Bongaarts, "A Framework for Analyzing the Proximate Determinants of Fertility," *Population and Development Review* 4 (1978), pp. 105–32.

7. N. O. Tsuya, "Japan's Fertility: Effects of Contraception and Induced Abortion after World War II," *Asian and Pacific Population Forum* 1, no. 1 (1986), p. 7. See also "Japan: Declining Fertility Due Mainly to Marriage Trends, Birth Control Use," *International Family Planning Perspectives* 13, no. 1 (March 1987), pp. 28–29.

8. Fabian Drixler, "Fertility Decline in Japan," in preparation.

9. Ibid.

10. Tiana Norgren, *Abortion before Birth Control: The Politics of Reproduction in Postwar Japan* (Princeton, NJ, and Oxford: Princeton University Press, 2001), pp. 36–37.

11. Jesse F. Steiner, "Japan's Post-War Population Problems," *Social Forces* 31, no. 3 (March 1953), p. 249.

12. Norgren, *Abortion before Birth Control*, p. 37. Norgren provides numerous references to such concerns expressed in the Diet and elsewhere by Japanese political leaders.

13. Warren S. Thompson, "Future Adjustments of Population to Resources in Japan," *Millbank Memorial Fund Quarterly* 28, no. 2 (1949), p. 198.

14. Ibid., p. 202.

15. Deborah Oakley, "American-Japanese Interaction in the Development of Population Policy in Japan, 1945–52, *Population and Development Review* 4, no. 4 (December 1978), p. 619.

16. Ibid., pp. 622–23.

17. Ibid., p. 619.

18. Norgren, *Abortion before Birth Control*, p. 38.

19. M. Thiery, "Pioneers of the Intrauterine Device," *European Journal of Contraception and Reproductive Health Care* 2, no. 1 (March 1997), p. 17.

20. Norgren, *Abortion before Birth Control*, p. 38.

21. Ibid., p. 39.

22. Ibid., pp. 39–40.

23. Matthew Connelly, *Fatal Misconception: The Struggle to Control World Population* (Cambridge, MA, and London: Harvard University Press, 2008), p. 137.

24. Oakley, "American-Japanese Interaction," p. 618.

25. Ibid., p. 624.

26. Quoted in ibid., p. 625.

27. Ibid., pp. 627–34.

28. Connelly, *Fatal Misconception*, p. 70.

29. Norgren, "Abortion before Birth Control," p. 87.

30. Oakley, "American-Japanese Interaction," p. 628.

31. Helen M. Hopper, *A New Woman of Japan: A Political Biography of Kato Shidzue* (Boulder, CO: Westerview Press, 1996), pp. 224–25; also cited in Connelly, *Fatal Misconception*, p. 136.

32. Oakley, "American-Japanese Interaction," p. 631.

33. Warren Thompson, *Population and Peace in the Pacific* (Chicago: University of Chicago Press, 1946).

34. Connelly, *Fatal Misconception*, p. 137.

35. Ibid., p. 139.

36. Norgren, *Abortion before Birth Control*, p. 93.

37. Connelly, *Fatal Misconception*, p. 139.

38. Norgren, *Abortion before Birth Control*, pp. 44–45.

39. Ibid., p. 46.

40. Ibid., pp. 48–49.

41. Ibid., pp. 5–7.

42. Connelly, *Fatal Misconception*, p. 139, quoting Thompson interview with MacArthur, 9 April 1949.

43. Ibid., p. 140.

44. John Dower, *Embracing Defeat: Japan in the Wake of World War II* (New York: W. W. Norton, 1999).

45. Chris Rohlfs, Alexander Reed, and Hiroyuki Yamada, "Causal Effects of Sex Preference on Sex-Blind and Sex-Selective Child Avoidance and Substitution across Birth Years: Evidence from the Japanese Year of the Fire Horse," *Journal of Development Economics* 92, no. 1 (May 2010), pp. 82–95.

46. United Nations, Department of Economic and Social Affairs, Population Division, *World Population Prospects: The 2010 Revision,* http://esa.un.org/unpd/wpp/index.htm.

47. Government of Japan, National Institute of Population and Social Security Research (NIPSSR), "Population Statistics of Japan 2008," table 4.3, http://www.ipss.go.jp/p-info/e/psj2008/PSJ2008.html.

48. Ibid., table 4.24.

49. Ibid., table 4.19.

50. Ibid., table 6.12.

51. Indeed, among those aged twenty to twenty-four, 88.7 percent were never married. Ibid., table 6.22.

52. Stephanie J. Ventura and Christine A. Bachrach, "Nonmarital Childbearing in the United States, 1940–99," *National Vital Statistics Reports* 48, no. 16 (18 October 2000), p. 15; available online at http://www.cdc.gov/nchs/data/nvsr/nvsr48/nvs48_16.pdf.

53. NIPSSR, "Population Statistics of Japan 2008," table 4.16.

54. Drixler notes that this is an interesting change from even the 1920s, when in parts of Japan (especially the southwest), illegitimacy rates were still very high and many marriages were only made official after a child had been born. Fabian Drixler, personal communication, February 2011.

55. Shigemi Kono, book review of *The Political Economy of Japan's Low Fertility,* in *Social Science Japan Journal* 11, no. 1 (Summer 2008), p. 177.

56. Landis MacKellar and David Horlacher, "Population Ageing in Japan: A Brief Survey," *Innovation* 13, no. 4 (2000), p. 418. See also N. Ogawa and R. D. Retherford, "Care of the Elderly in Japan: Changing Norms and Expectations," *Journal of Marriage and the Family* 55, no. 3 (1993), pp. 585–97; and N. Yashiro, "The Economic Factors for the Declining Birthrate," *Review of Population and Social Policy* 7, pp. 129–44.

57. Gavin W. Jones, "Delayed Marriage and Very Low Fertility in Pacific Asia," *Population and Development Review* 33, no. 3 (September 2007), pp. 453–78; available online at http://www.jstor.org/stable/25434630.

58. Ibid., p. 454.

59. Ibid., p. 458.

60. Ibid., p. 460.

61. Shigemi Kono, "Relationship between Population Ageing and Immigration in Japan," unpublished research paper, p. 15. See also Jones, "Delayed Marriage," p. 465.

62. Keiko Osaki, UN Population Division, personal communication, September 2003.

63. Kono, book review of *Political Economy,* pp. 177–78.

64. Jones, "Delayed Marriage," pp. 464–66.

65. MacKellar and Horlacher, "Population Ageing in Japan," p. 414.

66. Government of Japan, Statistical Handbook of Japan, chap. 2: "Population," table 2.3 and fig. 2.4; available online at http://www.stat.go.jp/english/data/handbook/c02cont.htm#cha2_2.

67. Government of Japan, Ministry of Health, Labour, and Welfare, *Abridged Life Tables for Japan 2009*, table 1, http://www.mhlw.go.jp/english/database/db-hw/lifetb09/1.html. See also L. Mayhew, "Japan's Longevity Revolution and the Implications for Health Care Finance and Long-Term Care," cited in MacKeller and Horlacher, "Population Ageing in Japan," p. 415.

68. Kaiji Chen, Ayşe İmrohoroğlu and Selahattin İmrohoroğlu, "The Japanese Saving Rate," *American Economic Review* 96, no. 5 (December 2006), p. 1851.

69. MacKellar and Horlacher, "Population Ageing in Japan," p. 419.

70. Alain de Serres and Florian Pelgrin, "The Decline in Private Saving Rate in the 1990s in OECD Countries: How Much Can be Explained by Non-Wealth Determinants?" Economics Department Working Paper no. 344 (Paris: Organisation for Economic Co-operation and Development [OECD]), 3 December 2002, ECO/WKP(2002)30, fig. 3; available online at http://www.oecd.org/officialdocuments/publicdisplaydocumentpdf/?cote=ECO/WKP(2002)30&docLanguage=En.

71. Ibid., fig. 4.

72. MacKellar and Horlacher, "Population Ageing in Japan," p. 419.

73. Sheldon Garon, *Beyond Our Means: Why America Spends while the World Saves* (Princeton, NJ: Princeton University Press, 2012), pp. 255–56.

74. Garon, *Beyond Our Means*, pp. 266–68.

75. Ibid., pp. 271–73.

76. OECD, "IV. Saving and Investment: Determinants and Policy Implications," *OECD Economic Outlook* 70 (18 December 2001); available online at http://www.oecd.org/dataoecd/2/40/2726831.pdf.

77. Garon, *Beyond Our Means*, p. 290.

78. MacKellar and Horlacher, "Population Ageing in Japan," pp. 421–22.

79. Nippon Keidanren (Japan Business Federation), "Trade in Services Negotiation on WTO Proposal Concerning the Movement of Natural Persons," 18 June 2002, provisional translation, http://www.keidanren.or.jp/english/policy/2002/036/proposal.html#2.

80. Government of Japan, *A 2009 Declining Birthrate White Paper* (English summary), p. 19, http://www8.cao.go.jp/shoushi/whitepaper/english/w-2009/index.html.

81. Sawako Shirahase, "Marriage as an Association of Social Classes in a Low Fertility Rate Society," in *Social Class in Contemporary Japan*, ed. Hiroshi Ishida and David Slater (London and New York: Routledge, 2010), p. 57.

82. For a more detailed summary of these measures, see Government of Japan, *A 2009 Declining Birthrate White Paper*, p 54.

83. Ibid., p. 9.

84. Jones, "Delayed Marriage," pp. 464–65.

85. NIPSSR, "Population Statistics of Japan 2008," table 10.1.

86. Yasuhiko Ota, "Is Japan Set for More Immigrants?" *Nikkei Weekly*, 19 June 2006, published originally in *Nihon Keizai Shimbun*, 4 June 2006.

87. Government of Japan, Ministry of Internal Affairs and Communications, Statistics Bureau, Director-General for Policy Planning (Statistical Standards) and Sta-

tistical Research and Training Institute, *Historical Statistics of Japan*, chap. 2: "Population and Households," table 2–1; available online at http://www.stat.go.jp/english/data/chouki/index.htm.

88. "This Is the New Japan: Immigrants Are Transforming a Once Insular Society, and More of Them Are on Their Way," *Newsweek*, International ed., cover story, special report, 11 September 2006.

89. Nippon Keidanren, "Trade in Services Negotiation."

90. Apichai I. Shipper, "Criminals or Victims? The Politics of Illegal Foreigners in Japan," *Journal of Japanese Studies 31, no. 2* (Summer 2005), pp. 299–327. See also "Magazine Plays to Japanese Xenophobia," *Financial Times Information Unlimited,* 2 February 2007.

91. "Can Japan Absorb Foreign Influx?," *Japan Times,* 24 January 2006. A longer version can be found at www.japanfocus.org.

92. In its 1971 Immigration Act, the British government uses the term *patrials* to refer to a similar concept of persons born outside the United Kingdom but whose parents had been born there. See Christian Joppke, *Selecting by Origin: Ethnic Migration in the Liberal State* (Cambridge, MA: Harvard University Press, 2005), p. 98.

93. Joseph Coleman, "Japan Mulls Importing Foreign Workers," Associated Press online, 20 January 2007.

94. "Entertainment of a Kind: Making it Harder to Abuse Younger, Prettier Immigrants to Japan," *Economist,* 3 March 2005; available online at http://www.economist .com/node/3723066?story_id=3723066.

95. United Nations, Population Division, Department of Economic and Social Affairs, *Replacement Migration: Is It a Solution to Declining and Ageing Populations?* (New York: United Nations, 2001), ST/ESA/SER.A/206; available online at http://www .un.org/esa/population/publications/migration/migration.htm

96. Among the projection assumptions is that the "structure of the migration streams is the average age and sex structure of migrants into Australia, Canada and the United States . . . selected because they are the three major traditional countries of immigration. . . . The projection methodology also assumes that, after the immigrants arrive in a country, they experience the average fertility and mortality conditions of that country. While this is typically not the case, especially when immigrants come from a country that differs greatly demographically from the receiving country, this assumption permits computations to be more straightforward and also facilitates comparisons between countries and regions." United Nations, *Replacement Migration,* p. 17.

97. Calculated from ibid., tables IV.4 and IV.7; available online at http://www .un.org/esa/population/publications/migration/migration.htm.

98. Michael S. Teitelbaum, "The Media Marketplace for Garbled Demography," *Population and Development Review 30,* no. 2 (June 2004), pp. 317–27.

99. United Nations, *Replacement Migration,* p. 1.

100. Ibid., p. 4.

101. Organisation for Economic Co-operation and Development (OECD), *Pensions at a Glance 2011: Retirement-Income Systems in OECD Countries: Online Country*

Profiles, Including Personal Income Tax and Social Security Contributions, Japan, http://www.oecd.org/dataoecd/34/3/47272780.pdf

102. Organisation for Economic Co-operation and Development (OECD), *Ageing and Employment Policies: Japan* (Paris: OECD, 2006), p. 75, table 3.1; available online at http://213.253.134.43/oecd/pdfs/browseit/8104051E.PDF.

103. Ibid.

104. "70 or Bust" and "Falling Short: A Special Report on Pensions," *Economist*, 9 April 2011l; available online at http://www.economist.com/node/18502013.

105. OECD, "OECD Thematic Follow-up Review of Policies to Improve Labour Market Prospects for Older Workers: Japan (situation mid-2012)," Employment Policies and Data: Ageing and Employment Policies (Paris: OECD, 2012); available online at http://www.oecd.org/employment/employmentpoliciesanddata/ageingandemploymentpolicies.htm.

106. Organisation for Economic Co-operation and Development (OECD), Directorate for Employment, Labour, and Social Affairs, *Live Longer, Work Longer: A Synthesis Report, Ageing and Employment Policies, Statistics on Average Age of Retirement* (Paris: OECD, 2006); available online at http://www.oecd.org/document/47/0,3343,en_2649_34747_39371887_1_1_1_37419,00.html.

107. OECD, *Ageing and Employment Policies: Japan*, p. 14.

SEVEN North America and NAFTA

1. The UN's "North America" category includes three large sub-categories: "Northern America," "Caribbean," and "Central America." The UN subcategory "Northern America" includes the United States and Canada (plus three small island countries), while Mexico is defined as part of the subcategory "Central America." United Nations, Statistics Division, "Composition of Macro Geographical (Continental) Regions, Geographical Sub-Regions, and Selected Economic and Other Groupings," http://unstats.un.org/unsd/methods/m49/m49regin.htm#ftnb.

2. See for example, "NAFTA: A Decade of Strengthening a Dynamic Relationship," http://www.international.gc.ca/trade-agreements-accords-commerciaux/assets/pdfs/nafta10-en.pdf.

3. All of the total fertility rates cited in this chapter are based on the interpolated total fertility rate database kindly made available by the United Nations Population Division. United Nations, Department of Economic and Social Affairs, Population Division: *World Population Prospects DEMOBASE extract. 2009.*

4. For example, see US Census Bureau, Population Profile of the United States, Dynamic edition, Age and Sex Distribution in 2005, http://www.census.gov/population/www/pop-profile/files/dynamic/AgeSex.pdf. For discussion of the US baby boom in relation to other countries, see Teitelbaum and Winter, The *Fear of Population Decline*, (Orlando, FL, and London: Academic Press, 1985), pp. 68–75.

5. Ansley J. Coale, "Population Growth and Economic Development: The Case of Mexico," *Foreign Affairs* 56 (1977–1978), pp. 415–29.

6. Ibid., p. 423.

7. See Michael S. Teitelbaum, "The Population Threat," *Foreign Affairs* 71, no. 5 (Winter 1992), pp. 67–68.

8. Gustavo Cabrera, "Demographic Dynamics and Development: The Role of Population Policy in Mexico," *Population and Development Review* 20, supp.: *The New Politics of Population: Conflict and Consensus in Family Planning* (1994), p. 105.

9. Ibid., p. 113.

10. Ibid.," p. 106.

11. For contrasting views published in the same edited volume, see Jesus F. de la Teja, "The Colonization and Independence of Texas: A Tejano Perspective," and Josefina Zoraida Vazquez, "The Colonization and Loss of Texas: A Mexican Perspective," both in Jaime E. Rodriguez O. and Kathryn Vincent, *Myths, Misdeeds, and Misunderstandings: The Roots of Conflict in U.S.—Mexican Relations*, (Wilmington, DE: Scholarly Resources, 1997.)

12. The Republic of Texas's declaration of independence contributed to the later war between Mexico and the United States from 1846 to 1848, in which the United States prevailed. The war ended with ratification of the 1848 Treaty of Guadalupe Hidalgo, under which the Mexican government not only agreed to US sovereignty over Texas but also ceded (in return for substantial monetary payments from the US government) its large though sparsely populated northern territories of Alta California and Nuevo México, thereby reducing its area by more than 50 percent. These ceded territories today comprise much of the US Southwest and other regions, including all or parts of what later became the US states of California, Nevada, New Mexico, Arizona, Utah, Colorado, Oklahoma, Kansas, and Wyoming. See for example: Enrique Krauze, *Mexico: Biography of Power: A History of Modern Mexico, 1810–1996*, trans. Hank Heifetz (New York: Harper Collins, 1997).

13. Cabrera, "Demographic Dynamics," p. 108.

14. Jan Lahmeyer, "Populstat," compiling data before 1950 from B. R. Mitchell, *International Historical Statistics* (ed. 3, 4) and from 1950 onward from United Nations, *Demographic Yearbook*, http://www.populstat.info/Americas/mexicoc.htm.

15. Dirección General de Estadística, 1970 Population Census of Mexico, cited in Cabrera, "Demographic Dynamics," p. 113.

16. For a fine analysis of the evolution of Mexico's policies on population, see Francisco Alba and Joseph E. Potter, "Population and Development in Mexico since 1940: An Interpretation," *Population and Development Review* 12, no. 1 (March 1986), pp. 47–75. Discussion of the dramatic policy changes during the Echeverría presidency can be found at pp. 61–62.

17. The Institutional Revolutionary Party (in Spanish, Partido Revolucionario Institucional, or PRI) ruled Mexico for fully seventy-one years, from 1929 to 2000, when its presidential candidate was defeated for the first time.

18. Cabrera, "Demographic Dynamics," p. 113.

19. Ibid.

20. Victor L. Urquidi, personal communication, 1980.

21. John S. Nagel, "Mexico's Population Policy Turnaround," *Population Bulletin* 33, no. 5 (December 1978), pp. 1–40.

22. Hanna Rosin, Annals of Broadcasting, "Life Lessons," *New Yorker*, 5 June 2006, p. 40.

23. U.S. Department of Commerce, Census Bureau, International Data Base, http://www.census.gov/population/international/data/idb/country.php.

24. United Nations, Department of Economic and Social Affairs, Population Division, *World Population Prospects: The 2010 Revision*, http://esa.un.org/unpd/wpp/index.htm.

25. Jeanne Batalova and Aaron Terrazas, "Frequently Requested Statistics on Immigrants and Immigration in the United States," Migration Policy Institute, December 2010; available online at http://www.migrationinformation.org/USfocus/display.cfm?ID=818#3.

26. World Bank, *Migration and Remittances Factbook 2011* (Washington, DC: World Bank Group, 2011), pp. 3, 5; available online at http://www-wds.worldbank.org/external/default/WDSContentServer/WDSP/IB/2010/11/16/000333038_20101116005627/Rendered/PDF/578690PUB0Migr11public10BOX353782B0.pdf.

27. For a full list of these "top emigration countries" by percentage of population, see ibid.

28. Campbell Gibson and Emily Lennon, US Census Bureau, Working Paper no. 29, *Historical Census Statistics on the Foreign-Born Population of the United States: 1850 to 1990* (Washington, DC: US Government Printing Office, 1999), table 3; available online at http://www.census.gov/population/www/documentation/twps0029/tab03.html.

29. A variety of terms are used by legislators, by statistical agencies, and by the many advocacy groups that are active in the US immigration scene: *undocumented migrants, illegal immigrants, illegal aliens, unauthorized migrants, irregular migrants*, and many other variations can be found. None is entirely satisfactory, and each has its vocal critics. For example, the word *illegal* is offensive to some (a person cannot be illegal), while *undocumented* offends others as a euphemism. The term *immigrant* implies permanent settlement that may not occur, while *migrant* implies nonpermanence, which may not be the case. The word *alien*, which is used in relevant US law, has otherworldly connotations to some. In this volume, we used such terms interchangeably, without any connotations intended.

30. Jeffrey S. Passel and D'Vera Cohn, "Trends in Unauthorized Immigration: Undocumented Inflow Now Trails Legal Inflow," Pew Hispanic Center, Washington, DC, 2 October 2008, p. 3; available online at http://pewhispanic.org/files/reports/94.pdf.

31. Alan Riding, the former *New York Times* bureau chief in Mexico, captured this nicely in the title of his 1984 book about Mexico: *Distant Neighbors: A Portrait of the Mexicans* (New York: Knopf, 1984).

32. Michael S. Teitelbaum, personal communications, 1987.

33. Peter H. Smith, *Mexico: The Quest for a U.S. Policy* (New York: The Foreign Policy Association, 1980), p. 26. See also Michael S. Teitelbaum, "Right versus Right: Immigration and Refugee Policy in the United States," *Foreign Affairs* 59 (1980), p. 46.

34. This provision was incorporated by the government of Mexico into the International Convention on the Protection of the Rights of All Migrant Workers and Members of Their Families. See discussion later in this chapter. The full text of the convention may be found at http://www.un.org/documents/ga/res/45/a45r158.htm.

35. Ana Minian, "Superfluous Persons: Migration from Michoacan to the United States from the 1960s to the Present" (PhD diss., Yale University, 2011).

36. Michael S. Teitelbaum, personal communications , 1997.

37. Philip Martin, "Mexico-US Migration," in *NAFTA Revisited: Achievements and Challenges*, ed. Gary Hufbauer and Jeffrey Schott (Washington, DC: Institute for International Economics, 2005), pp. 441–86.

38. Passel and Cohn, "Trends in Unauthorized Immigration," p. ii.

39. United Nations General Assembly, "The Universal Declaration of Human Rights," Paris, 10 December 1948; available online at http://www.un.org/en/documents/udhr/index.shtml.

40. United Nations General Assembly, "International Convention on the Protection of the Rights of All Migrant Workers and Members of Their Families," Adopted by General Assembly resolution 45/158 of 18 December 1990; available online at http://www.un.org/documents/ga/res/45/a45r158.htm.

41. Ibid., article 87.

42. Jay Winter and Antoine Prost, *René Cassin* (Paris: Fayard, 2011), pp. 340–44.

43. "Everyone has the right to leave any country, including their own, and to return to their country." Universal Declaration of Human Rights, 1948, article 13. As has oft been noted, this declaration of a human right to exit one's own country is not accompanied by a parallel right of entry into another state.

44. Gus Ranis and Jay Winter, "Global Citizenship and Migration," report of Hewlett Foundation Project, Yale University, 2010, pp. 1–111.

45. NAFTA did not attract the required two-thirds support from the US Senate for approval of a "treaty" under the US Constitution. Its proponents therefore arranged for its passage as a "congressional-executive agreement" (CEA); CEAs can be passed with only a simple majority from both houses of Congress.

46. In the interest of full disclosure, one of the authors (MST) was a member of the US Commission for the Study of International Migration and Cooperative Economic Development, which was the first official US government entity to recommend negotiation of a free trade agreement with Mexico. See United States, Report of the Commission for the Study of International Migration and Cooperative Economic Development: Hearing before the Committee on Foreign Affairs, House of Representatives, 101st Congress, 2nd sess., 24 July 1990 (Washington, DC: US Government Printing Office, 1990).

47. The proposed NAFTA was vigorously opposed during the 1992 presidential campaign by third-party candidate Ross Perot. Indeed, in the second presidential debate held on 15 October 1991, Perot argued that the agreement would produce what he then called "a job-sucking sound going south": "We have got to stop sending jobs overseas. . . . If you're paying $12, $13, $14 an hour for a factory worker, and you can move your factory south of the border, pay $1 an hour for labor, . . . have no health care— that's the most expensive single element in making the car. Have no environmental controls, no pollution controls and no retirement. And you don't care about anything but making money. There will be a job-sucking sound going south"; available online at http://www.pbs.org/newshour/debatingourdestiny/92debates/2prez1.html. In the end, Perot won 19 percent of the presidential vote, the best showing for a third-party candidate since Theodore Roosevelt. Subsequently he continued to campaign against passage of NAFTA.

48. The final vote on NAFTA in the US Senate was 61–38 with 1 member not voting. Of the 61 supporting, the majority (34) were Republicans. Public Citizen, "Final Senate Vote on NAFTA," http://www.citizen.org/trade/article_redirect.cfm?ID=15960. The final vote in the House of Representatives was 234 in favor, 200 opposed. Of the 234 in favor, the majority (132) were Republicans. Public Citizen, "Final House Vote on NAFTA," http://www.citizen.org/trade/article_redirect.cfm?ID=15959.

49. Major Garrett, "NAFTA defended as Way to Slow Influx of Illegals," *Washington Times*, Sunday, 26 September 1993, p. A1.

50. Ibid.

51. See for example David J. Lynch, "Jobs Could Solve Some Mexico Woes," *USA Today*, 29 May 2006; available online at http://www.usatoday.com/money/world/2006 -05-29-mexico-jobs-usat_x.htm.

52. Jorge A. Bustamante, Testimony before the Subcommittee on International Law, Immigration, and Refugees, Hearing on "Immigration-Related Issues in the North American Free Trade Agreement," Committee on the Judiciary, US House of Representatives, 103rd Congress, 1st sess., 3 November 1993 (Washington, DC: Government Printing Office, 1994), pp. 197–98.

53. The INS was a Department of Justice agency that was folded into the Department of Homeland Security after the September 11, 2001, attacks on New York City and Washington by Al-Qaeda agents who entered the United States with lawful temporary visas.

54. Doris Meissner, Testimony before the Subcommittee on International Law, Immigration, and Refugees, p. 30.

55. Rufus Yerxa, Testimony before the Subcommittee on International Law, Immigration, and Refugees, pp. 14–15.

56. US Commission for the Study of International Migration and Cooperative Economic Development, *Unauthorized Migration: An Economic Development Response. Final Report. Washington, DC: July 1990*, p. 33. One of the current authors (MST) was a member of this federal commission.

57. Wayne A. Cornelius and Philip L. Martin, "The Uncertain Connection: Free Trade and Rural Mexican Migration to the United States" *International Migration Review* 27, no. 3 (Autumn 1993), p. 506.

58. David Clark Scott, "Free Trade and Mexican Migrants," *Christian Science Monitor*, 15 June 1992, p. 7.

59. Ruth Ellen Wasem, "CRS Report to Congress: Unauthorized Aliens in the United States: Estimates since 1986." Congressional Research Service, updated 14 January 2007, Order code RS21938, 6 pp., fig. 2, p. CRS-5; available online at http://www.ilw.com/immigdaily/news/2007,0315-crs.pdf.

60. See US Commission for the Study of International Migration and Cooperative Economic Development, *Unauthorized Migration*.

61. Jorge A. Bustamante, Testimony before the Subcommittee on International law, Immigration, and Refugees, pp. 197–198.

62. David Bacon, "Displaced People: NAFTA's Most Important Product," Report: Mexico II, *NACLA Report on the Americas*, September–October 2008, pp. 23–27.

63. Philip L. Martin, personal communication to MST, May 2011.

64. The Pew Research Center for the People and the Press and Pew Hispanic Center, "America's Immigration Quandary: No Consensus on Immigration Problem or Proposed Fixes" (Washington, DC: Pew Research Center, 30 March 2006); available online at http://www.people-press.org/2006/03/30/americas-immigration-quandary/.

65. Chicago Council on Foreign Relations, *Worldviews 2002: American Public Opinion and Foreign Policy* (Chicago: Chicago Council on Foreign Relations, 2002), p. 72; available online at http://www.worldviews.org/detailreports/usreport.pdf.

66. Chicago Council on Foreign Relations, *Worldviews 2002: American Public Opinion and Foreign Policy*, p. 72.

67. Centro de Investigación y Docencia Económicas, Consejo Mexicano de Asuntos Internacionales, and Chicago Council on Foreign Relations, *Global Views 2004: Comparing Mexican and American Public Opinion and Foreign Policy* (Mexico City and Chicago: Chicago Council on Foreign Relations, 2004), 36 pp; available online at http://www.ccfr.org/UserFiles/File/POS_Topline%20Reports/POS%202004/2004%20US_Mexico%20Comparative%20Global_Views.pdf.

68. The US public opinion data come from an Internet survey of 1,195 American adults drawn by a random sample of an established respondent panel managed by Knowledge Networks, Inc. (KN). The estimated margin of sampling error is approximately 3 percent. The Mexican public-opinion data come from face-to-face interviews with a sample drawn from a probabilistic design of the adult Mexican population aged eighteen and older. The interviews were conducted face-to-face due to limited penetration of telephone and Internet. The sampling error for a 95 percent confidence interval is estimated at plus/minus 4 percent. For further methodological details, see Chicago Council on Foreign Relations , *Global Views 2004*, pp. 33–34.

69. Chicago Council on Foreign Relations, *Global Views 2004: Comparing Mexican and American Public Opinion*, p. 29.

70. Ibid., p. 30.

71. US Constitution, article 1, section 1, clause 4.

72. This doctrine increasingly is being challenged by new state laws requiring state officials to enforce federal immigration law, an approach that has attracted legal challenge from the US Department of Justice. See, for example, *United States of America v. the State of Arizona*, et al., Order on the Preliminary Injunction, in the United States District Court for the District of Arizona, case 2:10-cv-01413-SRB, doc. 87, filed 28 July 2010, 36 pp., issued 28 July 2010; available online at http://www.azd.uscourts .gov/azd/courtinfo.nsf/983700DFEE44B56B0725776E005D6CCB/$file/10–1413–87 .pdf?openelement.

73. Brian G. Slocum, "Canons, the Plenary Power Doctrine and Immigration Law," *Florida State University Law Review* 34 (Winter 2007), p. 3; available online at Social Science Research Network: http://ssrn.com/abstract=933372.

74. Ibid., p. 6, fn. 22.

75. In the interest of balance it is worth noting that the US Constitution grants similar "plenary powers" to the president, for example, the power to grant pardons, under article 2, section 2. Such actions by the president are not reviewable or reversible by Congress or the courts. This constitutional grant of plenary power too has been criticized, most recently following the controversial pardons granted by President Clinton as he left office, but it remains well established nonetheless.

76. Examples include the California Avocado Commission, http://www.avocado .org/; the California Grape and Tree Fruit League, http://www.cgtfl.com/Main.asp; and many others.

77. See, for example, the lobbying positions on immigration promoted by the American Hotel and Lodging Association, the industry association that describes itself as the "leading voice of the lodging industry for 100 years" and as "Uniting 11,000 hospitality executives, AH&LA is the only national organization dedicated to serving the interests of hoteliers on the front line, behind the scenes, and on Capitol Hill," http:// www.ahla.com/issuebrief.aspx?id=18190.

78. See lobbying positions of the National Restaurant Association, self-described as "Founded in 1919, the National Restaurant Association is the leading business association for the restaurant industry," http://www.restaurant.org/government/Issues/Issue .cfm?Issue=immigration.

79. One of the authors (MST) became an at-large member of this board in 1982 when it was described by Rick Swartz as a nonadvocacy organization. When it became clear that the forum was, contrary to its claims, very active in advocacy activities, MST tendered his resignation from its board.

80. See National Immigration Forum, "About the National Immigration Forum," http://www.immigrationforum.org/about.

81. John Heilemann, "Do You Know the Way to Ban José?" *Wired* magazine 4, no. 8 (August 1996), p. 7; available online at www.wired.com/wired/archive/4.08/ netizen_pr.html.

82. The 2012 Executive Committee and Board of Directors of the National Immigration Forum are listed as follows on the forum Web site, http://www.immigration forum.org/about/board:

Executive Committee
Dr. Warren H. Stewart, Sr., Chair, First Institutional Baptist Church [Phoenix, AZ]
Craig Regelbrugge, Vice Chair, American Nursery & Landscape Association
Esther Lopez, Treasurer, United Food and Commercial Workers Union
Sayu Bhojwani, Secretary, The New American Leaders Project

Board of Directors
Jeb Bush, Jr., Jeb Bush & Associates, LLC
Margie McHugh, Migration Policy Institute
Fred Niehaus, Interactive Global Services, LLC
Peter Orum, Midwest Groundcovers, LLC
Laura Reiff, Greenberg Traurig, LLP
Denyse Sabagh, Duane Morris, LLP
Angelica Salas, Coalition for Humane Immigrant Rights of Los Angeles
The Most Reverend Jaime Soto, Bishop of the Roman Catholic Diocese of Sacramento
Felicia Wong, The Roosevelt Institute

83. See http://www.ufcw.org/. Claims concerning abusive employment practices by meat processors in the Midwest are too numerous to cite. The most heavily covered recent case was that of Agriprocessors, Inc., the nation's largest kosher meat processor, whose Postville, Iowa, processing plant was raided by federal agents on 12 May 2008. The action resulted in the arrest of nearly four hundred unauthorized workers (about half the plant's workforce); http://www.manufacturing.net/article.aspx?id=160918. By early 2009 more than one hundred federal criminal indictments were made against the company's CEO and three other executives. Grant Schulte, "More Fed Charges against Agriprocessors Exec," *Des Moines Register*, 16 January 2009; http://www.desmoinesregister.com/article/20090116/NEWS/90116011/-1/ENT05.

84. See Coalition for Humane Immigrant Rights of Los Angeles, http://www.chirla.org/.

85. Jeb Bush Jr. is son of Jeb Bush, the former Republican governor of Florida and brother of President George W. Bush. Bush Jr. is CEO of Jeb Bush Associates, LLC (providing "a variety of consulting services, focused primarily on business development and strategic advisory work") and president of Bush Realty, LLC; http://sunpacfl.com/about-2/board-of-directors/.

86. See Web site of American Nursery & Landscape Association, http://www.anla.org/index.cfm?area=&page=Content&categoryID=91.

87. See Web site of Duane Morris law firm, http://www.duanemorris.com/attorneys/denysesabagh.html.

88. The Greenberg Traurig law firm also is well known as the employer from 2001 to 2004 of Jack Abramoff, the powerful Republican lobbyist who, during the late 1990s, had represented Microsoft and the Commonwealth of the Northern Marianas on immigration legislation. In 2006 Abramoff pleaded guilty to three felony counts— conspiracy, fraud, and tax evasion—and his former employer, Greenberg Traurig, made a payment of an undisclosed amount to some of his former lobbying clients. See Susan Schmidt, "Abramoff Ex-Firm Settles With Tribe: Former Lobbyist Was Paid Millions on Both Sides of Casino Issue," *Washington Post*, 12 February 2005, p. A02; available online at http://www.washingtonpost.com/wp-dyn/articles/A17529-2005Feb11.html. The court filing against Abramoff before the US District Court for the District of Columbia is available online at http://www.npr.org/documents/2006/jan/abramoff_charges.pdf.

89. For a discussion of the lobbying activities of the US Chamber of Commerce, see Eric Lipton, Mike McIntire, and Don Van Natta Jr., "Top Corporations Aid U.S. Chamber of Commerce Campaign," *New York Times*, 21 October 2010; available online at http://www.nytimes.com/2010/10/22/us/politics/22chamber.html?_r=1&pagewanted=1.

90. For a more detailed discussion, see Michael S. Teitelbaum, "Advocacy, Ambivalence, Ambiguity: Immigration Policies and Prospects in the United States," *Proceedings of the American Philosophical Society* 136, no. 2 (1992), pp. 208–25.

91. The ancestors of even Native Americans (or American Indians, depending upon one's usage preferences) appear to have migrated from Asia.

92. Personal communication to MST, July 2007.

93. B. Lindsay Lowell and Micah Bump, *Projecting Immigrant Visas: Report of an Experts Meeting* (Washington, DC: Institute for the Study of International Migration, Georgetown University, October 2006), p. 3.

94. Ruth Wasem, Congressional Research Service, oral comments at Experts Meeting on Projection Immigration Visas, Institute for the Study of International Migration, Georgetown University, September 2006. For a written summary of this Experts Meeting, see ibid.

95. Jay Winter, "Human Rights as Lived Experience," in Helle Porsdam, ed., *Rights Talk* (London: Frank Cass, 2012), pp. 30–66.

APPENDIX A UN Projections of Total Fertility Rates for Selected Countries

1. Adrian E. Raftery, Leontine Alkema, Patrick Gerland, Samuel J. Clark, Francois Pelletier, Thomas Buettner, Gerhard Heilig, Nan Li, Hana Sevckova, "White Paper: Probabilistic Projections of the Total Fertility Rate for All Countries for the 2010 World Population Prospects," http://esa.un.org/unpd/wpp/Documentation/EGM-RFTF_P16 _Raftery.pdf.

2. L. Alkema, A. Raftery, P. Gerland, S. Clark, F. Pelletier, T. Buettner, and G. Heilig. "Probabilistic Projections of the Total Fertility Rate for All Countries." *Demography* 48, no. 3 (2011), pp. 815–39.

3. Raftery et al., "White Paper," p. 13.

4. Ibid., pp. 10–11.

5. Ibid., p. 18.

6. Joseph Chamie, "Global Population of 10 Billion by 2100?—Not So Fast," *Yale-Global Online*, 26 October 2011, http://yaleglobal.yale.edu/content/global-population-10-billion-not-so-fast.

7. United Nations Population Division's Projections of Total Fertility: Median, 80 percent /95 percent prediction intervals, and High / Low fertility variants. Special tabulations kindly provided by Drs. Patrick Gerland and Gerhard K. Heilig, Demographic Estimates and Projections Section, United Nations Demographic Division, March 2012.

APPENDIX B Effects of and Adaptations to Changing
Demographic Composition

1. Portions of this appendix were presented by MST at the 2011 Legatum Prosperity Symposium, Brocket Hall, Hertfordshire, UK, June 2011; available online at http://www.li.com/FullPapers2011.aspx

2. There are some exceptions, especially in countries in which international migration represents a large fraction of demographic change.

3. The classic 1958 book by Coale and Hoover focused heavily upon such age-structure effects of fertility declines from high levels. See Ansley J. Coale and Edgar M. Hoover, *Population Growth and Economic Development in Low-Income Countries: A Case Study of India's Prospects* (Princeton, NJ: Princeton University Press, 1958).

4. Michael S. Teitelbaum and Jay M. Winter, *The Fear of Population Decline* (Orlando, FL, and London: Academic Press, 1985), chap. 2.

5. Sauvy was the most influential French demographer of his generation: the founding director of the leading demographic research institution, INED, a position he held for seventeen years; founder and editor of the main international demographic journal *Population* from 1946 to 1974; and the official French representative to the UN Population Commission from 1947 to 1974. Sauvy was also a leading public intellectual in France, writing regular articles in newspapers and magazines, such as *Le Monde* and *l'Observateur*. In a 1952 article in the latter, Sauvy coined the concept of the "third world" (*tiers monde*), which became popular in the 1960s but has now passed out of favor. Alfred Sauvy, "A propos de ... Tiers-Monde," *L'Observateur*, 14 August 1952; available online at http://sauvy.site.ined.fr/fr/tiers_monde/.

6. Alfred Sauvy, "Population Changes: Contemporary Models and Theories," *Research in Population Economics* 3 (1981) p. 234.

7. Robert Debré and Alfred Sauvy, *Des Français pour la France: La problème de la population* (Paris, Gallimard, 1946), p. 58.

8. Alfred Sauvy, quoted in M. S. Teitelbaum, "Aging Populations," in *Encyclopaedia Britannica Yearbook 1978* (New York and London, 1978), pp. xx–xxi.

9. There is a large economics literature on this topic. See, for example, F. Modigliani, "Life Cycle, Individual Thrift, and the Wealth of Nations" (Nobel Lecture delivered in Stockholm, Sweden, 9 December 1985), *American Economic Review* 76, no. 3, pp. 297–313; L. J. Kotlikoff and L. H. Summers, "The Role of Intergenerational Trans-

fers in Aggregate Capital Accumulation," *Journal of Political Economy* 89, no. 4 (1981), pp. 706–32; J. M. Poterba, ed., *International Comparisons of Household Saving* (Chicago and London: University of Chicago Press, 1994). See also Mauro Baranzini, "Modigliani's Life-Cycle Theory of Savings Fifty Years Later," *Banca Nazionale del Lavoro Quarterly Review 58*, no. 233–234 (June–September 2005), pp. 109–172.

10. Warren Sanderson and Sergei Scherbov, "Rethinking Age and Aging," *Population Bulletin* 63, no. 4 (December 2008), p. 7.

11. Ibid., p 4.

12. Ibid., p. 10, table 2.

13. Warren C. Sanderson and Sergei Scherbov, "Despite Aging, Proportions of Older Populations with Disabilities in Developed Countries Unlikely to Increase Much," unpublished manuscript dated 28 February 2011, International Institute for Applied Systems Analysis, Laxenburg, Austria, p. 2.

14. See discussion in Baranzini, "Modigliani's Life-Cycle Theory."

15. See Sheldon Garon, *Beyond Our Means: Why America Spends While the World Saves* (Princeton, NJ: Princeton University Press, 2011), chap. 9.

16. John Bongaarts, "Population Aging and the Rising Cost of Public Pensions," *Population and Development Review* 30, no. 1 (March 2004), pp. 1–23.

17. There has also been some evidence from Vietnam of a "reverse" marriage squeeze, attributable to the differential wartime losses among males.

18. In some Asian countries, such as Japan, these involve women trafficked in from lower-income Asian countries by organized-crime networks.

Index